DECISION SUPPORT IN THE DATA WAREHOUSE

ISBN 0-13-796079-4

90000

9 780137 960798

THE DATA WAREHOUSING INSTITUTE SERIES FROM PRENTICE HALL PTR

Planning and Designing the Data Warehouse by Barquin and Edelstein

Building, Using, and Managing the Data Warehouse by Barquin and Edelstein

Data Mining: A Hands-On Approach for Business Professionals by Groth

Decision Support in the Data Warehouse by Gray and Watson

Solving Data Mining Problems Through Pattern Recognition by Kennedy et al.

Parallel Systems in the Data Warehouse by Morse and Isaac

DECISION SUPPORT IN THE DATA WAREHOUSE

Paul Gray

Hugh J. Watson

To join a Prentice Hall PTR Internet mailing list, point to:
http://www.prenhall.com/mail_lists

Prentice Hall PTR, Upper Saddle River, New Jersey 07458

Library of Congress Cataloging-in-Publication Data

```
Decision Support in the Data Warehouse/Paul Gray, Hugh J.
Watson
     p.      cm.
  Includes index
  ISBN 0-13-796079-4
  1. Data warehousing. 2. Decision support systems I. Gray,
Paul.  II. Watson, Hugh J. III. Title
QA76.9.D37G73 1998
658.4'03'00285574--dc21                              97-38991
                                                        CIP
```

Acquisitions editor: Mark L. Taub
Editorial assistant: Tara Ruggiero
Production supervision: Kerry Reardon
Cover design: Anthony Gemmellaro
Cover design director: Jerry Votta
Copyeditor: Barbara Zeiders
Manufacturing manager: Alexis R. Heydt

 © 1998 Prentice Hall PTR
Prentice Hall, Inc.
A Simon & Schuster Company
Upper Saddle River, New Jersey 07458

Prentice Hall books are widely used by corporations and government agenices
for training, marketing, and resale.

The publisher offers discounts on this book when ordered in bulk quantities.
For more information, contact Corporate Sales Department, Prentice Hall PTR,
One Lake Street, Upper Saddle River, NJ 07458. Phone: 800-382-3419; FAX: 201-
236-7141; email: corpsales@prenhall.com

All product names mentioned herein are the trademarks of their respective owners.

Printed in the United States of America

10 9 8 7 6 5 4 3 2 1

ISBN 0-13-796079-4

Prentice-Hall International (UK) Limited, *London*
Prentice-Hall of Australia Pty. Limited, *Sydney*
Prentice-Hall Canada Inc., *Toronto*
Prentice-Hall Hispanoamericana, S.A., *Mexico*
Prentice-Hall of India Private Limited, *New Delhi*
Prentice-Hall of Japan, Inc., *Tokyo*
Simon & Schuster Asia Pte. Ltd., *Singapore*
Editora Prentice-Hall do Brasil, Ltda., *Rio de Janeiro*

To A. G. Lockett
1940-1997
Scholar, Gentleman, Colleague

Contents

VIII ■ CONTENTS ■

Series Foreword

Most data warehousing practitioners have come to the field from the database community. Yet there is a sizable group -- including myself -- that came to data warehousing from the DSS/EIS (Decision Support Systems/Executive Information Systems) fold. In effect, decision support and data warehousing have long been perceived as parallel and complementary concepts. Hence this is a very timely book addressing the many issues that come to mind when we look at decision support in the context of data warehousing. What is the relationship of decision support systems and data warehousing? What type of decision support applications do we see linked to data warehouses? What are the tools that best allow you to build decision support systems in a data warehousing environment? What are the costs involved? Who has done it? With what staff?

From its early beginnings in the late sixties and early seventies, decision support systems seemed to peak in the early eighties. After that they fell somewhat into a limbo. Why? Basically because the raw data necessary to drive the DSS was not there. They fell prey to the same problem of fragmented and disconnected data domains that eventually led to the emergence of data warehousing.

Once data warehousing emerged as a separate discipline, solving the problem of integration and facilitating access to previously inaccessible data, it was clear that these were the powerful and reliable supplies of information that could re-energize the whole field of decision support.

At the same time, data warehousing, like all emerging disciplines, brings along a challenging morass of concepts, terms, and acronyms which need to be explained to the novice. We need to clarify and demystify OLAP, ROLAP, MOLAP, multidimensional database engines, hypercubes, business views, universes, alert systems, and the like. And we need to do this soon, because the ultimate success of data warehousing depends on the end users; and they need to cut through the technical jargon quickly in order to get real value. That value comes shaped primarily in terms of decision support, hence the importance of this topic and the timeliness of this work.

The authors of this book -- Dr. Paul Gray (Claremont Graduate University) and Dr. Hugh Watson (University of Georgia) -- are recognized leaders and authorities on decision support and data warehousing. They are in a privileged position to write the book.

I've known Dr. Watson from the very earliest days of The Data Warehousing Institute. He was with us since the first conference and it was to him that we turned to launch the *Journal of Data Warehousing*, of which he is the founding editor. Furthermore, as the C. Herman and Mary Virginia Terry Professor of Business Administration at the University of Georgia, he has been one of the most prominent academic figures in the world of DSS; and was very quick to see the importance and links between data warehousing and decision support systems. For his valuable work in decision support in data warehousing environments he was named a Fellow of The Data Warehousing Institute.

Dr. Gray, a past president of The Institute of Management Science, is Professor of Information Science at the Claremont Graduate University and founding chair of its Program in Information Science. He, likewise, has excellent credentials to write on the topic of decision support and data warehousing. His pioneering work on group decision support systems, his previous book on decision support and executive information systems, and his book on the management of information systems, jointly with Prof. Watson, are indicative of the broad range of his knowledge and interests.

SERIES FOREWORD XI

Gray and Watson have produced a very solid work. *Decision Support in the Data Warehouse* is an excellent addition to the Prentice-Hall PTR Data Warehousing Institute Series.

Dr. Ramon C. Barquin
Chair, Advisory Board, The Data Warehousing Institute
President, Barquin and Associates

Foreword

Data warehousing is one of the hottest developments of the 1990's. In response to the need to provide decision makers with clean, consistent, and relevant data, an ever increasing number of organizations are developing data warehouses. These are expensive and time-consuming undertakings, requiring millions of dollars and many man years of effort. In return, organizations receive benefits such as higher quality decisions, freeing IS personnel from frequent ad hoc requests for data, and new insights about the purchasing behavior of customers.

Developing a data warehouse is a challenging experience because of the many issues involved. For example, funding for the project must be gained. Will the necessary dollars come from IS, a business unit(s), or a combination of the two? Development issues, such as determining the data requirements for the warehouse, must be handled. There are many technical issues such as what kind(s) of servers to use and whether parallel processing is required. And then there are the political problems such as those associated with a perceived loss of control over one's (i.e., a business unit's) data.

In response to the interest in data warehousing, a large number of conferences have been held and many books and articles have been written. Together, they provide a rich source of information about data warehousing. The problem, however, and our motivation for writing this book, is that the information needed to get a complete picture is not available in a single source. From our perspective, it is important to understand how to build and maintain a data warehouse, how to build applications that use the warehouse, the products and tools that are available for data warehousing, and examples of companies' data warehousing experiences.

What Is In This Book

To meet the goals stated above, the book is divided into four parts:

1. Overview
2. Creating the Data Warehouse
3. Supporting Decisions in the Data Warehouse Environment.
4. Data Warehousing Products for Decision Support.

Part 1, Overview, consists of Chapter 1, *Data Warehousing: The New Decision Support Environment*. It describes the major issues in data warehousing and in decision support in summary form.

Part 2 demystefies data warehousing's technical jargon and provides a framework for building and maintaining a data warehouse for decision support. This part integrates the building and operating of a data warehouse and shows which are the right warehousing tools to use. It pays attention to such details as how to extract, cleanse, process, and load source data; and how to maintain relational and multidimensional data warehouses and data marts. Part II consists of Chapter 2 *Fundamentals of Data Warehousing* and Chapter 3 *Building and Maintaining the Data Warehouse*.

Part 3 explains the development of decision support applications that use a data warehouse. It describes the use of decision support tools for the warehouse, ranging from query response to on-line analytic processing (OLAP) to data mining and database marketing. It also describes the role of World Wide Web technology as an integrating interface for decision support. It shows, step by step, how to build decision support applications in a data warehouse environment. Finally, this part contains practical information: what can go wrong, a survey of current practices, and developments that can be anticipated. The three chapters in this part are entitled *Decision Support Tools* (Chapter 4), *Building Decision Support Applications* (Chapter 5), and *Final Thoughts Before Building a Data Warehouse* (Chapter 6).

Part 4 consists of seven chapters contributed by some of the leading vendors in the field. The vendors are:

- NCR Corporation
- Oracle Corporation
- Red Brick Systems, Inc.
- Platinum technology, inc.
- Brio Technology
- Comshare, Inc.
- Seagate Software

Each vendor describes their data warehouse and decision support products and services, and presents case studies where their product has been used successfully. By reading these chapters, the reader will be able to compare these vendor offerings to determine which are best suited for their specific needs. These chapters have been carefully edited so that they are factual statements about capabilities and outcomes. The contents of these chapters is the responsibility of each of the contributors.

In summary, this book is the first book that focuses on data warehousing from a decision support point of view. Furthermore, it is unique in that it contains chapters from major vendors that allow the reader to compare vendor offerings in a single place.

Role of the Data Warehouse

Like all innovations, data warehousing is progressing through a life cycle. It is still in its rapid growth stage but will soon enter a maturity stage as more and more companies successfully implement data warehouses. The basic need for a warehouse will not change, however, because there will always be a need for data to support decision making. Based on current trends, such as increased competition, shortened product life cycles, and the need to have a closer relationship with customers, it can be argued that data warehouses will be even more critical to businesses in the future. To meet these needs, warehouses will be larger, more comprehensive, and contain data approaching real time. Also coming into play will be technological advances such as multimedia databases, object-oriented technology, and the ability to maintain and use huge databases. We can expect data warehousing to continue to be a major area of importance to IS.

Acknowledgments

This book was made possible through the help of many people. Our appreciation to The Data Warehousing Institute and to Ramon Barquin for giving us the opportunity to present this book in The Data Warehousing Institute series.

We would like to thank the seven vendors who contributed chapters to this book. The authors of these chapters (and their companies) are Ron Swift (NCR), Michael Ault (Oracle), Fred Wee (Red Brick), David Gleason (Platinum), Will Hansen (Brio), Dr. David King and Doug Hockstad (Comshare), and James Lucy (Seagate).

We are particularly grateful to a number of our students who developed basic material that appears in this book. They include Barbara J. Haley, Yong Tae Park, David Petrie, Mumtaz Shamsuden, and Bamphot Vanatansombut.

Production of this book resulted from the extraordinary work of Ms. Nancy Back of Claremont Graduate University, Ms. Roxanne Kling and Neil Crane of the University of Georgia, and the professionals with whom we worked at Prentice Hall PTR: Mark Taub, editor, Lisa Iarkowski, Kerry Reardon, and Gail Cocker-Bogusz.

Paul Gray

Hugh J. Watson

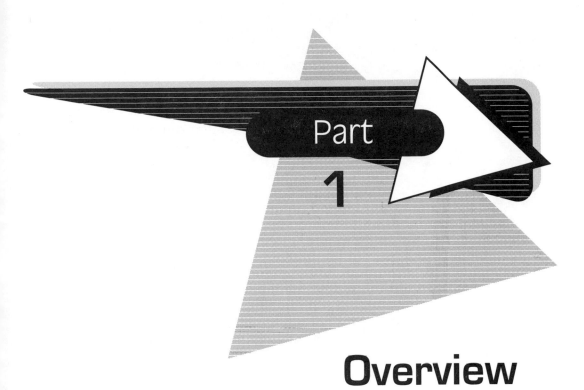

Part

1

Overview

Chapter 1

Data Warehousing: The New Decision Support Environment

1-1 INTRODUCTION

[handwritten margin note: Since the 70s recognition of need separated data for decision support because. — easy access — ↑ response time — ↑ data integrity]

Computers are used to process transaction data and to provide information to support decision making. As early as the 1970s the merits of placing specially prepared data on separate platforms for decision support purposes were recognized. This approach provides easy access to needed data, improves system response time, and enhances data integrity and security (Sprague and Watson, 1996). Decision support systems were the first applications to use this approach. The emergence of end-user computing saw many other applications (e.g., executive information systems) benefit from having specially prepared and staged data.

In the 1990s, many organizations developed data warehouses to provide end users with decision support data. There are, however, important differences from earlier efforts that attempted to serve these needs. One is the use of special-purpose software that facilitates extracting, cleaning and scrubbing, and loading data into a data warehouse (or data mart). Depending on the application, a variety of server software can be used as the data store; multidimensional data-

[handwritten margin note: Differences — specialized sw to load data — data store — Enhanced access tools]

3

base, Lotus Notes servers, and Web-based servers joined relational databases as options. Enhanced data access tools make it easier for end users to access, analyze, and display information, for example, without having to write SQL queries.

Forces pushing DW.
- technological advances
- bussinss presures

Concurrent with technological advances, business pressures and opportunities sparked management's interest in data warehousing. Today's turbulent, high-velocity environment led to shorter decision-making cycles that need to be supported by information technology. Many organizations are becoming increasingly customer focused and recognize that their large databases of customer-related data can be mined to provide information for business advantage. In addition, in many organizations, the only way for users to obtain timely decision-support information is to do their own analysis because downsizing decreased the availability of information systems personnel to do it for them.

1-2 DATA WAREHOUSING

Role of the Data Warehouse

DW objective

The fundamental role of a data warehouse is to provide data for supporting decision making. In some cases, the kinds of applications for which data warehouses are used have existed for some time (e.g., executive information systems). However, data warehouses have added new life to them by improving and expanding the scope, accuracy, and accessibility of data. They have also led to or facilitated other applications, such as on-line analytic processing (OLAP) based on relational or multidimensional database technology and data mining.

DSS and EIS Legacy

Definition
DSS

Decision support systems (DSS) was the name given in the 1970s to information systems designed to help managers in making choices. These systems used models and data to solve

1980s DSS
↓
simplified
↓
1990s EIS

managerial problems ranging in complexity from budget decisions using simple spreadsheets to optimal site location using integer programming. The original concept was that managers would be able to create and operate such systems on their own. This assumption proved false. Most managers did not have the sophistication, the skills, or the time needed. Therefore, starting in the early 1980s, a number of organizations and vendors offered simplified information systems, called executive information systems (EIS).

EIS
internal +
external
information

The basic assumption in EIS was that managers wanted standard information about their firms and the external environment. This information included the time history of processes and outputs in the organization as well as prediction of their future state. The idea was that a manager could turn to his or her EIS and know instantly what was going on. The EISs included information on financials, on production history, current status, and plans, on personnel, and on external events such as information on competitors, electronic mail, and more. The original EISs did not have the analytical capabilities of a DSS. As Rockart and DeLong (1988) said: An EIS is used by senior managers to find problems; the DSS is used by the staff people to study them and offer alternatives.

EIS and DSS
required
their own
Database

Although extremely useful, the EISs and DSSs often lacked a strong database component. As is almost always the case, information gathered for one purpose cannot be used directly for another. Specifically, most organizational information gathering was (and is) directed to maintaining current (preferably on-line) information about individual transactions and customers. Managerial decision making, however, requires consideration of the past and the future, not just the present. As a result, most DSS and EIS builders had to create their own databases, an area which was not their prime expertise. This activity was also demanding and time consuming.

The vendors of DSS and EIS software were quick to pick up on the opportunity offered by data warehousing. DSS and EIS had become "old news" and it was increasingly difficult to generate interest and sales. Furthermore, general-purpose programming languages such as Visual Basic and Power Builder emerged to provide low-cost solutions for companies wanting to build applications with attractive, easy-to-use front ends, such as those associated with EIS. By refocusing the product offerings through in-house-developed extensions, the acquisition of new capabilities to include in their products (e.g., data mining), and forming business partnerships (e.g., with a multidimensional database provider), vendors had "new news" to offer as they stressed capabilities such as OLAP and data mining.

Database Legacy

Databases for
- Transactional: current
- Analytical: historical

Database developers long understood that their software was required for both transactional and analytic processing. However, their principal developments were directed to ever-larger transactional databases at the expense of informational databases. This process occurred even though operational and analytic data are separate, with different requirements and different user communities.

The 1980s were a heady time, in which the relational model, introduced in the previous decade reached its full flower. The market for relational databases for on-line transaction processing was immense, and the coming of the client/server computer architecture increased the demand. There was little need to move beyond transactions.

As is the case for most new technology solutions, once everyone had one, databases became a steady replacement rather than a growth market. At this point, the database developers began looking at new directions for using the knowledge they had acquired. They hit upon the idea of storing not just current data but historical data as well. They also knew that the data in their systems was often not as accurate or as consistent as it could be. Perhaps even more important, they saw that when complex analysis queries were posed to existing databases, the time required to respond was much too long and often tied up the relational systems so that they could not perform their intended transaction functions.

Once these differences were understood, new databases were created specifically for analysis use. These databases are called data warehouses because they store huge amounts of data, far beyond what had been the case previously, and the data is to be kept and used for long periods of time.

DW
- large amounts of data stored

Data Warehouse Users

A data warehouse serves two classes of users:

- direct users and
- application owners.

Direct users are power users such as marketing analysts or financial planners who need access to data in order to perform their jobs. Working through simple software such as Excel or Access, they access data in the warehouse directly. Once they have the data, they manipulate it further. These users require a good understanding of what data is available in the warehouse, how it is stored, and how to access it.

Direct users
- access the DW directly

An application owner is responsible for making an application available to a number of users. For example, in many organizations, much of the data provided through an EIS comes from a data warehouse. For EIS users, the source of the data, whether from a warehouse or a set of separate files, is largely transparent. Unless there is a problem with the data or the response time is slow, they neither care nor worry about how the data is prepared or stored; they need to know little about the data warehouse. The application owner, however, must know a lot about the warehouse because it is probably the primary data feed for the application.

Application owner
- makes application available to others

What Is a Data Warehouse?

A data warehouse is typically a dedicated database system that is separate from the organization's on-line transaction

Differences from OLTP
- *stores transaction but*
- *longer time horizon*
- *data defined uniformly*
- *optimized for complex queries.*

processing (OLTP) systems. It differs from operational systems in that:

- It covers a much longer time horizon than do transaction systems.
- It includes multiple databases that have been processed so that the warehouse's data are defined uniformly (i.e., "clean data").
- It is optimized for answering complex queries from direct users and applications.

DW varieties
- *DW*
- *D Mart*
- *Operational datastore*

Data warehouses come in at least three varieties:

- A conventional *data warehouse* which provides data on and supports the entire enterprise.
- A *data mart*, which is a miniature data warehouse designed to support a particular business unit or department.
- An *operational data store* which applies data warehousing techniques to transaction systems.

Definitions

Definition DW.

Data warehousing has been defined in a number of ways. Inmon (1992) defined a data warehouse as a:

- subject oriented
- integrated
- time-variant
- nonvolatile

collection of data in support of management decision processes.

Inmon is credited by many as being the "father" of data warehousing. The definition is useful because it defines data warehousing in terms of measurable attributes. We discuss each of these attributes in detail in the sections that follow.

Inmon's definition of a data warehouse makes two implicit assumptions:

1. A data warehouse is physically separated from operational systems.
2. Data warehouses hold both aggregated data and transaction (atomic) data for management separate from the databases used for on-line transaction processing.

Assumptions
- separate from operational systems
- hold both aggregated and transaction data

Some alternative definitions, which take a DSS point of view, are also of interest.

Imhoff (1995) defined a data warehouse as:

other DW definitions

- a collection of integrated, subject-oriented databases designed to support the DSS function, where each unit of data is relevant to some moment of time.

- a collection of databases optimized for decision support.

Ralph Kimball, the founder of Red Brick Systems, has called the data warehouse a place where people can access their data, (Kimball, 1996).

Oracle Corporation, in the book by Corey and Abbey, (1997) defined the data warehouse as:

- A collection of corporate information, derived directly from operational systems and some external data sources. Its specific purpose is to support business decisions, not business operations.

Babcock, 1995, writing in *Computerworld* stated that:

- A data warehouse is a repository of data summarized or aggregated in simplified form from operational systems. End-user orientated data access and reporting tools let users get at the data for decision support.

Babcock goes on to add that a data warehouse is:

- informational, not operational

- analysis and decision are support-oriented, not trans-action-processing oriented
- usually client/server, not legacy host-based

Characteristics of a Data Warehouse

Table 1-1 summarizes the characteristics of a data warehouse. These characteristics are discussed in detail later in the chapter.

Characteristics

Table 1-1: Characteristics of a Data Warehouse

CHARACTERISTIC	DESCRIPTION
Subject oriented	Data are organized by how users refer to it.
Integrated	Inconsistencies are removed in both nomenclature and conflicting information; that is, the data are "clean".
Nonvolatile	Read-only data; data are not updated by users.
Time series	Data are time series, not current status.
Summarized	Operational data are aggregated, when appropriate, into decision-usable form.
Larger	Keeping a time series implies that much more data is retained.
Not normalized	Data can be redundant.
Metadata	Data about the data for both users and data warehouse personnel.
Input	Operational data ("legacy systems") plus external data as needed.

Subject Orientation

In a data warehouse, data is organized around major subjects of the enterprise (e.g., sales) rather than individual transactions. That is, the organization is by subject areas across the enterprise rather than on an application-by-application basis. The reason for this difference is that applications are typically designed around processes and functions, each of which has its specific data needs, but many of the data elements are local to that function. These operational data requirements relate to the immediate needs of the application and are based on current business rules. A data warehouse, on the other hand, contains data that is oriented to decision making. The data spans time and allows for more complex relations.

Data Integration

In the data warehouse, the information should be:

- Clean
- Validated
- Properly aggregated

By clean we mean that the same piece of information is referred to in only one way. Unfortunately, legacy systems have many ways of referring to the same piece of data. Thus you can have gender referred to as M,F in one system; Male, Female in a second system; and 0,1 in a third. Similarly, some systems use two digits for calendar year (creating the year 2000 problem), while others use four digits.

When data is brought into a data warehouse, it is integrated, so it is referred to in only one way, and has the same format and the same units for measuring attributes. Thus, in a data warehouse, the data is stored in a single, globally acceptable fashion even though sources may differ.

Similarly, the data has to be correct. Errors slip into databases and, once there, tend to remain there forever unless some external event occurs. Similarly, pieces of information may be left out. Specific steps are needed to make sure that the data in the data warehouse has been validated. Some data in the warehouse is aggregated. Care has to be taken to make certain that the aggregation is correct. If these operations are performed correctly, the users can focus on using the data, not its credibility or consistency.

Nonvolatile Environment

In an operational environment, updates, (inserts, deletes, changes) are made regularly on a record-by-record basis as they occur. Data warehouses are not updated in this way. Rather, data is loaded into the warehouse on a scheduled basis, after which users have access. This approach results in a much simpler technical environment. There is, in fact, little or no redundancy between the operational and data warehouse environments except where operational data is replicated.

When new data is loaded into the warehouse, it is filtered and transformed. Only data needed for decision support is stored. In addition, some calculations are performed to create summary data not found in operational data. For example, the warehouse may include weekly figures obtained from aggregating daily sales to create summary data not found in operational data. Such summarization improves the response time for warehouse users.

Time Series

In an operational environment, decisions are made on-line (e.g., do I grant credit to the customer on the phone?). Therefore, data must be accurate at moment of access. This is not the case for a data warehouse. The data is accurate at some moment in time but not necessarily "right now." Typically, the data is completely accurate when the data is being loaded into the warehouse.

The data warehouse typically has a 5- to 10- year horizon on the data that it contains. Operational data, on the other hand, typically covers 60 to 90 days.

In a data warehouse, the data is organized so that the key always contains the unit of time (such as day, week) being referred to. Furthermore, correctly recorded warehouse data *cannot* be updated by users.

Data Warehouse Structure

A data warehouse contains five types of data:

- Current detail data
- Old detail data
- Lightly summarized data
- Highly summarized data
- Metadata

These data are not necessarily stored in the same medium. However, the software is such that access can be obtained to each. Note that a key issue to be decided in the design of the data warehouse is the amount of detail to be included, that is, the "granularity" of the data. Raw data, as kept in the organization's transaction processing systems, is usually the most detailed.

Current Detail Data

Current detail data reflects the most recent happenings. This data can become very voluminous if stored at the lowest level of granularity. This information usually requires very rapid access and hence is usually stored on disk. Often, it is simply a replication of the current transaction data which has been cleaned and then loaded. However, not all fields kept in the transaction systems may be moved to the warehouse. Note that although referred to as "current", this data is up to date only to the time it was removed from the transaction system.

Many decision support questions involve using data that can be obtained directly from the detail records on transactions. For example, how many units did we sell today? What is the week-to-week trend in hardware sales? In returns? The reason the detail data is replicated in the warehouse is to make it possible to query it without bringing the transaction system down or stopping the transaction system for extensive periods of time while such legitimate queries are answered.

[handwritten margin notes: maybe be stored in different media; Definition Granularity: level of detail; most recent happenings; querying without interfering the performance of transactional systems]

Old Detail Data

Most warehouses have rules that state that when detailed data reaches a certain age, it is moved from disk to a mass storage medium. Although still retrievable in detail form, the access time is a little longer because it has to work with a slower medium. This information is the same, however.

[handwritten margin note: Usually stored in slower medium]

Lightly Summarized Data

Many decision support applications are based on summarizing the transaction data. Experience shows that, by summarizing the data in a form that anticipates requests for these standard quantities, the responsiveness and use of the warehouse are improved.

[handwritten margin note: improves response]

From the point of view of the designer, two decisions are required:

1. Selecting the attributes to summarize
2. Selecting the unit of time for summarization

[handwritten margin note: Decisions in summarizing]

Both these questions involve trade-offs. The trade-off is that the computations do not have to be performed over and over, but more storage space is needed. Clearly, attributes and combinations of attributes that are often queried should be summarized, whereas those that are rarely queried should not. Once the attributes are selected, the next question is how frequently should each particular attribute be summarized. For example, do we summarize sales daily? weekly? monthly? and store the results? The unit of time has to be answered for each attribute selected for summarization. The answer should be driven by user requirements.

[handwritten margin note: trade-off storage - performance]

[handwritten margin note: Driven by user requirements]

Highly Summarized Data

Some information, particularly that required by very senior managers, should be available in compact and easily accessible form. This information typically includes the information consulted over and over. This information goes beyond summarizing the transaction data being kept. It includes the ability to keep summary data over long time periods so that trends can be established. By storing highly summarized data, response times for that information are also improved.

Metadata

Metadata is defined as data about the data. It is information kept about the warehouse rather than information provided by the warehouse. Metadata turns out to be essential for both the staff and the users of the data warehouse. Each group requires different information. For the data warehousing staff, metadata includes:

- *A directory of what is in the warehouse.* The directory indicates where data is being stored. It is an index used when a query is posed to find the right information.

- *A guide to mapping data from operational to warehouse form.* When data is loaded into the warehouse, the data must be in standard form and must follow the conventions of the warehouse. That is, the data must be clean. The guide provides instructions on how each particular set of data is to be transformed so that it is in the correct form. For example, if American Telephone and Telegraph is stored as AT&T in one data set and ATT in another, it makes sure that the data warehouse records them in only one form.

- *The rules used for summarization.* For the users of the data warehouse, metadata includes:

  - The business terms used to describe the data.

  - The technical names corresponding to the business terms which can be used to access the data.

  - The source of the data, the rules used to derive it, and when it was created.

Form of Data

The concept of normalizing data in a transaction system, long popularized in relational data bases, is not applicable to data warehouses. In transaction systems it is considered desirable to eliminate redundancy so that, for example, all data about a given transaction are in the same place. The idea is to organize data fields into a group of tables that are easy to use and make sense. There is also a sense that storage space is expensive and that it should not be wasted.

The philosophy in the data warehouse is to arrange data so that it is useful and so that it can be retrieved quickly. Redundancies are perfectly all right.

Redundancy allowed to improve performance [handwritten margin note]

Flow of Data

As shown in Figure 1-1, almost all data enters the warehouse from the operational environment. The data is then cleaned and moved into the warehouse. The data continues to reside in the warehouse until one of three actions is taken:

1. The data is purged.
2. The data, together with other information, is summarized.
3. The data is archived.

Figure 1-1: Data Flow

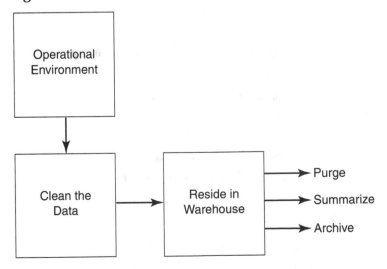

An aging process inside the warehouse moves current data into old detail data. The summarization process is based on the detailed data.

Warehouse Architecture

[handwritten note in margin: Typically 3 tiers architecture but can be 2 or 1 tier]

Typically, the data warehouse architecture has three components (or tiers) (Figure 1-2).

1. The data warehouse itself contains the data and associated software
2. Data acquisition software (back end) which extracts data from legacy systems and external source, consolidates and summarizes the data, and loads it into the data warehouse
3. The client (front end) software which allows users to access and analyze data in the warehouse.

Figure 1-2: Data Warehouse Three-Tier Architecture

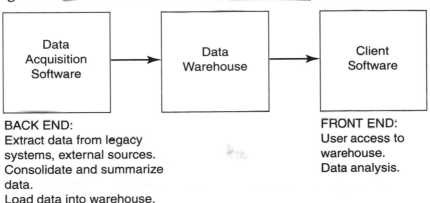

BACK END:
Extract data from legacy systems, external sources.
Consolidate and summarize data.
Load data into warehouse.

FRONT END:
User access to warehouse.
Data analysis.

Figure 1-3 expands on Figure 1-2 and shows many of the possible data sources, software, and users associated with a warehouse. The data sources (shown on the left) include internal, external, and transaction information. The data warehouse management software is used to acquire the information for the warehouse. The data stores include not only the warehouse but a variety of data marts and servers. Data

Figure 1-3: Data Warehouse Architecture in Practice

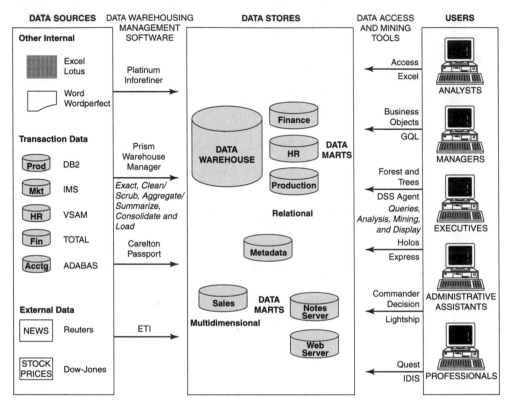

access and mining tools provide user access and data analysis capabilities.

Other architectures can also be used. For example, in a two-tier environment, the application engine and the client are on the same computer while the data warehouse and the data acquisition software resides on a different computer. A stand-alone one-tier architecture, in which all three functions are on the same physical machine, is sometimes used when the amount of data is limited and the number of users is small.

Why a Separate Data Warehouse?

Throughout this chapter, it is tacitly assumed that the data warehouse is separate from the on-line transaction processing system. Such separation is, in fact, the case. The four reasons for this separation are:

1. *Performance.* The peaks and valleys of requests for access degrade the performance of the OLTP system. Data in OLTP systems are oriented to operational rather than decision support issues. As a result, even seemingly simple queries can cause great disturbances in the OLTP system.

2. *Data access.* Organizations often maintain multiple databases which serve different OLTP functions. The data warehouse, being an integration of all of the enterprise's data, combines all these data sources and adds external data sources. The data for decision support applications use these multiple sources. The typical warehouse user doesn't care where the data are stored. They need and want access to data irrespective of which OLTP system has it.

3. *Data formats.* The data in the warehouse include summary data and time-based data which are not kept in OLTP systems. Furthermore, because the data in the warehouse are integrated, information is kept in a single, standard format.

4. *Data quality.* The data in the warehouse is clean, validated, and properly aggregated. It has been gone over to make sure that only one value is stored in the warehouse for each data item. The basic concept in the warehouse is that it contains the "official" value. Thus, when people meet or when they use the warehouse, they spend their time trying to understand what the data means, not arguing about what the correct value of the data is. The warehouse provides "the single version of the truth."

Fact Tables and Dimension Tables

The data stored in a data warehouse are optimized for retrieval for on-line analytic processing (OLAP; discussed in

How data is stored
1. MOLAP
2. ROLAP
2.1 Star
2.2 Snowflake

Section 1-3). The data are therefore organized either as multi-dimensional databases (called MOLAP) or as relational databases (ROLAP). In both cases, the objective is to speed data retrieval so that an analyst whose query, for example, involves the number of units of product A sold in Michigan at a discount to retailers during September can be answered quickly.[1] In this section we discuss the use of special forms of the relational database so that it can handle multiple dimensions.

Specifically, to make relational databases handle multidimensionality, two kinds of tables are introduced: fact tables and dimension tables.

- The *fact table* contains numerical facts. If all the data are stored in a single fact table, the result is a very large table.

- The *dimension table* contains pointers to the fact table; it shows where the information can be found. A separate table is provided for each dimension.

Fact tables are long and thin; dimension tables are small, short, and wide. In a query, the system first accesses one or more dimension tables (in our example, five dimension tables), and then accesses the fact table. This arrangement is called a *star structure* or *schema*. The star structure allows the data to represent a "virtual" rather than a physical data hypercube since the pointers in the dimension table allow the information to be organized in a different way than the query. A classic star schema is shown in Figure 1-4.

In a star schema, each dimension is described by its own table. Facts are arranged in a single large fact table. The fact table is indexed by a multipart key that includes the individual keys of each dimension. Thus, in Figure 1-4, the store, product, and period key are included, as are the dollars, units, and price at which the goods were sold.

---

[1] Note the five dimensions: product, state, terms of sale, customer class, and time.

Figure 1-4: Star Schema

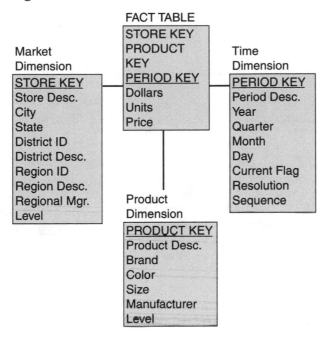

The *snowflake schema,* shown in Figure 1-5, is an alternative to the star schema. It is used when the database includes a large number of categories and the dimensions are large (high cardinality). The snowflake schema creates tables for attributes within a dimension table. This schema allows more rapid data retrieval for high dimensionality.

In the simple illustration of the snowflake schema in Figure 1-5, three fact tables rather than one are used. Each fact table (store, district, region) has its own associated dimension table as well as sharing the product and period dimensions. Notice that if the query is by district, there is no need to deal with either the region or store fact tables.

[handwritten margin note: Snowflake allows more rapid data retrieval for high dimensionality]

Figure 1-5: Snowflake Schema

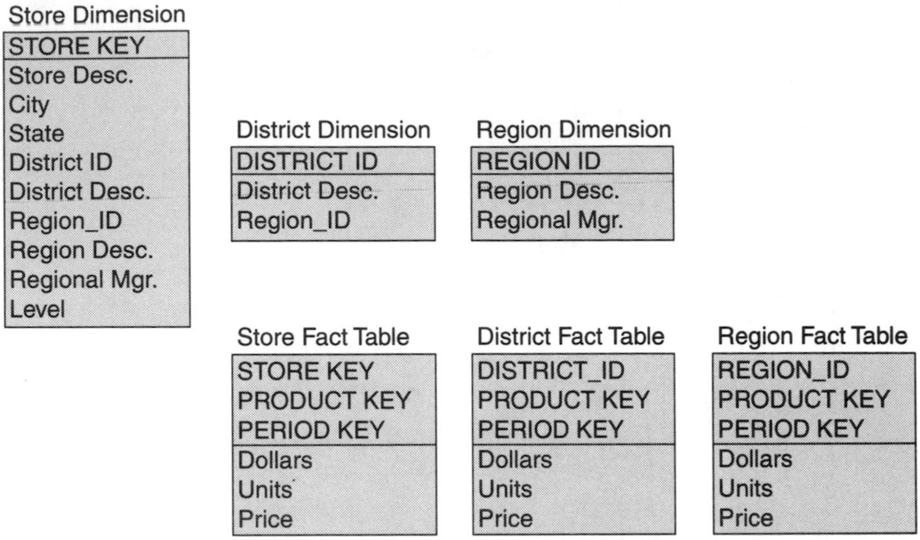

Store Dimension

STORE KEY
Store Desc.
City
State
District ID
District Desc.
Region_ID
Region Desc.
Regional Mgr.
Level

District Dimension

DISTRICT ID
District Desc.
Region_ID

Region Dimension

REGION ID
Region Desc.
Regional Mgr.

Store Fact Table

STORE KEY
PRODUCT KEY
PERIOD KEY
Dollars
Units
Price

District Fact Table

DISTRICT_ID
PRODUCT KEY
PERIOD KEY
Dollars
Units
Price

Region Fact Table

REGION_ID
PRODUCT KEY
PERIOD KEY
Dollars
Units
Price

Using the Warehouse: Summaries and Indexes

Like any software product, a data warehouse is of value to the organization only if it is used regularly. Experience with warehouses shows that:

↑summarize ↑use
↑summarize ↑performance

- The higher the level of summarization, the more the data is used.

- The more summarized the data, the quicker it is to retrieve.

As a result, warehouses routinely create and store summaries of the data accessed most frequently. Pre-calculations not only speed up responses to queries that ask for summarized data, but also speed the response to other queries because they reduce the busy time of the warehouse.

Data highly summarized can be indexed and restructured

Note that data at higher levels of summarization can be indexed and restructured for ease of use. However, data at lower levels is too voluminous to index or change structure. In addition to data from inside the organization, summary data for (or from) outside sources, such as company's SEC filing or competitor stock prices, are also kept in the warehouse.

Cost and Size

[handwritten margin note: Fact DW implementation cost]

Data warehouses are expensive undertakings. Multimillion dollar costs are common. One study reported a mean cost of $2.2 million (Watson and Haley, 1966). *[handwritten: 1997]*

[handwritten margin note: Fact storage size]

Because they are designed for the enterprise so that everyone has access to a common data set, they are large and increase in size with time. Typical storage sizes run from 50 gigabytes to over a terabyte.

Because of their large size, some firms use parallel computing to speed data retrieval. Parallel computers, although coming down in price, are also not cheap. Furthermore, they require support from programmers who are skilled in parallel computing, a group that earns more than normal programmers.

Data Marts

[handwritten margin note: Definition DMart used - to learn - as a "proof of concept"]

The high cost of data warehouses limits them to use by large companies. An alternative being used by many firms is to create a lower-cost, scaled-down version of the data warehouse called the *data mart*. A data mart is a small warehouse designed for the strategic business unit (SBU) or department level. It is often a way to gain entry to data warehousing and provide an opportunity to learn. It can also be used to provide a "proof of concept." The major problem encountered with data marts is that they often differ from department to department. Hence integrating them enterprise-wide can be difficult if a comprehensive warehouse is attempted after the fact.

[handwritten margin note: integration problems Approaches: 1:step-by-step]

Two approaches are being used to overcome the integration problem:

1. Some firms start with stand-alone data marts but have a plan in place for integrating them later. This is

2. Distributed Dmarts [handwritten margin note]

a step-by-step approach, with the goal of eventually having an enterprise-wide system.

2. Other firms build a complete warehouse in the form of distributed data marts assigned to individual units. The advantage here is that the data marts are smaller and more tuned to local needs; the disadvantage is that it becomes more difficult to obtain enterprise-wide solutions.

Information silos [handwritten margin note]

Data marts can lead to reinforcing information "silos," which currently plague many organizations. To avoid this problem, some organizations first create a data warehouse and use it to populate data marts. This approach results in the user having an enterprise view of the data, but with the performance characteristics of a data mart.

DW + Dmart
- Enterprise view
- higher performance [handwritten margin note]

Data warehousing vendors initially promoted the creation of enterprise-wide warehouses. However, many organizations were unwilling to commit the resources required for such a large undertaking without some experience with a smaller project (i.e., with a data mart). Responding to this market imperative, many vendors now offer a data mart strategy or solution as well as one for a full-blown warehouse.

Size of the Industry

Fact (1998)
Percentage of companies with DW. [handwritten margin note]

Data warehouses are a major industry. Estimates vary, but it is clear that many more than half of the Fortune 500 have data warehouse projects under way or planned. Table 1-2 lists some of the major vendors (in alphabetical order) of database and decision support software. Some vendors offer products in both categories.

Table 1-2: Representative List of Major Vendors

DATABASE VENDORS	DECISION SUPPORT VENDORS
Arbor	Andyne
Carleton	Arbor
IBM	Brio
Informix	Business Objects
NCR	Cognos
Oracle/IRI	Comshare
Red Brick	Pilot
Sybase	Planning Sciences
	Platinum
	SAS
	Seagate

Market

Facts
outdated.

Making market predictions is a blood sport among consulting firms. The following are typical of estimates made in 1996: The Butler Group (U.K.) estimates that data warehousing is a $9 billion business in 1997. International Data Corporation (IDC) says that the United States had a 57% share of world market in 1995.

IDC ran a study in 1996 entitled "Financial Impact of Data Warehousing." The results were based on 62 organizations with data warehouses. They found the (very positive) results shown in Table 1-3 for these firms.

Table 1-3: Financial Impacts Of Data Warehouses

Average 3 year return on investment (ROI)	401%
25% had ROI	>600%
Median payback	1.67 years
Median ROI	167%
Average payback time	2.3 years
Average investment	$2.2 million

Worldwide Market

Based on an IDC 1996 White Paper, estimated total revenues from the data warehouse market worldwide are shown in Table 1-4 and in Figure 1-6. Like forecasts about the reduction in the national debt, most of the increases are in the out years.

Table 1-4: World-wide Market Forecast for Data Wareouse Revenues (Millions of dollars)

Year	1993	1994	1995	1996	1997	1998	1999	2000
Market	800	1100	1500	2000	2600	3700	4600	5600

Figure 1-6: Plot of Projected Sales Given in Table 1-4

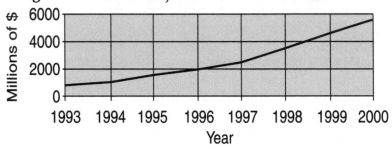

1-3 ON-LINE ANALYTICAL PROCESSING

In 1993, on-line analytical processing (OLAP) was introduced by E. F. Codd, who is often credited with being the father of relational databases. In a major article in *Computerworld*, Codd concluded that relational databases for OLTP had reached their maximum capabilities in the views of the data they provided the user. The problem stemmed principally from the massive computing required when relational databases were asked to answer relatively simple SQL queries. He also came to the view that DSS people had known for a long time: namely, that operational data are not adequate for answering managerial questions.

Codd therefore advocated the use of multidimensional databases. Codd's conversion to the DSS viewpoint gave legitimacy to data warehousing because of its role in OLAP. The basic idea in OLAP is that users should be able to manipulate enterprise data models across many dimensions to understand changes that are occurring.

Multidimension

Codd (1993) put forth a set of 12 rules for OLAP, which are summarized in Table 1-5 and in the Appendix. Codd based his rules on the assumption that the data used in OLAP would be in the form of a multidimensional cube (MOLAP) rather than in the form of a star or snowflake schema (ROLAP). Most decision support vendors claim to be OLAP compliant. Many have some but not all the rules implemented. Some simply relabeled what they had to be OLAP.

Codd's rules for MOLAP

Table 1-5: Codd's 12 Rules for OLAP

1. Multidimensional view	7. Dynamic sparse matrix handling
2. Transparent to the user	8. Multiuser support
3. Accessible	9. Cross-dimensional operations
4. Consistent reporting	10. Intuitive data manipulation
5. Client/server architecture	11. Flexible reporting
6. Generic dimensionality	12. Unlimited dimensions, aggregation

When to Use OLAP

We now know enough about OLAP to be able to state categorically the conditions under which OLAP should be used:

Analytical Processing

- Requests for data are analytic, not transactional in nature.

- The information being analyzed is *not* at its first point of entry into the enterprise.

- Significant calculations and aggregations of transaction-level data are involved.

- The primary type of data element being analyzed is numeric.

- Cross-sectional views of data are often required across multiple dimensions and along multiple consolidation paths.
- Elements that identify data points remain relatively static over time.

Multidimensional versus Relational Databases

The multidimensional databases (MDDB) used in MOLAP are not new. For about 20 years, the EXPRESS software package has featured a MDDB. By the early 1990s a number of other vendors were aboard. The definition of OLAP gave these vendors a boost. Relational database vendors responded by upgrading their products so that they could also handle multiple dimensions. Specifically, they used the star and snowflake schema described previously.

MDDBs store data as an n-dimensional cube. This arrangement implies very sparse matrices. It lets you deal simultaneously with data views defined by such combinations of quantities as product, region, sales, actual expenses, and budget. More important, MDDB adds time as a dimension.

MDDBs advantage over relational databases is that they are optimized for speed and ease of query response. That is, an MDDB is faster than a star or snowflake schema in presenting information. MDDBs disadvantage is that, as of mid-1997, they were limited to warehouses under approximately 50 gigabytes (GB). Above that size, only relational schema could be used. This 50-GB limit is expected to increase to hundreds of gigabytes over time.

Both the MOLAP and ROLAP versions of OLAP are being pushed by vendors. For example, the OLAP Council includes vendors such as Arbor and Pilot Software, which offer MDD products for OLAP. However, these vendors must compete in a world in which the predominant legacy databases are relational. Consequently, IS personnel feel more comfortable using the better-known and better-understood

MOLA P
- sparse matny
- optimized for speed and ease
- limited storage

relational database products. The relational database vendors are protecting their client base by working to improve the star and snowflake schema to make relational multidimensional databases more competitive.

At present, the final form of multidimensionality, that is, whether MOLAP or ROLAP will dominate, is unclear. Table 1-6 compares MOLAP and ROLAP.[2] Here the characteristics expected of multidimensional databases are listed, and for each characteristic, a judgment is presented of which form is superior. However, relational database vendors are "covering their bets" by developing or acquiring multidimensional databases.

It is clear from examining Table 1-6 that neither MOLAP or ROLAP is superior in add dimensions. The choice depends on what the characteristics of the problem and the data are. For example, MOLAP does much better if the warehouse applications involve high calculation intensity and complexity, frequent database update, quick response time, low network impact, and consistency and reliability.

Decision Support Tools

Decision support applications can be developed in a variety of ways: using vendor-supplied software solutions; mixing and matching different software, plus writing some code; or custom building. In most cases it makes little sense to build everything from scratch; rather, the most effective and efficient way is to acquire one or more tools to use in building the application.

---

[2] We are indebted to Bamphot Vatanasombut for this comparison.

Table 1-6: Comparison of MOLAP and ROLAP for Multidimensional Databases Used in Data Warehousing

CHARACTERISTIC	PREFER	CHARACTERISTIC	PREFER
Calculation intensity; complexity	MOLAP	Standards, interoperability	ROLAP
Data sparsity	ROLAP	Query response time	MOLAP
Row-level calculations	MOLAP	Consistency, reliability	MOLAP
Database update	MOLAP	Data loading time	ROLAP
Data volatility	ROLAP	Security	ROLAP
Maximum no. of dimensions	ROLAP	Network impact	MOLAP
Volume of data	ROLAP	Vendor stability	ROLAP
Development time, learning curve	ROLAP		

Many tools are available for building decision support applications. Vendors such as Comshare and Oracle IRI have offered DSS tools for many years (Commander Decision and Express, respectively). They also offer EIS and OLAP tools, as do many other vendors, such as Seagate and SAS.[3] There are also vendor-supplied tools for implementing managed query environments and data mining. Many organizations are developing decision support applications using Web-based tools. Recognizing this trend, vendors are making their products Web enabled. At a minimum, applications can be accessed using a Web browser. For the variety of decision support applications, there are a variety of tools for building them. Decision support tools and applications are discussed more fully in Chapters 4 and 5.

DSS
−Web-based

---

[3] See Table 1-2 for a larger list of DSS vendors.

1-4 CONCLUSIONS

The data warehouse concept has changed the nature of decision support. The warehouse is the link between the data (which was previously scattered in separate databases but is now unified) and the application.

Data warehouses differ from on-line transaction processing databases in that they are a:

- subject oriented
- integrated
- time-variant
- nonvolatile

collection of data in support of management decision processes. At this time, data warehousing is an expensive, large-firm solution. However, smaller, more affordable data marts, designed for strategic business units or departments, are common.

Codd made decision support legitimate for the database world through the OLAP concept. However, OLAP exists in two flavors, relational (ROLAP) and multidimensional (MOLAP). Currently, a fight exists between ROLAP and MOLAP for dominance. The winner is not clear at this time.

The three interrelated fields of data warehousing, OLAP, and data mining (discussed in Section 4-4) are all in the early stages of their development. Many products are on the market from both small and large vendors. However, these products, like the fields, are still far from mature. All three areas present an opportunity for expanding the horizons of information systems.

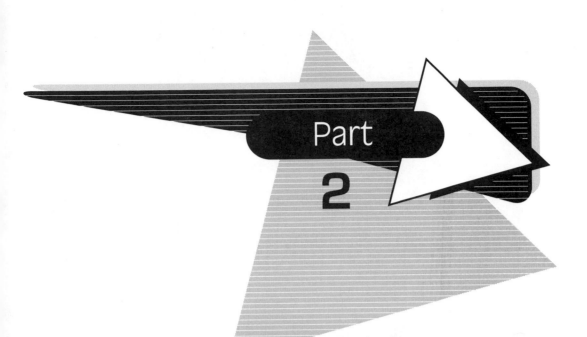

Part
2

Creating the
Data Warehouse

Fundamentals of Data Warehousing

2-1 INTRODUCTION

This chapter expands on the concept of the data warehouse presented in Chapter 1. It begins with a detailed discussion of the architecture of the warehouse, including the number of tiers, storing the data, the DSS, and the application development engine (Section 2-2). The architecture discussion also introduces the idea of the use of parallel computing, which speeds warehouse operation, and indicates some of the challenges faced in selecting architecture.

A second important consideration is the data in the warehouse. Here such topics as "cleaning" and summarizing the data, the important design choice of data granularity (Section 2-3) and the metadata (Section 2-4) are considered. Since the data in the warehouse are multidimensional, the advantages of alternative ways of representing this information (through relational and multidimensional databases) are discussed in Section 2-5. Finally, consideration is given to the interface to warehouse data, particularly the use of browsers, which have gained such popularity in Internet, intranet and extranet applications (Section 2-6).

2-2 PHYSICAL ARCHITECTURE[1]

The focus of this section is to identify the major components in a data warehouse architecture and to describe the physical infrastructure on which the data warehouse resides. Many organizations fail to differentiate between architecture and infrastructure. Architecture (Hildebrand 1995) defines the functions and responsibilities for each component of an application. The infrastructure specifies the hardware and software used to implement each component. The function of these components in a data warehouse architecture include:

- Components to transfer operational data to the data warehouse
- Components to manage and store data in the warehouse for easy retrieval
- Components to connect, access, analyze, and present data for decision making

In addition, designers implementing a data warehouse find components to design, define, and set up the data warehouse environment are valuable.

Three-, Two-, and One-Tiered Architectures

A data warehouse is generally implemented in a clientserver environment. In this environment, data warehouses can be built in three-, two-, and one-tier architectures. Figure 2-1 shows the key components of a *three-tier* data warehouse architecture where the operational systems (legacy systems) that contain the data and the software for cleaning the data are one tier, the data warehouse is another tier, and the third tier includes the decision support engine (i.e., the application server) and the client. The advantage of this architecture is the separation of the functions of the data warehouse. An

---

[1] We are indebted to Ms. Mumtaz Shamsudeen for most of this section.

ideal use of this architecture is for a data mart (Section 3-4). Data may be stored in an enterprise-wide data warehouse and "retailed" to a data mart for departmental use. Alternatively, summarized data can be "retailed" for analysis to DSS engines that, in turn, support clients. The client can be a "thin" client with very little processing capability of its own. In this case, the DSS engine would have the resources to perform the OLAP functions (Section 5-2), thereby reducing network traffic.

In a *two-tier* environment, the data warehouse resides on one of the other tiers. The two-tier architecture is a common architecture supporting data warehouses in organizations today (McFadden, 1996).

Figure 2-1: Enterprise-wide Data Delivery Architecture

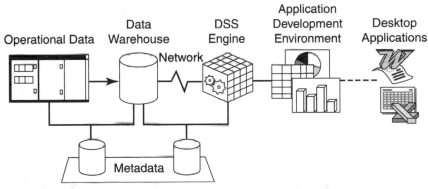

Source: Mircostrategy Inc. "Relational OLAP: An Enterprise-Wide Data Delivery Architecture" MicroStrategy White Paper, 1994.

A *one-tier* architecture, with all three functions on the same physical machine, may be applicable for a small data mart with a few users and a limited set of data. The one-tier architecture is essentially a stand-alone rather than a client/server architecture.

Operational Data Transfer

Very large quantities of data are transferred to the warehouse from the on-line transaction processing systems (OLTP) during initial implementation, followed by periodic "refreshing" when additional or updated information is loaded into the warehouse. In addition, data may be acquired from sources external to the organization. Extraction tools need to operate within the appropriate window of time to ensure the availability of data for decision support.

The tools for transferring the data from one location (OLTP systems) to another (the warehouse) are available from vendors such as Prism, Carleton, and ETI. Most data warehouse vendors have a third-party relationship with one or more of these vendors (Butler Group, 1995).

Storing the Data

The resulting data is stored in a data warehouse. Due to its analytical intensity, decision support data needs to be optimized for query performance. The data warehouse is modeled to facilitate retrieval and ad hoc querying. A key component of the data warehouse are the metadata files (Section 2-4), which function as a bridge to OLAP applications. In this capacity, metadata may contain the following information (Inmon, 1995):

- The location and description of the servers, databases, tables, names, and summarizations in the data warehouse
- Descriptions of original data sources and transformations
- Rules for automatic drilldown through and across business dimensions such as charts of account, markets, and products
- Information generated by end users, including:
  1. Custom names or aliases
  2. Rules for custom calculations
  3. Personal, work group, and enterprise security for viewing, changing, and distributing custom summarizations, calculations, and other analytics.

The DSS Engine

The DSS engine is part of the third tier in the three-tiered architecture (Figure 2-2). This figure is generic. The functions by the DSS engine will vary from vendor to vendor.

DSS Engine components

- *Computation engine*: retrieves data from the warehouse, performs calculations, and sends the answer back to the user.

- *Resource manager*: off-loads work from the client workstation to run in the background at scheduled times.

Figure 2-2: DSS Engine Functions

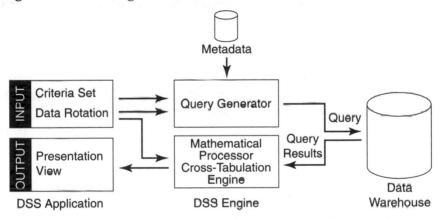

Source: Microstrategy Inc. "Relational OLAP: An Enterprise-Wide Data Delivery Architecture," MicroStrategy White Paper, 1994.

- *Multidimensional database*: data from the data warehouse is made available to end users. The end users are analysts and application owners.

The components to facilitate retrieval of data from the data warehouse, perform the analysis, and transmit the results to the end user may include: a dynamic SQL query generator, a multidimensional data analysis engine, a mathematical equation processor, and a cross-tabulation engine.

The Application Development Environment

ADE
tools for the
construction of
applications

The application development environment (ADE) consists of a suite of tools for the construction of applications. The following are typical examples of the functions performed by such tools:

- Specify, save, and retrieve data from the warehouse.
- Format the view of the query results for presentation.
- Rotate the data to view different dimensions.
- Sift through data in the warehouse looking for patterns (i.e., data mining; Section 4-4).
- Seek information for decision making based on user-predefined criteria.

Desktop Applications

use data from OW
- directly
- through ADE

Desktop applications are typical GUI clients that can use data either directly from the warehouse or through the DSS engine, or using ADE tool sets to integrate the desktop to improve personal productivity. The integration is done through standard APIs (application programming interfaces) such as ODBC, DDE, OLE, and MAPI or through use of a Web browser.

The Database

Database
- Flat files
- Relational DB
- Multidimensional DB

The database can be flat, relational, or multidimensional. A flat file is simply a table with unlimited rows. Flat files become cumbersome to manipulate and maintain as the files become large. Relational databases improve on flat file structures because each table is a relation with rules for creating, updating, modifying, and purging data. E. F. Codd (1970) defined normalization rules that eliminate redundancy and maintain data integrity. Relational database management systems (RDBMS) were designed to facilitate transaction processing. Their features include checks and balances to ensure transaction integrity. For the nonvolatile data warehouse, where updates occur infrequently, the overhead associated with RDBMSs is costly. Query response times can be long and complex for even seemingly simple questions because of the need to join many tables. However, relational data bases are well established, are understood by programmers in nearly all organizations, and have had recent improvements to make them simpler to use in data warehouse applications.

Multidimensional databases (MDDBs) have aspects of both a flat file and a relational database. MDDBs take advantage of Codd's rules where appropriate to maintain integrity while reducing the number of tables required by reintroducing redundancy associated with flat files. MDDBs are optimized for query processing with the tables organized around subjects and frequently accessed data for easy retrieval. The nature, advantages, and disadvantages of multidimensional and relational databases are discussed in Section 2-5.

Parallel Computing

Parallel Computing to ↑ speed

Because of the large size of the data warehouse, some firms use a parallel computing architecture to speed data retrieval and processing. Implementation of parallel computing dates back to 1985 when NCR shipped its first parallelized DBMS. Initially, parallel computing was used in solving scientific problems. In recent years, it has also been applied to problems in finance and securities. However, except for these niche applications, it had not been a standard tool of business computing until data warehousing came on the scene. The size of the data warehouse has made parallel computing a particularly attractive option for the DSS engine. Parallelism can be achieved in hardware as well as software.

Parallelism in sw & hw

Parallel computers, although coming down in price, are not cheap. Furthermore, they require support from programmers who are skilled in parallel computing, a group that earns more than normal programmer. Nonetheless, a major shift has occurred and parallel computing is now standard for many data warehouses.

The basic idea behind parallel computing is quite simple. The classic von Neumann computer architecture is sequential. That is, computations are performed one after the other on a single central processing unit (CPU). Thus, even if two computations are completely independent in terms of the data they use or the computation to be performed, they cannot be handled simultaneously. In parallel computing the situation is different. Two alternative approaches are used:

1. Pieces of the problem are worked on simultaneously by two or more CPUs and the results are then combined.
2. Multiple CPUs are used sequentially (an arrangement called *pipelining*).

Computers with multiple CPUs processing in parallel are divided into three categories (*IBM Dictionary of Computing*):

1. *Fine-grain* parallel computers may use thousands of processors, usually in the range from 1024 to 256,000.
2. *Medium-grain* parallel computers have about 32 to 1024 processors.
3. *Coarse-grain* parallel computers usually have 2 to 16 processors.

Connectivity among processors varies considerably; many have connections only among neighboring processors. Four hardware architectures are available for parallel computing:

1. Shared memory multiprocessors (SMP)
2. Clusters
3. Nonuniform memory access (NUMA)
4. Massively parallel multiprocessors (MPP)

Of these architectures, the two most frequently used are the SMP and MPP arrangements. Clusters are hybrids of the two arrangements. The four architectures are described later in a sidebar.

Parallel computing is required because some data warehouses are exceptionally large. The Data Warehousing Institute's Terabyte Club[2] has many members. The Meta Group (DePompa, 1996) recommended the following server size to accommodate varying capacity requirements:

WAREHOUSE SIZE	SERVER REQUIREMENTS
5-50 GB	Pentium PC > 100 MHz
50-500 GB	SMP machine
>500 GB	SMP or MPP machine

Table 2-1 describes the advantages and disadvantages of the four parallel computing approaches for data warehousing

Serial versus Parallel Loading

Loading the data into the warehouse (Section 2-3) provides an example of the differences between serial and parallel computing. As shown in Figure 2-3, in loading the data, either a serial or a parallel architecture can be used. A serial load allows only a single process (called a *thread*) to perform the entire load function, while a parallel load breaks the task into multiple threads to improve the efficiency and speed of the load function.

The key issue is loading speed, since OLTP systems can be interrupted for only a brief time if they are to remain effective. By dividing the task among processors, parallel computing allows data from various transaction systems to be loaded concurrently. Thus, the window of time required to load data into the warehouse is reduced and the availability of

---

[2] That is, organizations whose data warehouses store more than a terabyte (10^{12}) of data.

Table 2-1: Advantages and Disadvantages of Parallel Computing Architectures

TECHNOLOGY	ADVANTAGES	DISADVANTAGES
SMP	Warehouse performance can be increased by adding CPUs Applications do not have to be architected to run in the SMP environment	Operating system must be architected for multiprocessing Too many CPUs slow performance because of memory bus bottlenecks
Clustering	Improved warehouse performance with each node added to a shared database High availability	Systems administration more complex Database must be architected
NUMA	Warehouse performance improved Applications run unaltered but scale better if multithreaded and tuned to architecture	Operating system must be architected for NUMA Not much experience in commercial environments
MPP	Steep performance increases Single-system view of all shared nodes	Operating system, utilities, tools, and applications must be architected Very expensive

J. Vijayan,"Scaling Up Your Warehouse," *Computerworld*, April 21, 1997, p. 71. Http://www.computerworld.com

Figure 2-3: Serial versus Parallel Loading

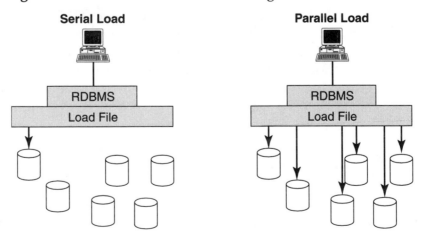

Four Approaches to Parallel Computing

SMP. In an SMP computer, a single memory is shared among all the CPUs, which are typically physically located in a single box. These computers are usually referred to as *shared-everything* machines. They are relatively easy to configure and administer. The CPUs can be Intel or UNIX-based systems. Because they share memory, SMP computers are limited by the memory bus to handle at most a few dozen CUPs. Thus, SMP systems are useful for gigabyte, but not terabyte databases.

MPP. In an MPP computer, each CPU has its own associated memory and the computers are distributed. These computers are usually referred to as *shared-nothing* nodes. A collection of PCs working in parallel would be an MPP computer. MPP systems are more expensive than SMP systems because they usually require more complex software, very fast switching, and scalable interconnect technology, and are more difficult to manage. A key problem in data warehousing is scalability, and here MPP excels. In a data warehouse, the amount of data, the number of users, and the functionality all tend to increase with time. Thus the warehouse must be scalable if it is to have a long, useful lifetime.

Clusters. Clusters are a way of expanding SMP systems. Connecting two or more SMP machines eliminates the single-memory problem. However, the maximum number of SMP machines that can be interconnected without sacrificing speed is currently limited to eight.

NUMA is a hybrid approach between SMP and clustering. NUMA arranges multiple processors in a server in small groups of processors. NUMA allows you to connect more processors in one box than SMP. For example, a 32-processor server can be arranged into eight nodes with four processors each. Currently, one manufacturer (Sequent Computer Systems Inc.) can support up to 252 Intel processors. Like SMP, NUMA provides for scalability, in that additional processors can be added without databases and applications requiring change.

data is increased. ~~ity of data is increased~~. Done properly,[3] a separate thread is created for each subtask that executes in parallel. The parallel computer software optimizes the use of resources by allocating and deallocating resources while processors are in wait mode.

Table Partitioning

The records within a table can be organized to optimize retrieval using one or more of the following partitioning strategies: range partitioning, round-robin partitioning, or expression partitioning.

- In *range partitioning*, record ranges such as A - F may be stored on one disk, H - Q on another, and R - Z on a third disk.

- In *round-robin partitioning,* record storage rotates from disk to disk. For example, three disks are used with records 1, 4, and 7 on disk 1, records 2, 5, and 8 on disk 2 and records 3, 6, and 9 on disk 3.

- In *expression partitioning,* a hashing algorithm is used, for example, to indicate that all "or" portions of an SQL expression are stored in one disk, all "and" portions on another, and the remainder on a third disk.

Architecture Considerations and Challenges

In preceding subsections, the components of a data delivery system were discussed. In this section the data delivery process or pipeline through which data flows is described within the context of the data warehouse's physical architecture. At each phase in the process of moving the data from the transaction system through the data delivery pipe, issues relating to performance, connectivity, and technology are addressed.

---

[3] To avoid contention for CPU, Ram, and other hardware resources, an MPP or SMP architecture may be employed with what is called "dynamic mutithreading." (Christman, 1995).

Loading Data

The first process in the data warehouse pipeline is loading the data from various transaction systems. Data must be identified, scrubbed, and cleaned either prior to loading or during the loading process or both (Section 2-3). At the receiving end, the data warehouse may use various indexing and table partitioning schemes along with dynamic multithreading to send data about the transfer process and other relevant information to the metadata and warehouse files. The data may be loaded "all at once" (initial load) or in a "trickle feed" (periodic updates). The data may be further cleaned, scrubbed, and indexed to facilitate easy access once it reaches the warehouse.

In most cases the warehouse component is a relational DBMS. While the data warehouse may start out small, it can grow exponentially in a short time. Where justifiable, the underlying hardware architecture may use MPP or SMP components to improve performance and scalability of the data warehouse.

In a three-tier architecture, a DSS engine generally requests large amounts of data from the warehouse in response to user queries. The window of time to retrieve this data needs to be within some acceptable threshold since the purpose of on-line analytical processing is defeated if data is not available when needed. The end user may as well revert to batch reports if the information is not available on demand. The response time from the data warehouse to the DSS engine and the bandwidth requirements when transmitting the data must be addressed in the design. If the DSS engine is located at a distant remote site, transmitting large quantities of data would cause traffic congestion. To avoid such bottlenecks, the DSS engine should be placed close to the warehouse database.

Three tiers architecture - network load

In a two-tier architecture, it is possible to have the DSS engine reside on the same platform as the warehouse. However, this arrangement can lead to hardware and processing resource constraints since the loading and storing of warehouse data, and the DSS engine's analysis functions are both resource intensive. In most two-tier environments, the DSS server functions are performed on the client. This approach, of course, causes network traffic bottlenecks. A way around the traffic congestion problem is to consider loading the most frequently used data onto the client during off-peak times for analysis at a later time or to precompute the most frequently asked queries. If the user requirements are not consistent, this solution is not feasible. Adding more hardware resources to the warehouse platform may be the answer. The important thing is to consider the trade-off in increased network traffic versus the need for hardware resources when designing a two-tier architecture. This design consideration raises the issue of whether a two- or three-tier architecture is preferable for a data warehouse.

Two tiers
network vs. hw
load

Three-Tier versus Two-Tier Architectures

A three-tier architecture eliminates the resource constraint issues in a two-tier architecture. Having the processing done by the DSS engine allows the organization to reduce the cost of "fat clients," one that requires more intelligence, processing capability, and storage. The trade-off is the cost of many fat clients versus one relatively expensive server to perform the DSS server functions. The network traffic would consist only of answers for the query being transmitted back to the client. The client may include software to improve the presentation of the answer received from the DSS server; and to manipulate this data further. Data manipulation may include calculations, graphing, and pivoting and rotation to view the data across different dimensions.

three tiers
— fat client vs
servers
— Dependent Dmarts

Another advantage of three-tier architecture is that the DSS engine and specialized databases can be distributed among various departments or business units to function as data marts (see Section 4-3). Data in a preaggregated form (summarized data) relevant to the business unit is transmitted during off-peak hours, perhaps at night, and made available for analysis during the day. This strategy violates one of Codd's 12 rules for OLAP (see Appendix) that only one copy of the database should be maintained.[4] In addition to major improvement in the data distribution process, the cost of data storage decreased steadily as storage technologies improved. Furthermore, the data in the warehouse is nonvolatile. Updates to warehouse data occur only during the periodic loading, which is generally tightly controlled. The chances of data integrity problems in the distribution channel are thus limited. A benefit of having local data marts is reduced network traffic in an enterprise-wide data delivery architecture, especially in an organization with many remote locations. As discussed in Section 3-4, however, care must be taken that the data marts and the main data warehouse contain compatible data.

Conclusions

There is no one architecture or solution that will resolve all the problems of delivering data from the transaction system to the warehouse, the DSS engine, and the client computer to the end user. The delivery system architecture involves a series of trade-off decisions. Organizations must assess their needs against the financial, personnel, and technical resources and make these trade-off decisions in selecting the right physical architecture and the appropriate design for the data warehouse.

---

[4] It can be argued that the experience in the 1970s and 1980s with copy management and database replication issues such as dirty updates, out-of-sync databases, and the cost of data storage, resulted in this rule. In the 1990s, however, the techniques for copy and replication management and data integrity have improved significantly. For detailed descriptions of the copy management and replication processes for enterprise-wide connectivity, see Hackathorn (1993)

2-3 DATA INPUT

In this section we examine the considerations involved in moving data into the warehouse. We begin by describing the steps required to load the data. The input process is more than mechanical loading. First, it requires considering the quality of the data; specifically, the modifications needed to make the data in the warehouse correct and uniform. A second consideration is the level of summarization to be provided. The more levels of summary, the larger the amount of information stored but the easier the data is to use. Summarization is one aspect of the third consideration, the granularity of the data. Granularity refers to the smallest element of data stored in the warehouse and may reflect transactions or some larger level of aggregation. Finally, we consider the flow of data in and through the warehouse.

All of these elements of data input interact strongly with the metadata kept in the warehouse. Metadata is discussed in Section 2-4.

Loading the Data Warehouse

Internal and External data

The information in the data warehouse comes both from internal systems (mostly legacy systems) and from outside the organization. Not all information available in these sources is transferred into the warehouse. Only those items are loaded that are defined in the metadata as belonging in the warehouse.

Data Extraction

Automated data extract systems

Metadata contains rules of translation

In setting up and running a data warehouse, the complexity and resources required for extracting the information from its original sources and moving it to the warehouse are usually underestimated. Because of the large volume of data that has to be moved from the legacy systems to the warehouse, an automated data extract system is used. The metadata (see Section 2-4) contains the rules that define the translation from the original to the data warehouse.

[handwritten margin notes: translation to standard / Cleaning the data.]

Two major problems need to be resolved:

1. Converting data from different systems to a commonly agreed upon meaning and format
2. Cleaning the data to remove incorrect data and anomalies and to fill in missing data

For example, depending on the conventions in the source application, the "year" may be:

- Given by two digits (creating a year 2000 problem)
- Given by four digits,
- Embedded in a Julian calendar, or
- Expressed as an arbitrary number of days since a particular start date.

Furthermore, when the year is unknown, a code may be used to indicate that the data is missing. For example, 99 was often used together with a two-digit year. This choice made the year 2000 problem a year 1999 problem.

The process of data extraction involves the sequence of steps shown in Table 2-2. Note that the exact order in which the steps are performed may vary from warehouse to warehouse, but the function of each of these steps must be performed. In addition to the formal steps of moving data to the warehouse, consideration has to be given to the changing nature of the information. For example, some dimensions, such as product descriptions, may change slowly with time. Here attention has to be paid to make sure that it is possible to modify keys and to keep track of the changes made.

Data Cleaning

Data is recorded repeatedly and often in different ways in an organization. As a result, the same information may be referred to in different way in different places. Data warehouses, with their emphasis on data integrity, require that information be *cleaned* if it is to be uniform.

Table 2-2: Sequence of Steps in Loading the Data Warehouse

STEP	NAME	DISCUSSION OF PROBLEMS
1	Read the legacy data.	The legacy database may require cleaning.
2	Decide what changed.	Moving just the changed items reduces the amount of data that has to be moved; includes both newly obtained transaction information and changes in the legacy system that affect the metadata.
3	Combine separate sources.	A specific type of information may be scattered among several files and must be combined for use in the warehouse.
4	Create load record images.	Involves creating record-by-record images that are complete with data for all fields in a standard format.
5	Migrate data from source to the data warehouse server.	Copying the data to the warehouse could be done earlier or later than this point. Usually, cleaning the data on the source machine is easier than cleaning on the target machine.
6	Create aggregate records.	Aggregate records are summaries that can be obtained by using sorting on one or more attributes.
7	Bulk load with referential integrity.	
8	Process load exceptions.	
9	Index newly loaded records.	
10	Perform quality assurance.	
11	Publish.	

Source: R. Kimball "Mastering Data Extraction," DBMS, June 1996.

Table 2-3, which shows entries into a sales form, illustrates nine of the many ways that data can become non-uniform. Some of the errors result from recording the same type, of information in different ways (e.g., errors 7, 8, and 9). Others are more subtle. Multiple values (error 1) for an item result in the same event being counted multiple times. In the example, sales would be inflated. Multiple database records (error 2) can be created for a single customer because of a name change, an acquisition, a move to a different address, or

Table 2-3: Potential Data Problems

CATEGORY	INFORMATION RECORDED	POTENTIAL PROBLEM
Buyer	Jones James L.	
Contract	3033	1. Different departments record contract with different numbers
Company	James Jones, Inc.	2. Multiple database records for the same company 3. Commercial names combine with personal names
Address 1	JJI	4. Multiple names means query about JJI misses James Jones, Inc.
Address 2	c/o William Green	5. No c/o on customer information screen
Address 3	830 W. 10th St.	
City, state, zip	Los Angeles, CA 90001	6. Different departments use different customer location indicators
Country	USA	
Phone	213-555-3334	
Multinational	Yes	
Web site?	Y	7. Different format for same information
Total order last year	13,550	
Total order year-to-date	8531	
Bonus points last year	200	
Bonus points this year	$300	8. Meaningless information recorded
Overtime, sales	60 days	
Overtime, service	3 months	9. Different units for time

Adapted from: Byte, January 1997, p. 97.

combining personal and business names (e.g., doing business as) (error 3) .

Cleaning data so that it is suitable for the data warehouse requires a series of steps:

Cleaning steps

1. Analyzing the organizational data to find inaccuracies, anomalies, and other problems
2. Transforming the data so that it is accurate and represented consistently
3. Creating *referential integrity*
4. Validating the data
5. Creating metadata (see Section 2-4)
6. Documenting the process for future use

Referential integrity refers to the ability to identify correctly every instance of an object (e.g., product, customer, employee). It results in maintaining consistency of references between two related tables in a relational database. Validity refers to providing and image that is perceived to match reality. Metadata involves describing the data type, format, and meaning of each field.

Checking Validity

Data perceived as no valid then no used

If the data are not perceived to be valid, the information in the data warehouse will be ignored by users. For example, if the warehouse yields values that are very different from those in standard reports, either the warehouse data or the standard reports are not accurate. Managers typically assume that the checks are typically run. These checks include one or more of the following:

Checking validity procedures.

- Uniformity check
- Version check
- Completeness check
- Conformity check
- Drilldown (or genealogy check)

Figures 2-4 and 2-5 show where these validity checks are performed when loading data.

Figure 2-4: Initial Data Loading

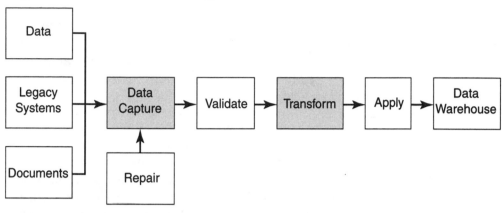

Source: R. Hackathorn "Data Warehouse Credibility Crisis," BYTE, August 1997.

Figure 2-5: Validity Checks after Initial Loading

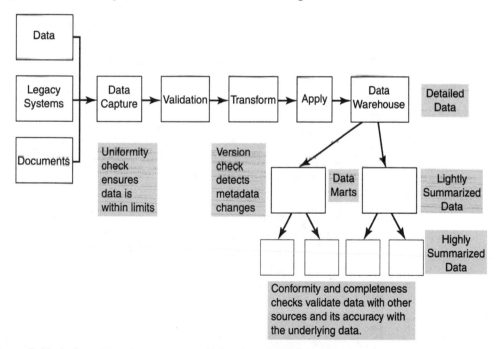

Source: R. Hackathorn "Data Warehouse Credibility Crisis," BYTE, August 1997.

During data capture, *uniformity checks* ensure that the data are within specified limits. *Version checks* are performed when the data is transformed through the use of metadata.

The version check makes sure the format of the original data has not changed. If it has (e.g., because of year 2000 updates, the incoming data now records four digits for year rather than the two digits used previously), the version check detects the change. Even with version checks, it is difficult to catch situations where differences exist across sources. For example, two subsidiaries may have different fiscal years.

Figure 2-5 shows the checks that are performed once the data is in the data warehouse and is being summarized. The figure indicates that the data in the warehouse undergoes a series of summarizations. The summarized data contain such information as totals and averages. To be meaningful, all the components that make up a total or an average have to be available. For example, if only four of the six stores in a region have reported sales, the sum of these four numbers does not reflect the total sales for the region invoked when a user questions the validity of the data. By reviewing the values that went into each summarized number and the rules used to transform the numbers to summary form, the user or the data warehouse specialist can follow the numbers back to their source.

- A *completeness check* makes sure that the summaries are correct and that all values needed to create the summary are included.

- A *conformity check* makes sure that the summarized data are "in the ballpark." That is, during data analysis and reporting, correlations are run between the value reported and previous values for the same number. Sudden changes (e.g., in sales or personnel expense) can indicate either a basic change in the business, analysis errors, or bad data.

- The *genealogy check* or *drilldown*[5] is a trace back to the data source through its various transformations. It is

---

[5] The term *genealogy check* is used by data warehouse specialists. *Drilldown* is the term used by people who work with decision support applications. For our purposes here, the terms are identical.

invoked when a user questions the validity of the data. By reviewing the value that went into each summarized number, the rules used to transform the numbers to summary form, the data warehouse specialist can follow the numbers back to their source.

Summarization

The data warehouse includes data at various levels of summarization. Although it is possible to store all data at the transaction level and summarize upon request, such an approach negates the purpose of storing data in the warehouse for managerial use.

Trade-offs in summarization

The levels of summarization kept in the warehouse are a design choice and require care in selecting. Summarizations involve trade-offs:

- The more levels of summary that are kept, the more storage that is required.
- The more the data is summarized, the faster it is to access.
- The more the data is summarized, the less information the summary contains.
- The level of summarization required by individual users depends on their area of the firm and/or their level in the organization.

A level of summarization becomes a database of its own. Like all databases, once a summary is defined it becomes difficult to add fields or change the structure. A rule of thumb is that the greater the level of summarization, the more the information is used. However, a well-known human phenomenon then enters. People periodically do not trust the summary they see and therefore ask to see more detail. This phenomenon, called "the intuitive statistician," is one reason decision support software typically provide a drilldown capability. Drilldown refers to the ability to click on a number on the screen and see its components. It is also possible to provide a drilldown on other things. For example, a screen might show a map with sales figures in each state. Clicking on the state of Texas, for example, might lead to a display showing the sales in each Texas sales region. Drilldown capability can be provided to several levels of increasing detail.

The usual approach in data warehousing is to store both lightly and highly summarized information, so as to make drilldown quicker. The summaries are updated automatically whenever data is loaded.

Granularity

Granularity refers to the level of detail provided by a data point in the data warehouse. The more detail, the lower the level of granularity Clearly, details of individual transactions serve as the lowest level. For example, if the warehouse is to be used in the grocery business for data mining based on individual items scanned with a bar code reader, such a level of granularity would be appropriate. Unfortunately, because data warehouses contain information over very long periods of time, high-transaction-volume businesses, such as groceries, quickly create very large databases if they maintain this level of granularity for all information.   For decision support applications, where the unit of decision is not at the transaction level, a higher level of granularity may be appropriate.

The choice of granularity is an important design issue because:

- The lower the level of granularity, the larger the amount of data stored in the data warehouse.
- The lower the level of granularity, the greater the level of detail for which queries can be answered.

Thus, the choice of granularity requires trading off volume of data for level of query detail.

A second trade-off is between the level of granularity and the amount of computing power required. For low levels

Handwritten margin notes:
- Definition, Granularity
- For DSS — ↑ granularity
- ↓ granularity
- ↑ amount of data stored
- ↑ level of detail for queries
- ↑ computing power

of granularity, there are large amounts of detailed data. For every query not concerned with that level of granularity, computing power is required to aggregate the information so that answers are presented quickly on the screen. Summarization also reduces the number of indices required.

Thus, the level of granularity affects the detail of the questions that can be answered. For example, suppose you work for an oil company that maintains a credit card system. At the lowest level of granularity, you can find every gas stop that was made by a cardholder and determine whether John Smith stopped in Pasadena on June 12. If only the total sales per month are kept (a higher level of granularity), you can find out how much gas was sold at the Pasadena station in June but not about John Smith's buying habits.

Data Flow

Data warehouses involve three tiers (Section 2-1):

1. Back end for data loading and cleaning
2. The warehouse, which is a database containing both data and metadata
3. Front end for user queries and interaction

These three tiers can result physically in a one-, two-, or three-tier architecture; however, all three tiers are present irrespective of the hardware arrangement. In this section we describe the flow of data into and out of each tier. Figure 2-6 taken from Figure 1-2) shows an overview of the three-tier architecture from a data flow perspective.

Figure 2-6: Overview of Data Flow

The data acquisition software that forms the back end is shown in Figure 2-7. Data initially resides in legacy systems

Figure 2-7: Acquisition Data Flow

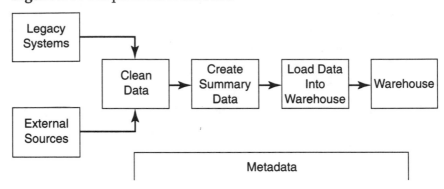

and external sources. Periodically, the data acquisition software is run. The first step is to perform data cleaning so that missing data is identified (and, hopefully, obtained) and so that discrepancies in nomenclature and format changes are taken care of. Then, as part of the backend work, the summarizations to be stored are computed. Some of these summarizations are based on the data being acquired. Others, however, involve updating the summary information kept in the warehouse. For example, for a department store, the summaries may include daily sales totals taken directly from the input data as well as updating the month-to-date and year-to-date sales as well as the average sales per day. The clean data and the summary data are then loaded into the warehouse.

Note that in Figure 2-7, metadata (which is actually stored in the data warehouse) guides the data acquisition process. It contains the rules for cleaning and summarizing the data and for determining where the data is to be loaded into the warehouse.

The organization of the data in the warehouse is shown in Figure 2-8. The warehouse contains data at different levels of detail. The old detail data is typically archived but retrievable. Physically it may be kept off-line, for example, on tapes that are mounted on request. The current detail data as well as data summarized at various levels are stored in the warehouse, together with the metadata.

[handwritten margin notes: meta data guides data acquisition]

[handwritten margin notes: DW - different levels of detail - old data is archived.]

Figure 2-8. Organization of Data in the Warehouse

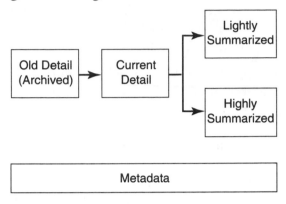

The user's frontend view of the warehouse is shown in Figure 2-9. Here the user working on a decision support problem works at a PC and directs queries at the warehouse through the metadata. The metadata also helps the user identify what information is available in the warehouse. The responses to the queries again flow through the metadata and become visible on the user's screen.

[handwritten margin note: Flow between users and DW through Metadata.]

Figure 2-9: User Software

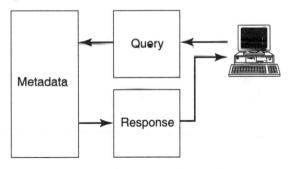

2-4 METADATA

[handwritten margin note: Metadata for users' understanding]

Metadata is data about data. A data warehouse requires a good metadata system so that the user understand's how the data was created and what it means. Although in concept it should be a simple matter to keep track of what is in the warehouse, in practice, creating the metadata is one of the most difficult of design tasks. The metadata issue is particularly acute for heterogeneous shops with hardware and software from a number of vendors.

For retrieve and navigate the information

Metadata provides the user with a way to retrieve the information in the warehouse. Because of the large amount of data it contains, users require the equivalent of a library catalog to navigate through the warehouse. The metadata provides the information needed for navigation.

Organizing the Metadata

Conceptually (and occasionally, physically) the metadata is organized into three components:

Components of Metadata.

COMPONENT	CONTAINS	USER
Technical directory	Information about the data	Data warehouse administrator
Business Directory	User's perspective on the data	End user
Information Navigator	Access to the business directory and the warehouse data	End user

Figure 2-10 shows how these components tie together. Of the three components, the technical directory is represented most strongly in existing implementations. Elements of the other two components are beginning to be implemented. In part, the emphasis on the technical directory comes from the needs of the warehouse creators and administrators to know what is included in the warehouse. The focus on end users' needs is the next direction for development.

Figure 2-10: Organization of the Metadata

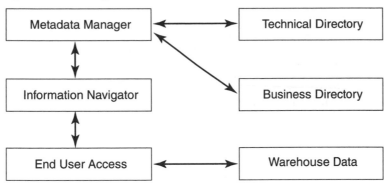

Technical Directory

—Sources
—transforma-
* tion rules*

The information in the technical directory tells the warehouse administrator about both the sources of the data and how the data is organized in the warehouse. It also explains the rules used to clean the data and to transform it for business use. Specifically, for each piece of data in the warehouse, the technical dictionary contains the information listed in Table 2-4.

Note that the source data (inputs) and the target data (what is in the warehouse) are often different and the metadata must keep track of both. For example, one source may use M,F for Male or Female, another 1,2, and a third 0,1, while the warehouse standardizes on 0,1.

Note too that metadata includes sections of the data interface program. Because data elements are frequently mixed from different sources to obtain the most accurate information possible, the metadata also contains information about how the data interfaces from these sources are integrated into the value presented to the user.

Business Directory

The technical directory, being oriented to the mechanics of the warehouse, does not meet the needs of end users to understand what is in the warehouse from a business perspective. The business directory should include:

Table 2-4: Contents of the Technical Dictionary

Data sources	File name and type (i.e., format) How The value is defined in the source (and aliases) When the data was created What system it came from Who owns the data Who is the steward of the data Which users are authorized to access the data Schema of the operational database
Data targets (i.e., the warehouse)	Field name and type How the value is defined in the warehouse (and aliases) Where the data is located in the warehouse Version Last update Frequency of update Who owns the data Who has access to the data Schema of the data in the warehouse End user access patterns
Cleanup rules	Record and field restructuring performed The mapping between data elements in the original data source(s) and the warehouse Rules used to supply missing field values Rules for data integrity Rules for consistency checking
Transformation rules	How time is to be recorded Algorithms (business rules) to determine derived values How data summaries are created
Mappings	Rules for filtering data and for merging data from different fields and sources

Handwritten margin notes:

Business directory
1. Business terms
2. Match between business and technical terms
3. Source, rules & date
4. data owner
5. Predefined reports & queries
6. Security information

1. The business terms used to describe the data
2. The technical names (and aliases) corresponding to the business terms that can be used to access the data
3. The source of the data, the rules used to derive it, and the date it was created

It should also contain:

1. Information on how to contact the data owner
2. Lists of predefined reports and queries available
3. Security information (who is authorized to access)

Note that some of this information overlaps the technical directory. However, it approaches the information from a different point of view. The warehouse administrator can usually create this directory by working with end users.

Information Navigator

For the IT professional involved in data warehousing, creating and maintaining metadata are just two of many functions performed. For DSS analysts and other users, the contents of the metadata and the ability to navigate it are central and immediate to their job. The information navigator provides the interface that allows the user to access the business directory and the warehouse itself. It provides the following capabilities to the end user:

1. Accessing and drilling down through the business directory
2. Creating new data by querying the warehouse
3. Requesting new data from the warehouse administrator
4. Transferring data from the warehouse to data marts or other users
5. Interfacing to warehouse data access tools.

For example, the business directory should be arranged so that it groups metadata into frequently used subject areas and so that it allows the end users to navigate the metadata though drilldown.

The Metadata Interchange Coalition

The Metadata Interchange Coalition was established in July 1995 to create standards for metadata, particularly for defining specifications for access and interchange of metadata among different data management tools. The members of the coalition include most (but not all) the major firms in the data warehouse business. The coalition has proposed a metadata interchange format (MIF). The coalition was originally facilitated by the Meta Group, although they are no longer involved formally.

2-5 DATA MODELING

A model is an abstraction of reality. Data modeling involves creating an actual database design from one or more models. In this section we discuss the modeling process, and in the subsections that follow, we describe the two data models used most often in data warehousing for OLAP: relational databases and multidimensional databases.[6]

The steps in creating a data model are:

steps for data modeling

1. Develop a conceptual model of the business activity or process to be supported by a database
2. Use this high-level model to create a *logical model* of the data. The logical model provides much more detail but is still independent of the implementation.
3. Transform the logical model into a detailed physical model which implements the database. The physical model is called a *schema*.

For a new database, the first step, defining the business activity or process, is often the most difficult and longest. It is a requirements definition stage. It involves data gathering (including detailed conversations with potential users) and understanding the business processes to be supported.

The conceptual model in OLTP is organized around entities (e.g., product, engineer), relationships (e.g., product engineer is to design) , and state transitions (e.g., from engineer to manufacturing supervisor). As a result, by the time such a conceptual model is implemented as a relational data base, it may contain hundreds of tables. In a data warehouse, the conceptual model is based on facts, dimensions, hierarchies, and sparseness. The information in a data warehouse is

DW conceptual model.

---

[6] We will define these terms later.

used to search through, summarize, and organize data for analysis. As a result, the design of the database is much simpler and hence much easier for users to understand.

The data warehouse information supports the needs of knowledge workers for analysis and reporting. It therefore has the following characteristics:

DW information characteristics

- Information is viewed in terms of a "time slice" rather than individual transactions.

- Information is presented in a globally consistent view of the enterprise. For example, there is only one chart of accounts.

- Information presents the big picture (e.g., will we make a profit?) rather than the details of a transaction (e.g., where is my shipment?)

The objective of data modeling is to convert business concepts into a form that can be developed into a physical data structure. Two kinds of data models used in data warehousing are:

1. A logical model
2. A dimensional business model

A logical model, which is a traditional form of data modeling, is sometimes (but not always) used in data warehouse development. Whether a logical model is created or not often depends upon whether such models are used customarily by the IS organization. For example, some organizations do not maintain a corporate data model whereas other organizations are heavily involved in creating and maintaining a data model. While helpful, creating a logical model is not a necessary condition for developing a data warehouse.

not needed for the whole organization

A logical model of the entire enterprise can be quite time consuming to create. With the typical changes that go on in enterprises today, by the time such a model is ready, it will tend to be obsolete. Therefore, it is usually appropriate not to attempt to develop a corporate data model for the entire enterprise at the start of a data warehouse project.

Most logical data models focus on current information for on-line transaction processing. As a result, they are two-dimensional and present a fully normalized data design. Data warehouses for decision support; however, always incorporate time as a third dimension so that the information can show trends over time. Time is often only one of many added dimensions. Therefore, the logical design requires some degree of denormalization.

dimensional view reflects users' thinking

The dimensional business model reflects the way the users think about their information. Users usually know:

1. What they want quantitative information about
2. The variables (and dimensions) in which they examine information
3. The relationships among the variables

That is, the users have a model of the business. The data warehouse should reflect this model in the way information can be retrieved by users from the system.

Models are created at increasing levels of complexity. There may be a top-level model that is as simple as the one shown in Figure 2-11, which dislays three kinds of information: sales, costs, and inventory. Each of these facts is described in terms of four dimensions associated with each item: time, product, logistics channel, and location. Note that even this simple model is multidimensional. Once a top-level model is drawn (and these models are typically graphical), the process is repeated at increasing levels of detail.

An important issue is how to represent the multidimensionality. Relational data tables for databases are two-dimensional. Hence other means must be used to represent additional dimensions. The two most common ones, MOLAP and ROLAP, are discussed below.

Figure 2-11: A Multidimensional Business Model

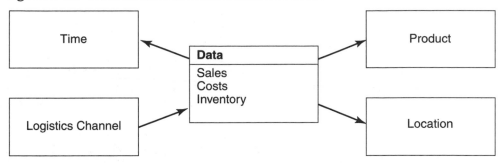

Gathering Requirements for Use in the Data Model

defining
requirements

The data model is created from verbal inputs from users as well as reports, requests of IT, spreadsheets, and PC and mainframe databases. It depends on inputs from users. Capturing requirements verbally is an art in itself. Some people go from one user to another and then aggregate the information obtained. A preferred method is to use facilitation. Gathering data requirements is discussed further in Chapter 5.

Data Dimensions

each dimension
– one variable
time is always
a dimension

The data in a warehouse has multiple dimensions. A dimension represents one variable. The data warehouse always includes time as a dimension, but has many others. For example, sales data might include at least these five dimensions:

1. Time
2. Product
3. Customer
4. Salesperson
5. Sales

Table 2-5 shows a sample of the data for these five dimensions. In the table a numerical data point reports the actual sales of Whammos to Alpha Corporation by Joe Jones in January ($300,000) and another Jones' sales quota under these conditions ($350,000).

Table 2-5: Sample Data

| | | | | Sales | |
Time	Product	Customer	Sales-person	Sales quota	Actual Sales
Jan.	Whammos	Alpha	Jones	300	350
Jan.	Nolos	Gamma	Jones	200	120
Jan.	Softies	Delta	Green	50	75
Feb.	Punchos	Beta	Jones	200	150
Feb.	Whammos	Alpha	Jones	250	220
Feb.	Softies	Delta	Green	80	60
Mar.	Whammos	Alpha	Jones	350	425
Mar.	Punchos	Beta	Jones	250	275
Mar.	Softies	Delta	Green	70	75

Note: Shading in headings denotes dimensions.

Multidimensionality
- Multidimensional
- Relational

Multidimensional data can be represented in two ways:

1. In a multidimensional database.
2. In a relational database as a set of two-dimensional tables

Either of these two approaches can be used to support on-line analytic processing (OLAP), which is discussed in detail in Chapter 4. The two approaches are named:

- **MOLAP:** multidimensional on-line analytic processing
- **ROLAP**: relational on-line analytic processing.

The two approaches have fierce loyalists. They are intertwined with the database and data warehousing markets, where vendors present either a MOLAP or a ROLAP solution. In the following subsections we discuss MOLAP and ROLAP and compare the two approaches.

In either MOLAP or ROLAP warehouses, users perform analyses of the data by selecting the dimensions of interest to them and directing a query. Some simple ones might be:

- "Tell me how much revenue Jones generated in January from all the products he sells?"
- "How many Whammos did the company sell in the central region in the first quarter compared to our sales quotas?"

Each of these queries requires a different "slice" of the data. In the first case, since the data are recorded by month, the result can be obtained directly. In the second case two new concepts are introduced: the central region and the first quarter. The software must be able to recognize which customers are in the central region and be able to add data for January through March. This can be done if rules exist defining which customer is in which region and which combinations of months constitute a quarter. The sidebar shows the answers to the two questions.

Solutions To Sample Queries

"How much revenue did Jones generate in January? "

Solution: 350 + 120 = 370

"How many Whammos were sold in the central region in the first quarter compared to our sales quotas?"

Solution:
First quarter = January + February + March
Central = Alpha + Gamma
Sales = 350 + 120 + 220 + 425 = 1115
Quota = 300 + 200 + 250 + 300 = 1050
Net sales above quota = sales - quota = 1115 -1050 = 65

Multidimensional OLAP

Clearly, both the data and the questions asked of it can become complex quite quickly as the number of dimensions increases. Since drawing four or more dimensions is difficult, consider only three of the dimensions [time (month), salesperson, and actual sales by salesperson] in Table 2-5. As shown in Figure 2-12, these three dimensions generate a cube. Each cell represents the number that applies to that intersection of the cube.

Figure 2-12: Three-Dimensional Cube

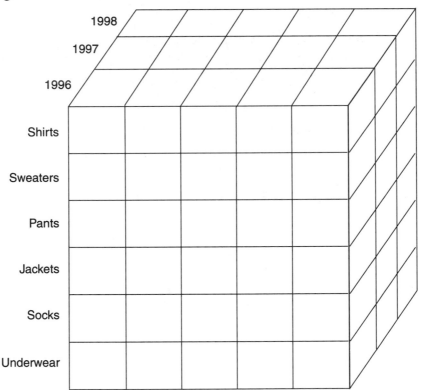

↑ variables ↑ dimensions
↑ size

Data cubes become *n*-dimensional (i.e., hypercubes) as more variables are added. They can become very large very fast because a separate cell must be available for each combination of data. For the data in Table 2-5, the number of cells required in the five-dimensional cube would be

3 months x 4 products x 4 customers x 2 salespersons x 2 sales

= 192 cells

Sparse data usually compresed.

where the sales values represents the columns for sales and quotas. Yet, there are only 9 records. That is, not every combination is filled in. The data are "sparse." Usually, a multidimensional database uses some form of compression to take care of sparse data.

Advantages

— More intuitive command

— faster response

From the point of view of the decision support analyst, the multidimensional model provides more intuitive commands for performing drilldown and other analytic operations. The reason is that data is physically transformed and stored in the cube structure according to the end-user's vocabulary of the business. In short, the user can concentrate on the business when creating a query rather than on the computer, which is required in SQL queries. In general, for data within the size limits (see below), MOLAP tends to be faster than ROLAP.

A single cube holds the answers to a number of requests. If preprocessing is done in batch mode, data does not have to be aggregated in real time as it does in normalized relational data models. As a result, consistent response time is achieved.

Limitations

- Need learning
- No standard query language
- No OBDC
- Constrained in scalability and size

The biggest limitation on MOLAP is that it is a new and expensive technology that must be learned by both end users and IS. It also has to be integrated into the organization's computing environment. There is no current standard for multidimensional database queries such as SQL for relational data bases. However, the work of the OLAP Council may overcome this limitation.

Similarly, the databases have proprietary application programming interfaces (API) and do not provide access through OBDC (open database connectivity). Other limitations include scalability and database size. The conventional wisdom is that multidimensional databases are limited to the order of hundreds of gigabytes. Extension to terabyte data-bases is expected but was not available in late 1997.

Data Transfer

MOLAP best aggregated
ROLAP best raw
Have both
transfer From
ROLAP to MOLAP

Multidimensional databases are at their best when storing and analyzing aggregated rather than raw data, where relational databases excel. To make use of this strength, it is necessary to move selected raw data in aggregated form from relational databases into multidimensional ones. This transfer has to be performed periodically because the large amounts of data and the multiplicity of dimensions result in long transfer times.

Operational Considerations

Figure 2-13 shows a typical MOLAP client/server architecture. The multidimensional database contains the data cube created within predefined dimensions. Keeping the data cube in memory provides faster response time but makes the MDDB use more resources (memory, storage, and processor) than in a relational database. The server receives data requests from end users and converts them into requests that are passed to the database. The GUI (graphical user interface) allows users to request data from the server.

Figure 2-13: MOLAP Client/Server Architecture

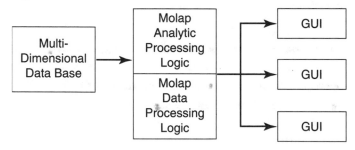

ROLAP

In their original article on OLAP, Codd and associates (1993), argued that relational databases would be replaced by multidimensional databases primarily because SQL queries for decision support were bringing transaction processes to their knees. The relational database vendors took this finding as a challenge and developed relational OLAP, or ROLAP, a modified form of relational data base specifically designed for OLAP[7]. While generally slower than MOLAP, ROLAP has the further advantage that it can be scaled to handle terabyte-sized data warehouses.

Most firms have:

- A large inventory of legacy relational databases
- Software licenses for relational databases
- Skilled programmers and database administrators of such databases

Thus, they are more familiar with relational databases and hence are more likely to adopt ROLAP than MOLAP.

Star Schema

Although still working with two-dimensional tables, ROLAP provides a different organization of the data. Table 2-5 showed a typical relational database table. ROLAP, using a *star schema*, reorganizes the information into multiple tables, called a *fact table* and *dimension tables*. The *fact table* contains the actual numbers. The *dimension tables* contain pointers to where the data are in the fact table. In terms of Table 2-5, the two columns of sales information provide the data for the fact table and the rest of the columns form separate dimension tables.

Figure 2-14 illustrates how Table 2-5 converts into the fact and dimension tables of the star schema. Note that the fact table is long and skinny in shape and the dimension

---

[7] Vendors of multidimensional products sometimes have fun by referring to ROLAP as *slowlap*.

tables tend to be short. In the dimension tables in Figure 2-14, the shaded elements indicate the type of information stored in each table (i.e., the key). A dimension table has a single key. The primary keys for the fact table consist of the keys for each of the dimension tables. Each dimension table contains, in addition to the names of the variables which are shown, the rows in the fact table that correspond to those variables. For example, Jan. has rows 1, 2, 3 associated with it. Punchos and customer Beta are both associated with rows 4 and 8. Similarly, Jones has rows 1, 2, 4, 5, 7, and 8 and Sales quota is shown in column 5.

When a query asks:

What was Jones' total sales quota for Punchos in February and March combined?

the system looks for the intersection of Jones, sales quota, Punchos, February, and March and finds it is column 5, rows 4 and 8, and adds up the numbers 200 and 250 to obtain a result of 450.

Figure 2-14: Fact and Dimension Tables

TIME
January
February
March

PRODUCT
Whammos
Nolos
Punchos
Softies

FACT TABLE		
TIME		
PRODUCT		
CUSTOMER		
SALESPERSON		
SALES		
	300	350
	200	120
	50	75
	200	150
	250	220
	80	60
	350	425
	250	375
	70	75

CUSTOMER
Alpha
Beta
Gamma
Delta

SALES
Quota
Actual

SALES PERSON
Jones
Green

Snowflake Schema

The star schema can be limiting from the point of view of the database designer. A more sophisticated alternative in this case is the *snowflake schema*. In the snowflake schema, the fact table is the same as in the star schema. However, the dimension tables are stored in the third normal form. This approach results in a larger number of tables since specific items become keys. For example, suppose that customer Beta has three divisions named Rho, Sigma, and Tau. The customer dimension table would then be shown as two tables to take care of the many-to-one relationship in the hierarchy.

In general, in a snowflake schema, each many-to-one relationship is shown as a separate table. Kimball (1996) recommends against the snowflake schema, arguing that while it may be satisfying to the designers, it makes browsing the data more difficult for the end user. Furthermore, he shows that because dimension tables are small relative to the fact table, there is little effect on storage requirements.

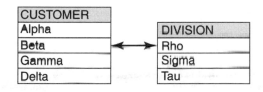

CUSTOMER		DIVISION
Alpha		
Beta	←→	Rho
Gamma		Sigma
Delta		Tau

Storage Requirements

The star and snowflake schemas use the sparseness of data to reduce the amount of storage needed. Although the potential number of cells explodes exponentially as the number of dimensions and the number of values associated with each dimension increases, in practice the actual cells required in the star schema are only a small fraction of these. Values such as 1% or 0.5% (referred to as 99% and 99.5% sparse) are not uncommon. The star schema achieves these numbers by not creating records for invalid combinations.

Handwritten margin notes:

Similar to star but dimension tables are in the third normal for.

Kimball's recommendation against snowflake. harder data browsing little effect on storage

use the sparseness of data to reduce the amount of storage needed

Operational Considerations

Figure 2-15 shows (the a) typical ROLAP three-tier client/server architecture. The ROLAP database (RDBMS) contains the data accessible in a star schema. The server, which contains the analytic and the database logic, receives queries from end users and converts them to the complex SQL queries requiredfor data warehouse access. The front end provides the GUI for the client's computer. It passes the requests for information to the server and receives replies from the server which it formats for presentation to the user.

Figure 2-15: Typical ROLAP Three-Tier Architecture

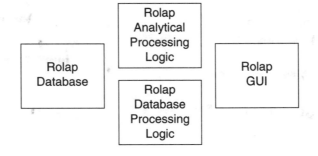

Indexing

Indexes for faster response time.

Indexing techniques are used in ROLAP implementations as a way to speed up the retrieval process for decision support queries. Popular techniques are the bit-mapped (also called bit vector) index and the join index. These indexes differ from those used with B-trees and hashes that are popular in conventional relational databases.

Bit-mapped indexes offer the advantage of keeping the index as small as possible. For example, if one column of a million-row database indicates gender by M or F, replacing these two possible values with 0 and 1 results in a savings. For a million records, this corresponds to approximately 125 kb, a small index by present standards. Comparison and join operations become binary arithmetic, which increases query speed. As the number of bits required to represent the number of possible values (e.g., 8 bits are needed for 256 values), the size of the index grows, reducing the value of the bit mapping. Bit mapping is generally used when the cardinality of the data (i.e., the number of possible values) is small.

Join indexes, sometimes implemented as B-trees, map the column values of the internal identifiers of rows in multiple relational tables. That is, join indexes locate the rows of one or more tables by arbitrary column values in another table. Because they are read-only indexes, they can be used in data warehouses, where values do not change over time. Of course, the indexes have to be recalculated when the warehouse is reloaded for updating.

Bit-maps and join indexes are relatively new ideas. They are needed to deal with the complexity of the queries usually encountered in decision support. Older indexing schemes tend to be larger and more complex, resulting in unacceptably long update cycles.

Performance in data warehouses is also improved if the software includes an index building process. These processes include:

- Incremental indexing, in which the existing indexes rather than the base tables are used as a starting point
- Parallelization

2-6 USER INTERFACE

importance of the interface

The human interface is important in data warehouse design because to the user, the system *is* the interface. If the interface is difficult to use or is unfamiliar, the systems it supports will not be used. A warehouse that is not used quickly becomes a failure.

interface use what is available.

The human interface selected for a data warehouse generally follows the interfaces available to users in an organization. Thus, an organization operating, for example, in Windows 3.1 or Windows 95 will provide the same interface for warehouse access. Where a existing decision support system or executive information system exists and is being augmented by putting the data into a warehouse, the existing high-quality interfaces may be kept because users are familiar with using them. As discussed in Section 5-4, because many organizations provide a browser interface for Internet or intranet access and because the browser interface is compatible with exploring complex databases, the browser interface has become popular for data warehouse use.

The three key questions about the interface delineated by Bennett (1983) for decision support systems apply to the data warehouse as well:

1. What do users see?
2. What do users have to know about what they see?
3. What can users do about what they see?

The first question refers to design decisions on what information is made available to users and to the way that information is displayed. This decision interacts with the second question because what information is displayed and how it is displayed affects what the user has to know about what the user sees. The third question refers to actions the user can take based on what they see. For example, one action is to drill down in the data presented; another is to launch a new query.

Overall, the trend is toward providing users with a browser interface. The reason is simple. With the popularity of the Internet, most users are experienced with this interface. It is simpler and less costly (in terms of training and support) to standardize than to introduce another look and feel. This trend toward the Web browser has reached the point where all, or almost all vendors provide this interface.

Chapter
3

Building and Maintaining a Data Warehouse

3-1 WHY BUILD A DATA WAREHOUSE

A data warehouse is typically constructed because a business has one or more of the following three needs:

Operational objectives

- *Creating a single version of the* "truth." Users need to find accurate, pertinent information for the analyses they do and the reports they write. A basic idea in the warehouse is that it contains information that everyone agrees is correct. A major savings results from people not spending endless hours in meetings and in discussions trying to decide what is the "correct" or "official" data.

- *Automating data collection and updating.* In most firms, data elements are stored in a variety of data structures and platforms. The data warehouse automates the collection and updating of data and makes the data conform to a single set of standards.

- *Off-loading analysis and reporting functions.* The efficiency of on-line transaction processing systems (OLTP) is reduced when they are also used for analysis and for reporting. By creating a separate data warehouse, the OLTP system is not interrupted, and hence its performance is not degraded by management and analyst queries.

The single truth is a priority of business units. Off-loading analysis is an information systems group priority in maintaining service levels. Automating data acquisition is a priority for both the business unit (which does not want to waste resources in gathering data) and information systems.

Although automating data collection and updating functions, off-loading analysis and reporting functions, and creating a single version of the truth are all good micro-objectives, given the size of the investment in a data warehouse, the issue a company faces is whether the investment is worthwhile at a macro level. That is, does the creation of a warehouse serve the strategic needs of the firm?

Needs strategic objectives

Strategic Use of Data Warehousing[1]

The decision whether to undertake a warehouse project at all is intertwined with the decision of whether to undertake a full-scale warehouse for the enterprise or to begin at a smaller level, such as a data mart. The purpose of this section is to explore the decision from the point of view of the organization's strategy. To do so, we create a *strategic grid* and indicate how this grid can be used in the decision process. The strategic grid is the result of analyzing 15 successful data warehouse implementations and of applying Porter and Millar's value chain (Porter and Millar, 1985).

Basic Questions

The basic questions are:

1. Will a data warehouse be beneficial for the organization as a whole or for one of its functional units?
2. What organizational conditions suggest promise for the data warehouse project?

---

[1] We are indebted to Y. T. Park for the concepts in this subsection. Much of this material originally appeared in Park (1997).

To explore this issue, Park (1997) considered 15 data warehouse cases. In five of them, he interviewed people in the firms involved directly; in the rest he used information available in the trade literature. The industries of the 15 cases are listed in Table 3-1. The firms included British Airways, Visa, Sumitomo Bank, Prudential, Wal-Mart, and GTE.

Table 3-1: Industries Providing Data Warehouse Cases

Airline	Investment
Apparel	Personal care
Banking (2)	Public sector
Credit card (2)	Retail (2)
Health care	Steel
Insurance	Telecommunications

Source: Y.T. Park, "Strategic Uses of Data Warehouses: An Organization's Suitability for Data Warehousing" *Journal of Data Warehousing*, Vol. 2, No. 1, January 1997.

Simplified Porter/Millar Value Chain

Figure 3-1 shows a simplified form of the Porter/Millar value chain. The chain indicates where value is added in bringing product to the customer. The chain includes product development, manufacturing, distribution, and marketing. The figure shows which industries used the warehouse to accomplish tasks along the chain. It is clear from the figure that the data warehouse is used for applications in each element along the chain. Which element is used depends on the industry. Note that data warehousing is most used in marketing where data provide trend analysis, buying patterns, and sales promotions. Table 3-2 describes representative companies' data warehouse experience.

Figure 3-1: Simplified Porter/Millar Chain

Product Development	Manufacturing	Distribution	Marketing
Airline	Airline	Apparel	Airline
Banking	Banking	Personal Care	Apparel
Investment	Health Care	Retail	Banking
Insurance	Investment		Credit Card
Telecom	Insurance		Investment
	Public Sector		Personal Care
	Steel		Retail
			Telecom

Source: Y.T. Park, "Strategic Uses of Data Warehouses: An Organization's Suitability for Data Warehousing" *Journal of Data Warehousing*, Vol. 2, No. 1, January 1997.

Table 3-2: Data Warehouse Experience of Representative Firms

AIRLINE INDUSTRY- British Air/US Air British Air built 200 GB warehouse for strategic IS Used to measure profitability, fleet deployment US Air tried to do data mining on frequent flier program off its OLTP Failed because OLTP system slowed down Created warehouse and solved problem	**STEEL INDUSTRY- Bethlehem Steel** Tracked thousands of variables but in different format; could not do analysis Data warehouse provides integrated operational data needed to maintain quality consistency Could find patterns in production that led to high-quality steel
PUBLIC SECTOR- DOD Data Center Built warehouse based on Pilot Software Used for executive information -environmental costs by state -transportation training, performance -foreign investments in U.S. firms Also used for access to internal and external data sources from legacy systems	**HEALTH CARE- Piedmont Hospital** 500-bed hospital in Atlanta 20 GB data warehouse for financial data, patient information Used by 40 managers to determine cost and effectiveness of treatments Data mining showed one surgeon's operating costs to be 20 - 30% higher because of OR supplies Used data in formulating bids for corporate accounts
BANKING INDUSTRY- Chase Manhattan Chase Manhattan built 500 GB data warehouse to support $10B credit card portfolio Manages 22 million records on 15M accounts on 1 database rather than 54 Using parallel computing, expect to reduce annual cost for credit card decisions from $18M/year to $4M/year	

The following are examples of strategic uses in product development and distribution:

Product development

Banking	Customer service
Credit card	New services for a fee
Insurance	Risk management
Telecom	New service promotions

Distribution

Apparel	Replenishment
Distribution	Distribution decision
Retail	Optimal distribution channel

Strategic Grid

Analysis of these results leads to a 2x2 strategic grid, similar in form to the famous Boston Consulting Group grid. As shown in Figure 3-2, the dimensions of this grid are:

- The intensity (number of transactions and frequency of occurrence) of the transaction data

- The strategic impact of the data warehouse

Figure 3-2: Location of Firms Studied on the Strategic Grid

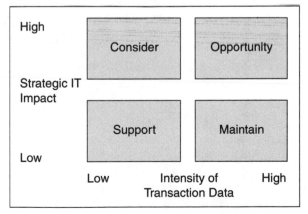

Source: Y.T. Park, "Strategic Uses of Data Warehouses: An Organization's Suitability for Data Warehousing" *Journal of Data Warehousing*, Vol. 2, No. 1, January 1997.

The four quadrants of the grid have been named *opportunity, consider, maintain*, and *support*, where these quadrant names are in decreasing order of the strategic importance of the data warehouse.

The *opportunity* quadrant includes firms where data warehouses can make a considerable difference. Typical characteristics include:

- There is a large volume of transaction data.
- Information systems are vital to business success.
- The information is used to support the relationship with the customer.
- It is possible to develop new information services through the warehouse.

Industries in which IS is vital to business success include banking, credit cards, retail, and telecommunications.

Firms in the *consider* quadrant are characterized by lower data intensity but data still has high impact. As a result, information systems play a strategic role in organizational success. Because of the lower data intensity, these firms may not need a full data warehouse, but can operate (at least initially) with a data mart. The data mart allows the firms to gain insights into their business while providing them with the experience needed to decide whether to upgrade to the warehouse.

The *maintain* quadrant is the diametric opposite of the consider quadrant. Here the data intensity is high but the strategic use of information technology is low. If a firm in the quadrant wants to maintain its current position in the market, it may want to consider data warehousing. The data warehouse allows the firm to gain value from the large amount of data it generates by providing insight into its operations.

Finally, in the *support* quadrant, typical firms have small numbers of transactions and make relatively little strategic use of information systems. As a result, the value added by the data warehouse is small.

Figure 3-3: Placement of Firms in Industries Studied on the Strategic Grid

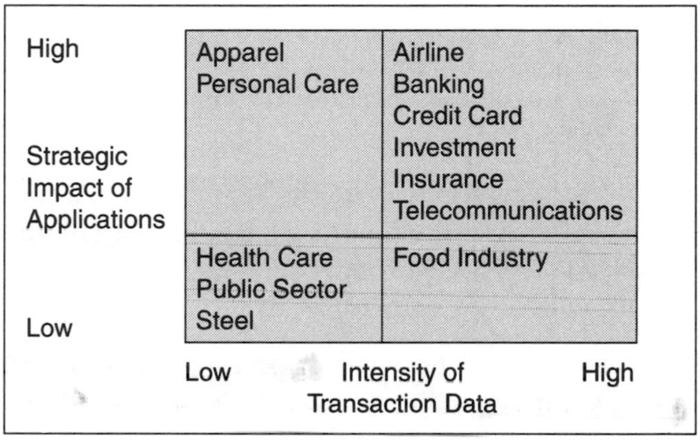

High	Apparel Personal Care	Airline Banking Credit Card Investment Insurance Telecommunications
Strategic Impact of Applications		
Low	Health Care Public Sector Steel	Food Industry

Low   Intensity of   High
Transaction Data

Source: Y.T. Park, "Strategic Uses of Data Warehouses: An Organization's Suitability for Data Warehousing" *Journal of Data Warehousing*, Vol. 2, No. 1, January 1997.

Limitations

The strategic grid was developed by considering only two variables (transaction intensity and strategic impact) for a sample of convenience. The data was obtained both by interview and from the published literature. The size and the nature of the organizations varied. The transaction intensity and the strategic impact were not based on quantitative measures; they are in the opinion of Mr. Park, who developed the grid. Despite these limitations, the logic of the grid appears compelling and allows senior managers to begin the process of assessing the strategic value of data warehousing for their firm.

Corporate Information Viewpoint[2]

The previous discussion took a strategic view of the data warehouse decision. An alternative is to take an information viewpoint. Conventional wisdom argues that more information is better. It is argued that more information results in:

- Better cost management
- Improved risk management
- Improved productivity
- Better customer management

Managers gain benefits from data warehouse information at the operational and tactical levels. Historical trends are used in decision support. Scenarios based on information support new strategic ideas.

However, there are pitfalls associated with corporate information available in a data warehouse:

Playing	using data to substitute for thought.
Price	creating a data warehouse is expensive.
People	managers lose instinctive decision skills.
Data mapping	making sure the data is clean.
Path finding	requires metadata to find the information.
Politics	groups need to agree what the data is and what data is to be recorded.
Security	deciding who has a need to know and making sure that operational systems are not compromised.
Privacy	for individuals and customers.
Paradigms	the decision on which data is stored depends on the paradigm of the organization. Data is "within the box."

Given these benefits and costs, a series of questions need to be resolved:

---

[2] This section is based on McKeen and Smith (1996)

1. Will the value received from the warehouse be greater or equal to that received from some other method of dealing with data?
2. Can users really leverage the information, or will they just play?
3. Do managers recognize the limits of data for strategy formulation?
4. Will the benefits outweigh the not inconsiderable costs of added hardware, software, and staff time?

Assuming that these questions are resolved positively, you would choose the data warehouse approach, provided that:

Conditions to install a DW

- You have a senior management mandate to proceed.
- You have support of a disciplined group of users.
- You are willing to invest the time and money (particularly, compared to alternative uses).
- You expect to reap benefits if the data are provided.
- The data will be used to implement corporate strategies.

These reasons for selecting the warehouse approach form a logical "and." That is, they must all be true for the implementation decision to be positive.

3-2 ORGANIZING FOR THE PROJECT

Having decided to create a data warehouse, the next step is to organize for what is usually a very large project. All the principles of project management apply. Critical success factors must be determined. A project leader must be chosen. A project plan must be developed, including allocation of funds, schedules, deliverables, and more. Staff must be assigned. In this section we discuss each of these topics.

Critical Success Factors[3]

Definition CSF

Critical success factors is a term introduced by Rockart (e.g., Rockart and Bullen, 1986) to refer to those things that must go right if an undertaking is to succeed. The critical success factors for data warehouses designed for decision support include the following:

1. *Set specific, achievable, and measurable goals.* This factor, while simple, straightforward, and applicable to any project, is particularly important for data warehouses. Being large projects, warehouses tend to suffer from "scope creep." Large sums of money are available. Users define new requirements as the project progresses. Additional users come on board, adding to the requirements. While each separate request for increasing scope may be valid, the sum of these requests leads to projects that are late and over budget. Thus, managing expectations and keeping the goals specific, achievable, and measurable helps ensure that the completed warehouse will be used by its intended audience.

2. *Involve everyone with a stake in the warehouse throughout the process.* This factor is linked with the preceding one. The stakeholders in a data warehouse come from throughout the organization and include business analysts and other users, sponsoring business executives, and IT. All of these people should be involved from the start and be kept informed of progress as the project proceeds. Warehouses are justified by business benefits and are technically complex. Keep everyone who needs to be "in the loop" informed and involved. A particular source of danger is that each of the three parties involved moves off in his or her own direction. Thus:

   •Business analysts may install and try to maintain

---

[3] This section is based, in part, on Stackowiak (1997).

their own data marts (Section 3-4).

•Sponsoring executives may become parochial and fail to resolve coordination problems across departmental boundaries.

•The IT group may try to define data to be provided in the warehouse without consulting the business analysts, thereby creating a warehouse that is limited in its capabilities and consequently remains unused.

3. *Keep an eye on the big picture as to why the warehouse exists.* The purpose of a warehouse is to provide answers to business problems, particularly those linked to new business initiatives. Care should be taken to avoid taking on other, more local agendas. Examples of such agendas are:

•Using "bleeding-edge" technology rather than proven simple solutions

•Searching for "best of breed" tools without considering the problems to be solved

•Establishing a perfect data model when the company's business continually changes

4. *Pay attention to the assumptions and the details.* A warehouse, with its large amount of data being used by a diversity of users, requires attention to the details. The details are affected by the assumptions made in creating the warehouse. Here are some of the pitfalls that can be encountered:

•Assuming that the sources of data are clean

•Assuming that summary data is adequate

•Assuming that users will not ask for detailed data later

•Assuming that development is on track

•Assuming that users have all the skills needed to use the warehouse and its tools

•Assuming consultants will be available on short

notice to solve last-minute problems

- Assuming IT has all the skills available to manage the project

Specific steps can be taken to overcome these pitfalls. For example, monitoring and updating of development schedules, continual feedback, and prototyping that involves executives and users will help ensure that development is on track.

5.   **Consider long-term strategy.** A long-term strategy for the warehouse should be developed early. It should include a fair amount of detail but should be flexible enough that the warehouse can accommodate changes such as those resulting from mergers and acquisitions. Tactical decisions often solve immediate problems but create long-term difficulties. The following are examples of tactical decisions that can affect strategy:

- Establishing individual data marts without considering a long-term warehousing plan or establishing enterprise-wide data definitions and standards

- Storing summary data only when transaction-level data will be needed in the future

- Not establishing who has data ownership and responsibility for data quality

- Using a platform that does not scale up as the business grows

- Not establishing metadata standards that make it possible to understand changes in the data and in the business over time.

6. *Learn from Others.* Data warehousing is relatively new. Firms just beginning to create a data warehouse have to struggle with the learning curve. Competing claims from vendors and consultants, all of whom are trying to sell their particular solution, make it difficult to separate the facts from the hype. The best approach is to learn from firms that have actually built a warehouse and used it. Networks can be estab-

lished at the many data warehousing conferences run each year around the country. These conferences bring together vendors, each of whom is demonstrating products, a few academics, and most important, people who have practical warehouse experience.

Project Staff

The data warehouse team should include:

- A technical staff, available for the whole project. This staff includes the project leader, a data analyst, a business analyst familiar with the business problems to be solved, a database administrator, and programmer/analysts.

- An "ad hoc" technical staff brought in as needed for specific project tasks. Functions include systems administration, technical support, technical writing, training, and help desk.

- An end-user staff which includes subject matter experts and future warehouse users.

- Corporate-level sponsors such as executives in the end-user and IT community, data stewards, and an executive steering committee.

Staffing is discussed in more detail in Section 3-8.

Project Plan

The sheer size of a warehouse project implies that good, careful planning must be done in advance if the project is to succeed. Two kinds of planning are involved:

- An overall plan for building the warehouse and its infrastructure

- Specific plans for each application that is to be included in the warehouse

The overall plan involves four major components (Mattison, 1996):

- Vision
- Validation and estimation
- Detailed planning
- Infrastructure planning

Vision

Vision refers to defining what is to be built. Different individuals in the organization may have different objectives. For example, the sponsor may want an improved executive information system; analysts better data sources for decision support; marketing the ability to do database marketing and data mining; and the IT organization a central, quality data facility that they control. Not all the objectives of the various groups involved can necessarily be satisfied simultaneously. The conflicting viewpoints of managers, operating people, and IT people must be resolved and consensus obtained before the project can move forward.

The output of the vision phase of project planning is typically a document that describes why the warehouse is being built, what is included and what is not (i.e., the scope of the project), a view of what the warehouse contains (infrastructure, hardware, software, data), and the value to be gained by having the warehouse. Value is added through specific applications. Hence, the vision must include discussions of these applications.

The sidebar contains a very brief vision statement. Note that this statement doesn't just say that a warehouse will be built to make things better. It calls out each of three applications being planned and the value that is anticipated from each.

Validation and Estimation

Starting in parallel with defining the vision of the warehouse and continuing on through the entire project planning phase, the anticipated costs, schedule, and resource requirements are estimated. The technical feasibility of each portion of the

SIMPLE VISION STATEMENT

The data warehouse is being build to support:
- The executive information system
- A new database marketing effort
- The work of managers and analysts in corporate planning

These three applications will become available in the order listed. The data available in the warehouse will provide the following: Both raw and summarized data on current operations obtained from the 15 legacy systems that we operate. The data will be a single, official source of information for use in answering managerial queries, will provide additional drilldown capability in our EIS, and make information available to managers and analysts in a more timely fashion. It is estimated that the savings from improved query response, from eliminating shutting down the legacy systems during queries, and from reducing the staff needed to support the EIS is of the order of $400,000.

A new database marketing effort will allow the company to target customers so that we make offers only to likely prospects. We anticipate storing 1 million names, with detailed data about each. We anticipate that as a result, a typical mailing will be 300,000 rather than 800,000 items as at present. At $1/item mailed, we will save $500,000 at least 12 times/year, which should result in more orders per mailing. Marketing estimates that their current response rate of 2% (16,000/ mailing from a mailing of 800,000) will increase to 6% (18,000/mailing from a mailing of 300,000) and that the average sale/response will increase by 50%.

External information will be placed in the data warehouse on competitors, technical and social developments and news events and so on. This environmental information should inprove the quality and timeliness of corporate planning.

plan, as well as of the plan as a whole, is also established. The technical feasibility is a validation step. Validation involves checking the assumptions and finding ways to minimize the risks associated with the development.

Estimation and technical feasibility are linked. Trade-offs may have to be made to achieve an end result that can be delivered in a reasonable timeframe within a reasonable budget, yet have sufficient value added to make the warehouse project worthwhile.

Detailed Planning

Detailed planning moves the project from the conceptual to the specific. The objective is to define budget, schedule, and intermediate and final deliverables for the warehouse. Project planning tools are used to allow managers to see the time sequence in which events occur, and kind of personnel will be assigned, and what software and hardware needs to be acquired and integrated. A well-structured

plan not only defines the warehouse but includes details on every step, from the sources of data, to how data are to be cleaned, to end-user training. The training portion of the plan considers not only teaching end users the mechanics of how to obtain information from the warehouse, but also the kind of information that can be obtained and the analyses that can be performed.

Infrastructure Planning

The infrastructure for a warehouse includes all the components that will be needed once the warehouse is in operation. Infrastructure includes the physical components (computers, terminals, or PCs), the software (database, extraction tools, cleaning tools, query handling), and the support staff available to users. The infrastructure for a warehouse often has to be built from scratch, and hence proper infrastructure planning is essential.

One planning approach with inherent appeal is to create a series of relatively short (3 to 9 month) projects, each of which adds another value component (Mattison, 1996). Some of these projects (such as the planning itself and the creation of the infrastructure in which the warehouse functions) are 'overhead' associated with creating the warehouse. The others are projects that deliver applications to end users.

Outsourcing versus Custom Building

The data warehouse, like all information technology developments, can be created in-house, outsourced in part, or outsourced completely. In pure economic terms, the outsourcing decision is a classic make versus buy decision. In real life, the decision is more complex.

Such factors as enhancing skills in-house, availability of knowledge of how the organization works, and using organizational memory that knows what data are available and where and how they are stored are considerations that push the decision toward in-house development. On the other hand, lack (or unavailability) of personnel with the right skills, availability of warehouse expertise from vendors, and lack of faith that the project can be accomplished in-house all contribute to decisions to outsource.

DW as a strategic system - → in-house

Because a data warehouse is usually considered a strategic application, the favored approach is to keep the warehouse project in-house, with the information systems group responsible for construction. However, outside consultants are used to help in the design and to cover areas beyond existing expertise within the firm. Independent consulting firms as well as consulting groups working for hardware and software vendors are available.

3-3 DESIGN CHOICES AND CONSIDERATIONS

A data warehouse is a major investment for an organization. The initial impulse, therefore, is to develop a firm set of requirements and a fixed design before starting to build. Unfortunately, this approach is not the best one. Data warehouses are created iteratively. At first, only a portion of the data eventually included is populated. The end user analysts, whether they are using the warehouse for decision support, data mining, or database marketing, will find that they need additional data and/or that some data is not beneficial and can be deleted. Furthermore, over time, a successful warehouse will attract new users who may have very different subject matter requirements than those of the initial user community.

Thus, the consensus is that the traditional approach of using the systems development life cycle (SDLC) is not appropriate for the warehouse. However, the other extreme, of building a series of prototypes and hoping that the process will scale to the eventual large warehouse, is also not desirable. A mixture of the two is more appropriate. That is, the best approach appears to be:

- Defining the general dimensions of the warehouse including its anticipated eventual content
- Making design choices about the warehouse
- Running a series of projects, each delivering additional working capability over time

As will be seen from Chapters 7 through 13, the range of design approaches is large. None had proven clearly superior by the end of 1997, when this book was written. Therefore, rather than trying to describe or recommend a particular design method, we discuss the warehouse designer's choices and considerations.

Decisions in Design

At the start, the designer is faced with a blank sheet. Anything is possible. As design decisions are made, the number of options still available decrease. It is much like concrete. Initially, the structure is quite malleable. Over time, however, the design solidifies and the options left to choose among become few.

As indicated in Section 2-2, the warehouse architecture has three components:

- Back end for data extraction
- The warehouse itself
- Front end for user interface

[handwritten margin notes: Traditional LC not applicable. think big and small at the same time.]

Although these components can be arranged in a three-, two-, or one-tier architecture, all three must be present. The critical decisions that must be made for these components, together with the overall issues involved in organizing the warehouse and those associated with maintaining the warehouse (Section 3-5) once it is operational, are listed in Table 3-3 through 3-7. These tables should be viewed as initial checklists. They indicate some of the major choices the design groups must make in undertaking the project. The specific choices will depend on such factors as the uses anticipated for the warehouse, the time and funding available, the level of technical expertise and experience of both the IS group and the user, the existing infrastructure, and more. Cross-references are presented to the sections where these design choices are discussed in more detail

Table 3-3: Design Decisions: Organization of the Warehouse

Capacity requirements	How much data is the warehouse expected to handle?
Number of tiers	This choice is dependent in part on the anticipated capacity requirements. Two- and one-tier architectures are more common for data marts than for enterprise-wide warehouses.
Enterprise versus data marts versus both	Should the warehouse be centralized and available for the entire enterprise? Should it be distributed among a series of data marts (Section 3-4) coordinated with one another? Should a mixed system be created with a central, enterprise-wide warehouse supplemented by individual data marts that serve local needs?
Data model	What level of data model (Section2-5) if any, will be used?

Table 3- 4: Design Decisions: Back End

Sources of data (internal, external)	This decision is linked with the data model decision (Table 3-4) and the subjects to be included in the warehouse (Table 3-6). The issue is which internal and external sources of data are to be included in the warehouse.
Relational DBMS or specialized extraction tools?	Relational DBMSs are quite sophisticated[a] in that they can support the extraction, data replication, needed to move transaction data to a warehouse and can do summarizations. However, they are not able to handle logical inconsistencies that may exist when multiple sources are used, or deal with the reorganization and transformation needed to make the databases clean for executive users.
How to do data loading (frequency, time of day, etc.)?	The interval between data loads determines the average age of the data. The more frequently data is loaded, the more up to date it is; however, the operating cost increases. Data loading also involves consideration of the time when the source database can be made available to the warehouse without interfering with OLTP transactions.

[a] Examples are Oracle, Sybase, Informix, and DB/2.

Table 3-5: Design Decisions: Data Warehouse

Subjects to be included	The data warehouse is subject oriented. Designers, working with users, need to consider which subjects will be included in the warehouse and the sequence in which they will be brought in.
ROLAP versus MOLAP	For decision support systems using OLAP, either a relational database (ROLAP) or a multidimensional database (MOLAP) can be chosen (Sec. 2-5).
Granularity	Granularity refers to the lowest level of aggregation to be found in the warehouse. Granularity involves a design trade-off between increased detail and speed of computation. Granularity is usually determined by the anticipated uses of the warehouse.
Summarization levels	A variety of summaries can be created from the input data. The designer must select the specific summaries to be provided.
Precomputing	To speed up response, some warehouses precompute the answers to frequently queries. The trade-off is extra storage for speed of response.
Aging the data	Data in a warehouse is moved from one level of summarization to another, depending on its age. Eventually, it is archived. The design decision involves the times when data is to be moved from one summarization level to another (Section 2-3).

Table 3-5: Design Decisions: Data Warehouse

Metadata	Metadata (Sec.2-4) has proven to be a difficult data warehouse task. The issues are what metadata to create and update from the point of view of both the user and the warehouse maintainer.
Serial versus parallel computing	The size of the warehouse and the type and frequency of queries all enter into the decision as to whether the warehouse should have parallel computing capability.
Levels of normalization, data redundancy	Although relational databases are typically in normal form and without redundancy, data warehouse information tends not to be. The extent to which normalization is retained and the effects of redundancy are design choices.

Table 3-6: Design Decisions: Front End

Metadata for users	What metadata are going to be available to the user, and how are they going to be organized?
How users navigate through the system (drilldown)	In decision support and executive information systems, users want to access increasing levels of detail; that is, they want to drill down into the data. Arranging the drilldown sequences and providing ways for users to move around the data are part of the design problem.
Selection of users to have access	Which users will have access to the warehouse, and which services will be provided to each? When the warehouse is being rolled out, the sequence in which users are given access also has to be decided.
Graphical user interface	The front-end interface (Section 2-5) is the user's prime point of contact with the warehouse. As such, it requires particular care in design.

Table 3-7: Design Decisions: Maintaining the System

Monitoring capabilities	Means for monitoring the operation of the warehouse should be included in the design so that operational problems that inevitably occur can be resolved and so that the needs for improvements, updates, and changes can be determined.
Adding or deleting subject areas	The subject areas covered by the warehouse will change as the business changes.
Adding or deleting metadata	Similarly, the metadata will change over time.
Security	Security needs to be built in during design, not added after the system is operational.

Other Considerations

The data warehouse, being a large project, requires consideration of

- complexity
- coordination
- costs and benefits

The large size of the project and its use of many techniques that are at the leading edge of data technology make warehouse projects complex. To deal with complexity, a large amount of coordination is required. The time spent coordinating cannot be used for design or construction. In fact, in some projects, people use so much time for coordinating and issue resolution that they have no time for design. As we know from Brooks' law,[4] simply adding people doesn't solve the problem.

Several actions can help cope with the interlinked complexity and coordination issues.

1. Break the project down into smaller parts, with each part having a clearly defined set of deliverables.
2. Make sure that the people involved in the process (systems developers, users, managers) understand what they are to do and what they are responsible for delivering on what time schedule.
3. Assign fiscal and managerial responsibility for each part.

A large part of the problem involves people. Each member of the design team wants to create a first-rate product. Many creative ideas are offered. Although these ideas should be encouraged, there has to be a common vision of the warehouse from the beginning, including its size, what is included (i.e., scope), how construction will be approached, and the

---

[4] Brooks' law states that adding people to a project can actually reduce the total effort (Brooks, 1996).

value of the warehouse to the organization. Failure to obtain buy-in from the start can be catastrophic later.

To make a warehouse happen, an infrastructure must be created. Technical design choices have to be made and the requisite hardware and software obtained. Again, the design team has to be in agreement on the physical design. Once an infrastructure is in place, it is possible to develop and implement applications. Typically, applications are brought into the warehouse one at a time. There is a plan for the sequence in which applications are added.

3-4 Data Marts

Definition
D mart

The term *data mart* is used to refer to a small-capacity data warehouse designed for use by a business unit or a department of a corporation. The dichotomy between a data warehouse and a data mart is partially dependent on the size of the organization. A large organization's data mart may well be a small organization's data warehouse. IBM's Visual Warehouse 1.2, with a capacity of 10 to 50 GB, is typical of the data marts on the market.

Advantages

Data marts have a number of advantages over data warehouses:

- The cost is low (prices under $100K are quoted).
- The lead time to implementation is short, often under 90 days (Digital Equipment Corporation claims 4 to 6 weeks with their product).
- They are controlled locally rather than centrally, conferring power on the using group.
- They contain less information than the data warehouse and hence have more rapid response and are more easily understood and navigated than an enterprise-wide data warehouse.

- They allow a business unit to build its own decision support systems without relying on (and waiting for) a centralized IS shop.

Integration

The key issue in data marts is not their data warehousing capability. That is usually a given. Rather, it is how individual data marts are integrated into the organization. The usual assumption is that an organization either has or will have several data marts. The data marts may:

- Be integrated into a distributed data warehouse
- Be a subsidiary of a centralized data warehouse
- Operate independently

distributed D marts

The first alternative, a distributed data warehouse, is the result of planning. Each data mart is assigned a specific set of information for which it is responsible. A central organization, such as IT, specifies the rules for the metadata so that the information kept by each mart is compatible with that provided by all the other marts. The central organization may also provide a corporate data warehouse. The distributed nature of the warehouse is transparent to a user posting a query. That is, a manager working on a particular problem can view information kept in several data marts and in the central data warehouse as if the data were all located in a single warehouse. This arrangement is sometimes referred to as a "virtual" data warehouse. Security is maintained by allowing access only to pertinent information on a need-to-know basis.

Dependent D marts

The second alternative is a centralized data warehouse off-loading a portion of its data to a remote data mart through replication. This arrangement is often referred to as a *dependent data mart*. Here the information provided to each data mart is determined by the local needs for centralized information. In addition, some locally generated and used information my be stored in the data mart. However, that information is never transmitted by the owner of the data mart to other portions of the organization. Data marts and the data warehouse use the same data, the same data definitions, measurements, and aggregations.

The third alternative is a laissez-faire alternative in which each department or division has its own data mart. This situation can result when vendors, unable to sell a data warehouse to the whole enterprise, sell scaled-down versions of their product as a data mart to an organizational unit. Different organizational units wind up buying different brands of data marts.

Stand alone Dmarts

While solving the problem of its owner, a stand-alone data mart can result in serious fragmentation problems for the organization. Specifically, when data marts are not integrated with one another, they can generate inconsistent and conflicting data. These differences can come from such simple things as different definitions of terms, reporting periods, and time lags in recording information. These are not significant problems until components of the organization try to interact with one another. The independent data marts have separate representations of the data and hence cannot be integrated with one another.

Limitations

A multiple data mart environment creates a number of limitations:

- Performance degradation over time
- Administration of multiple data marts
- Building and implementing the data marts
- Access to remote data marts

Each of these limitations is being addressed by vendors, although ideal solutions are not necessarily available for each of them.

Other Data Mart Considerations

Users expect more rapid response from a data mart than from a data warehouse. Unfortunately, performance decreases as data marts grow in size over time and as the number of interconnected data marts increases. Multiple data marts also complicate database administration. Issues such as the consistency and integrity of data and metadata, security where users have access to multiple marts, and versioning must all be resolved. Data marts have proven to be difficult to build quickly.

Performance

Performance requires trading off end-user response time and data loading. Faster response time implies storing more summary tables and aggregated numbers. However, increasing the amount of information stored increases the time required for data loading. Techniques for improving performance such as parallel processing and faster hardware are used mostly in data warehouses. Data marts, being small and cheap, generally, do not have these capabilities. However, the picture is not all bleak. New software techniques for more efficient query response, the use of multidimensional databases in which only changed cells are updated, and more exotic approaches such as fractal algorithms all promise to improve performance. Performance is also improved by reducing the amount of data kept in a data mart. This last approach requires strong self-discipline by both users and IT.

Administration

Good standardized data mart administration is required as the number of data marts grows in an organization. Security, versions, performance tuning, and consistency of data across data marts are all required. Coordination must be centralized to be effective.

Building and Implementing the Data Marts

Although a data mart's database is smaller and hence easier to install than a data warehouse, other issues, such as data loading, vendor performance, and software integration, can make building and implementing a data mart difficult. To minimize these problems, a number of vendors offer a "data mart in a box." These offerings provide all the needed components through one-stop shopping. The data mart in a box approach is also designed to reduce or eliminate the expensive amount of "hand-holding" that vendors must so that the can reduce their costs and the purchase price.

Data marts in a box do not solve all problems. Firms must still make decisions such as determining the logic of data extraction and creating consistent data definitions.

Access to Remote Data Marts

The Web browser has alleviated many of the problems associated with remote access in distributed systems with or without a central data warehouse.

3-5 OPERATIONAL DATA STORE

The operational data store (ODS) is a database for transaction processing systems that uses data warehouse concepts to provide clean data. That is, it brings the concepts and benefits of the data warehouse enjoyed by the planning groups to the operational portions of the business. It is used for short-term decisions involving mission-critical applications rather than the medium- and long-term decisions associated with the data warehouse. These decisions depend on much more current information. For example, a bank needs to know about all the accounts for a given customer who is calling on the phone.

As shown in Figure 3-4, the ODS works closely with legacy systems that feed it. As operational data ages, it is moved (and perhaps summarized) from the ODS to the data warehouse.

Figure 3-4: Relation of ODS to Legacy Systems and the Data Warehouse

The reason for creating an operational data store is to obtain a "system of record" that contains the best data that exists in a legacy environment as a source of information. Best is used here in the sense of being the information that is most:

- Complete
- Up to date
- Accurate
- In conformance with the organization's information model

Table 3-8 compares the operational data store with the data warehouse. The two systems are the same in the quality of the data (subject oriented, integrated), which implies that the data have been transformed to meet the quality standards of the data warehouse. However, they differ in all other respects. mostly as a result of the difference in emphasis on time. In fact, a key decision in designing an ODS is the choice of time at which the ODS is updated.

Three typical update schemes are:

- Synchronous with changes in legacy system
- Periodic but frequent update daily
- Periodic but at intervals of a day or longer

Cases 2 and 3 are basically store and forward systems. In these cases, the data is, on average, half the refresh period out of date, whereas in the first case, the ODS and legacy systems are in step. Clearly, the first case is the most difficult and

Table 3-8: Comparison of ODS and Data Warehouse Characteristics

OPERATIONAL DATA STORE	DATA WAREHOUSE
Subject-oriented data	Subject-oriented data
Integrated data	Integrated data
Volatile data	Nonvolatile data
Data is updated as it changes	Data remains fixed
Only current data	Current and historical data
Short time between data refreshing	Longer time between data refreshing
Detailed data only	Detailed and summary data
Is the system of record	Used for planning purposes

costly, and therefore rarely encountered. The longer time interval allows the updating to be done in a batch mode from the logs and journal tapes that are generated by on-line transactions.

An ODS must have a versatile database management system because it is expected to handle both complex on-line transactions and large sequential batch processing. The variety of tasks includes:

- Batch processing of the loading of information from legacy systems
- Preparing data for on-line processing
- Answering individual queries from users accessing small amounts of data
- Batch analytical processing for decision support

Unlike a data warehouse, a typical ODS does not contain summary data. With the data changing continually, the summaries quickly become out of date. When summary information is needed, it is recomputed. A decision that involves a client's bank balance needs the best possible information. Storing the balance from this morning may not be adequate for making a decision about a loan in the afternoon.

mine: Markus and Tan's argue that DW is the poor substitute of ENTRP. However it seems that is the ODS rather than a DW.

Metadata is not as central in an ODS as in a data warehouse. It is used principally to support the DSS analyst working in batch mode. The analyst who is working with live data tends to execute the same transactions repeatedly and does not need the metadata's roadmap capabilities.

3-6 OPERATING THE DATA WAREHOUSE

Until now we have concentrated on the design aspects of the data warehouse. However, when the warehouse is built and the initial loading is completed, it is time to start the operational phase. This phase involves administering and maintaining the warehouse. The basic principles are:

1. A warehouse must be someone's (or some group's) responsibility.
2. The warehouse is a living organism that changes over time. Hence it, like all software and hardware, requires maintenance and updating.
3. Procedures should be in place for routine operations that are done over and over. To the extent that these routine procedures can be automated, they should be.

Administering the Data Warehouse

The responsibility for administrating the data warehouse (or for data marts, for that matter) typically rests with the information systems (IS) department in an organization. One approach, proposed by Inmon and Hackathorn (1994), is to form (or use) a *data architecture group.* This group, which interfaces with all the concerned parties (management, IS, and the end user), is responsible for the data warehouse. Its duties include:

- Monitoring data warehouse operations
- Adding and deleting subject areas
- Supporting end users
- Maintaining the metadata

- Updating the warehouse content
- Upgrading the warehouse
- Updating the data model
- Capacity planning
- Maintaining security, including backup and recovery

These responsibilities require more than one person. The skills range from technical duties such as database administration and programming to personal interactions with managers and other end users.

Monitoring Data Warehouse Operations

This activity involves keeping track of how the warehouse is actually growing and how it is being used. Growth patterns will inevitably differ from those predicted when the warehouse was designed. Growth may be too rapid (extending the limits of the technology used) or too slow (resulting in stale data.) End-user activity is an indication of which data is useful and which is not. Monitoring end-user activity, however, can be a difficult technical task.

Monitoring also involves making sure that the data warehouse and the on-line transaction processing system are kept separate. End users are tempted to run operational data on the warehouse or to degrade the operational system by performing queries on the OLTP system. Both approaches reduce enterprise efficiency. IS's role here is that of a traffic cop who keeps the two data flows separate.

Adding and Deleting Subject Areas

As the business of a firm changes, its interests change. Since the warehouse is organized by subject area, major changes will typically involve the subject areas covered by the warehouse.

Supporting End Users

When end users start working with the data warehouse, they need training. Even after training they may need support for such simple tasks as logging on. Over time they become more experienced and their requests for help become more sophisticated. Whenever the system yields a "strange" result, such as returning too much data or no data, or not returning a response at all, the user asks for help.

Users also need help when planning and formulating complex queries. Here the role of IS is to help users by making them aware of what is easy and what is hard to do. If the user wants to execute queries on a regular basis, IS helps by building procedures to make running that query simple. IS keeps the users apprised of what data is in the warehouse, how to use the metadata, and of the addition of new subject areas as they become available.

Maintaining the Metadata

As the warehouse changes, the metadata about how the warehouse is loaded and what is in the warehouse changes. Tools for automatic upkeep of metadata are available. However, someone must still be responsible for auditing and editing the metadata.

Updating the Warehouse Content

In addition to routine loading of new data into the warehouse (Section 2-3), the data in the warehouse must be kept up to date. Actions include:

- Condensing data by summarizing information as it ages.
- Archiving data to bulk storage after it reaches a predetermined age (e.g., 1 year or 5 years, depending on its use).
- Purging data that is no longer needed. For example, a product is dropped or a facility is closed.

Utilities are used to perform these updating tasks.

Upgrading the Warehouse

A more complex form of updating occurs when the warehouse is changed to upgrade its contents and/or its performance. Successful systems result in increasing demands from users. There is a natural tendency to request that additional data be included. Furthermore, if the system is successful, its use will increase, thus making the system response time longer and leading to the need to upgrade hardware and software. To make performance and/or data upgrades typically requires shutting the system down. However, with increased use, it is harder to find time when the system can be shut down for an extended period to make the changes. Changes, of course, are fraught with danger because errors can occur. Thus, it is usually wiser to test upgrades on a separate test system before going live with them. The upgrades themselves will need to be done overnight or over the weekends.

Updating the Data Model

The changes that occur in the data warehouse need to be integrated with the data model (Section 2-5). One of the roles of IS is to make sure that changes in the warehouse are integrated into the data model. Changes occur one at a time. Some are easily accommodated by the existing model but others require revising the model or creating a new one.

Capacity Planning

Data warehouses grow over time. The amount of data increases, as does the number of MIPS of computing resources consumed. Growth also comes from adding subject areas. Warehouses that appear to be ample in size become too small. Capacity planning is needed so that additional hardware (and software) is obtained in time or so that the contents of the warehouse is modified to fit within the existing capabilities.

Maintaining Security

The data warehouse is like any other collection of data. Care must be taken to make certain that only people entitled to the information ("need to know," in military parlance) actually gain access to the information. The warehouse is, in many ways, more sensitive from a security point of view than the OLTP system. The warehouse contains aggregated information ready for management use. It contains precisely the information that competitors would like to obtain. Not much literature exists on data warehouse security. Yet, in many ways, it is one of the key issues that the warehouse operational group must resolve.

Log-in control is typical of routine security operations. Because people are given access privileges when they log in, care must be taken to make certain that individuals are not given too much or too little access for their needs and their responsibilities. Users with special privileges can cause inadvertent damage if they delete a table or a data file in a large warehouse. Such operations need to be done with menus that contain checks to prevent accidents.

Logging and tracing can consume large amounts of memory, yet must be kept for issues currently being worked on. To save disk space and to avoid having this information removed by automated housekeeping, some warehouses move log and trace data to a separate location

Security also refers to the need to make backups of the data and to provide plans for recovery if the data are lost due to any cause. Backups are typically made overnight. Because the data in the warehouse is "read only," it does not change much, if at all, during the day. Changes occur only when new data is loaded and new aggregations are run. Again, aggregations are typically done overnight.

Data losses occur as a result of computer crashes and natural disasters (e.g., fires, earthquakes, power outages). For a firm with an active on-line transaction system (such as a bank or a retailer), restoring the warehouse from backup information takes second priority to restoring the OLTP system since the latter is necessary for continued operation of the organization, whereas the warehouse for decision support is typically a staff operation.

Other Duties

The foregoing is a partial list of responsibilities for IS. Other duties include managing data loading, correcting errors that are detected after loading,[5] managing the query workload, interacting with DSS and EIS users to make sure their changing requirements are being met, and communicating warehouse failures and successes to management.

Conclusions on Operations

The basic message of this section is that the data warehouse is not a turnkey activity where the delivery of a wording package ends the activity. Rather, it is a continuing activity that requires human supervision. Warehouses change over time. The warehouse that is delivered is different from the warehouse that exists after one year and it, in turn, is different from the one after two years or after five years. Institutionalizing support for the data warehouse can help ensure its long life.

3-7 ECONOMICS OF DATA WAREHOUSING[6]

As discussed in Chapter 1, data warehouse projects are a significant business investment. However, data warehouses present an interesting paradox. The primary motivation to build these systems is to provide timely, useful information to decision makers so that they can make more informed deci-

---

[5] Remember that once data is entered in the warehouse, it is not supposed to change. However, if an error is detected, it must be fixed.

[6] The material in this section is based on an analysis by David Petrie. His input is gratefully acknowledged.

sions and rely less on intuition and "gut-feel" decision techniques. Yet these same organizations generally rely on intuition when evaluating proposals to invest in data warehouse systems. In this section we discuss some simple decision-making techniques that should help firms make informed data warehouse investment decisions.

What We Know

Key drivers of the demand for data warehouses are based on four business trends (Rymer, 1995):

- The data glut
- Time-critical competition
- Decentralization of decision making
- The shift to client/server open infrastructures

The primary approach to justifying data warehouse projects rests on the business value of the information retrieved from the system. Evidence exists that the value of business intelligence can be very high, leading to the *single query theory* which states that the entire data warehouse project can be justified with one key finding, followed by the appropriate business decision. (Grupe and Owrang, 1995; Haisten, 1995; Bull, 1995).

A second major approach to justifying data warehouses is reduced reporting costs from existing systems by offloading work from expensive host-based systems to new, less-expensive open platforms. A 30% savings in reporting costs is not unusual (Haisten, 1995). Purina Mills saved $100,000 per year in mainframe reporting costs (Harding, 1995). Stanford University saved $750,000 in processing/reporting in one year. (Janah, 1995). By using data warehouses, organizations maximize the return on their legacy mainframe investments while allowing themselves to move forward at their own pace to client/server computing.

There is general agreement that data warehouses are expensive and, as described in Chapter 1, that the claimed return on investment is amazingly large. However, statistics on actual projects are hard to come by and somewhat inconsistent. Note, however, that these statistics are typically after the fact and based on successful projects.

Benefit data are difficult to estimate before building the system. For example, it is difficult to evaluate EIS and DSS benefits since the systems provide "better, more timely information" or "a better basis for making a decision." Justifications tend to be based on an intuitive feeling that benefits exceed costs. User satisfaction and frequency of use after the fact by systems built by others serve as surrogate measures.

To overcome the weaknesses of the traditional cost/benefit approach to measuring IT value, Keen (1981) suggests focusing on value first and cost second, with particular emphasis on simplicity and robustness of the applications. Also important is reducing the uncertainty and risk with the introduction of technology. Radding (1995), for example, talks about firms using a gradual approach to avoid risk by using a multiphase (i.e., prototyping) approach in which they build an initial warehouse within a six-month period to prove principle and then iterate. Keen suggests Value Analysis, a methodology in which a project is evaluated on the expected benefits to be derived from the first prototype of the application. Once the initial version of the system is completed, an assessment of value is made, followed by a decision on whether or not to fund the next iteration of the prototype. Keen (1991) identifies three primary issues that must be addressed within the economics of information capital:

- Managing development and maintenance costs
- Managing benefits
- Managing risk exposures

3-8 PERSONNEL

Design and Construction

The job functions to be performed in building a data warehouse were described in Section 3-2. In brief, these functions are listed in Table 3-9. The table is based on the assumption that a full-size warehouse is to be built by personnel within the company. The skill sets required to build a warehouse may not be available within the organization, particularly the technical skills. As described below, it may not be possible to hire additional personnel directly. Hence, it may be necessary to rely on consultants and contractors.

Table 3-9: Project Staffing Functions for Building the Data Warehouse

TECHNICAL STAFF (ENTIRE PROJECT)	"AD HOC" TECHNICAL STAFF	CORPORATE AND END USER
Project leader	Systems administration	Executive sponsors
Data analyst	Technical support	Data stewards
Business analyst	Technical writing	Steering committee
Database administrator	Training	End-user subject experts
Programmer/analysts	Help Desk	Expected end users

The exact number of people required for each function depends on the size of the data warehouse. The distinction between "technical staff" and "ad hoc technical staff" made in the table refers to the fraction of the total development time that people spend with the project.

The specific technical skill mix required to support the project should match the hardware and software products selected. That is, people with experience and/or understanding of the selected:

- hardware   - database

- network
- operating system
- human interface

- program language(s)
- data mining tools

need to be available to support the project. That is, a wide-ranging set of talents are required. The reason is that, because the data warehouse architecture is inherently three tiered,[7] the skills needed in these three tiers differ and hence require different people to perform. For example, the people working with the legacy systems to extract and clean data need to understand how the legacy systems work and their relation to the business, whereas the people working on the front end need skills in the application area of the warehouse, be it decision support, or data mining, or database marketing.

Operation

Once the data warehouse is built, it must be managed, supported, and maintained just as any other application. Even if built mostly with vendor and consultant assistance, data warehouses cannot be installed and forgotten. They tend to grow in size over time. Decisions need to be made as to which data to add or delete, when and which hardware to obtain, what changes should be made in metadata, what the relations should be to data marts, and more.

A warehouse represents not only a large initial investment, but also a major mission-critical resource of the organization. Thus, the warehouse needs a project manager who is responsible for both the day-to-day operations and for planning and implementing upgrades in hardware and software.

---

[7] As described in Section 2-2, the actual architecture may be two-tier or one-tier. The smallest number of tiers are obtained by combining portions of the three-tier architecture.

The manager will need to be supported by analysts and programmers who can deal with the inevitable changes.

If the warehouse project is successful, it will inevitably create demands for growth in capacity and capability. The decisions on which improvements to make should not be the responsibility of the project manager alone. Rather, a formal change and maintenance procedure should be put in place and a steering committee formed. The role of the steering committee is to make the decisions that involve the user community and to approve technical decisions (e.g., hardware selection, metadata modifications) proposed by the project manager.

Skill Availability

People with data warehouse experience are becoming more scarce as demand increases faster than the number of people acquiring knowledge in the field. In late May 1997, Stedman (1997) reported that compensation for some full-time warehousing personnel was exceeding $100,000 and that top consultants were charging $1500 to $3500/day.

Because of the personnel shortage,

1. Workers who had built warehouses were being recruited actively by competing firms and by consulting houses.
2. Firms that did not have the skills internally were at a disadvantage. The need to keep finding and training people slows down development schedules.

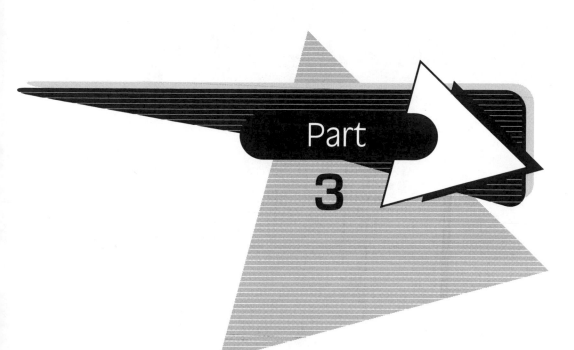

Part

3

Supporting Decisions in the Data Warehouse Environment

Chapter

4

DECISION SUPPORT TOOLS

4-1 INTRODUCTION

Decision support software dates back to the 1970s when DSS first became popular. A few of the vendors from that era (e.g., Comshare) remain in the marketplace, but with very different products. For example, command line (e.g., RUN, PRINT) interfaces have given way to Windows and Web-based approaches.

As decision support applications evolved and become the norm in organizations, products appeared from vendors to serve specific needs. It is possible to categorize these products as being for:

- Queries
- Managed query environments
- Decision support systems
- Executive information systems
- Data mining

While these categories are useful for discussion purposes, this list is a simplification since some products serve multiple purposes. For example, some software (e.g., Holos) can be used to build both DSS and EIS.

It is also important to recognize the role of the World Wide Web in decision support. Like all computing, Web-based technology affects how applications are developed and used. Many companies are building decision support applications that have a multitier architecture consisting of a browser, Web server, and database (Section 3-1). Recognizing the shift, vendors of decision support software have made their products Web enabled. Applications can now be accessed by browsers but still provide the capabilities long associated with decision support software.

Web interface for DSS

Another area of emerging importance is the use of information technology in marketing. It allows companies to conduct what is commonly referred to as *relationship* or *1-to-1 marketing*. Through it, a company knows enough about a customer's buying behavior and preferences to customize marketing efforts toward that person.

The purpose of this chapter is to cover the tools that are available for building decision support applications. It does not focus on specific vendors' products, but rather, the capabilities of the tools for specific applications (e.g., data mining). In Chapters 7 through 13, specific products are described.

4-2 OLAP

On-line analytical processing (OLAP) is at the heart of using data warehouses for decision support. OLAP is used for array-oriented applications such as market analysis and financial forecasting, where the objective is greater market share or better return on investment. Thus, the purpose of OLAP differs from that of on-line transaction processing (OLTP), which is oriented to dealing with individual records for billing, order entry, inventory, and accounting. Table 4-1 shows the differences.

Table 4-1: Comparison of OLAP and OLTP

Characteristics	OLAP	OLTP
Operation	Analyze	Update
Screen format	User-defined	Unchanging
Data transaction	Considerable	Little
Level of detail	Aggregate	Detail
Time	Historical, current, projected	Current
Orientation	Attributes	Records

OLAP is an analyst's tool used for planning and decision making. Codd and associates (1993) have defined four kinds of processing done by analysts:

Categorical:	static, historical view of data limited by database design
Exegetical:	drilldown to determine what happened
Contemplative:	what-if for change of a single variable
Formulaic:	what-if for changes in multiple variables

Categorical analysis uses the standard relational databases to do static analysis of what occurred in the past. The data is viewed according to how it is stored.

In *exegetical* analysis, the user still works with the existing data in the form in which it is stored, but is able to perform queries on the data. Typically, the queries are drilldown; that is, they ask how a number on the screen (e.g., total sales) was obtained (e.g., sales of individual business units). If the data of interest is multidimensional, these views must be created on the fly. EISs and spreadsheets are able to perform exegetical analysis.

Contemplative analysis allows the user to change a single variable (e.g., what if sales were doubled? what if sales were down 20%?). Such seemingly simple questions can result in changes in multiple dimensions.

Formulaic analysis involves changing an outcome in multiple dimensions. According to Codd, these models do not yet exist. They are the ultimate goal of OLAP.

As a result of Codd's 1993 paper, OLAP was initially associated with multidimensional databases (see Section 2-5). However, over time, the term has come to be applicable to both relational and multidimensional representations of multidimensional data. OLAP is designed to formulate data so that it can be optimized for data analysis. As presently constituted, the principal analyses performed with OLAP products are:

1. *Slice and dice.* Users can view from many perspectives. The term *slice and dice* refers to the idea that the user can extract portions of the aggregated data and examine it in detail according to the dimensions of interest. For example, if data show the total sales of soft drinks, the user can find out the value of sales by geography (e.g., in New York and Los Angeles) or by product (e.g., cola, diet cola, lemonade) or by a combination of product, geography, and time (e.g., sales of diet cola in Los Angeles this month versus last month).

2. *Drilldown.* Drill down refers to navigating through the data to obtain more detail and help answer "why" questions. Typically such questions are asked when a summary number is well below or above the expected. Thus, for example, if the total sales of soft drink are significantly lower this month than last, going to a finer level of detail (perhaps first to type of soft drink and then to market for each soft drink) will point out the reason for the decline. It is also possible to *drill up* (i.e., obtain consolidations) and *drill across* (i.e., obtain data at the same level but for a different quantity such as potato chips).

Slice and dice is equivalent to categorical?

4-3 QUERIES

Displaying data that fit conditions.

Many applications involve accessing a database. The user specifies the search conditions, and all data that meet the conditions are displayed. For example, a human resource application might allow a user to request the names of all electrical engineers who speak Spanish.

If an organization does not have a separate data warehouse or data mart, decision support analysts have to access the on-line transaction processing systems to obtain answers to their queries. Because many queries are large and complex, requiring a long time to execute, individual queries can interrupt the on-line systems for unacceptably long periods and even bring a system down. The warehouse/mart environment ameliorates this problem. However, even with a data warehouse, attention has to be given to making queries efficient.

SQL

SQL standard language for queries

Structured Query Language (SQL) is the standard for conducting queries. It originated as the SQUARE language in IBM's System R project, later was revised and renamed SEQUEL, and then was revised and renamed again as SEQUEL2. Its current name SQL (still often pronounced as "sequel" rather than SQL) was the result of legal issues surrounding the name "SEQUEL." International standards for SQL were put forward by organizations such as the American National Standards Institute (ANSI), and vendors have largely complied with the standards.

1. Stand-alone write the query
- needs knowledge

SQL is used for database definitions, manipulation, and control. Database administrators use its database definition and control capabilities. Users such as analysts employ the manipulation capabilities to access data.

2. Embedded mode.
- preprogrammed no knowledge need
- limited to preprogrammed queries.

SQL can be used in either a stand-alone or an embedded mode. In the former, the user writes SQL statements such as

```
SELECT QITEM.ITEMNAME, ITEMTYPE, QDEPT.DEPTNAME,
 DEPTFLOOR
FROM QITEM, QSALE, QDEPT
WHERE QSALE.ITEMNAME = QITEM.ITEMNAME
AND QSALE.DEPTNAME = QDEPT.DEPTNAME
```

This code executes a three-table join,[1] where for each item, its type, the departments that sell the item, and the floor location of these departments are provided (Watson, 1996). Products like Access and Excel support the use of SQL to access data.

In embedded mode, SQL is part of a larger application that might use software such as Visual Basic or PowerBuilder. In this situation, the user is given a graphical front end that allows search conditions to be specified through, for example, the use of radio buttons or pull-down menus. The user does not need to know SQL and may not ever know that it is embedded in the application. Queries are relatively easy to perform in this way but are limited to those that are preestablished.

Managed Query Environment

There are many potential problems with SQL; in particular, with stand alone use. SQL requires the user to know both the often cryptic table names used in the database and the contents of these tables. Users also have to be able to write SQL statements correctly. This task is frequently error-prone, especially for more complex queries. And then there is "the query from hell," which requires so many executions that it ties up the system for long periods of time. Embedded SQL applications (e.g., a company travel specialist working on arranging discount rates to identify the percent of company travel on different airlines) avoid the problems just mentioned, but queries are limited to those that were preplanned.

---

[1] A join is a relational database operation in which two or more tables with a common domain are combined into a single table.

A managed query environment (MQE), described below, is designed to reduce or eliminate the problems associated with stand-alone SQL queries. Experience with products such as Brio (from Brio Technology), GQL (Andyne Computing), and Business Objects (Business Objects), which provide such a managed query environment, shows that both users and IS benefit.

Users in a Managed Query Environment

Users of an MQE operate through a graphical user interface and point-and-click objects that have been established for them. The objects have names that correspond with business terms (e.g., customer, sale) that are used in day-to-day operations and are much easier to recognize and use than list-based data descriptions. These names provide a semantic layer between the user and names used in the databases. Each object has an underlying SQL statement(s). An object can be as simple as "customer's last name," which is a single field in a table and is defined as customers.last_name, or as complex as "sales revenue," which is an equation that draws upon multiple fields in multiple tables.

To execute a query, a user points-and-clicks on the objects that have been defined. For example, if a sales manager wants to know "all customers in Ohio who purchased more than $5000 in goods," the manager would specify:

- The objects to be used (in this case, customer, name, state, and sales revenue)

- Any conditions the query must satisfy (Ohio and over $5000)

- The sorting specifications for the information generated, such as list customers in alphanumerical order

The results from a query can be received and processed further in a variety of ways. The information can be presented in predefined or user-defined reports that integrate data, text, and image. A large variety of charting options exist. Executive buttons can be created to automate routine queries and report writing. This provides a low-level EIS capability and illustrates how decision support software crosses boundaries that might be defined. Alerts can be set to detect and report important conditions. Output information can be further manipulated (e.g., pivoting) or exported to HTML pages, a spreadsheet, or some other application. A drilldown capability can be provided that allows users to access underlying detail data. Wizards support the use of the MQE.

Role of IS in a Managed Query Environment

In an SQL environment, complex queries result in users calling upon IS to write the queries. The result is that IS personnel are tied up for considerable periods of time in what is, for them, a nonproductive task. With an MQE, users can perform most of their own queries. IS works with users to define objects and to create predefined queries and reports. Consequently, IS can use their skills to create new applications rather than writing queries for users.

An MQE provides security. The objects that are created control what data can be accessed and users are only given access to those objects that they are authorized to use. This is all handled through the MQE software.

The MQE also allows IS to control and schedule how queries are executed. Limits can be set on the size of the result set and execution times. Queries can be prioritized and defined to run at certain times. For example, queries can be set to run (and perhaps be posted to an intranet) at scheduled times (e.g., weekly) or when the user signs on to the network (thus providing the most current data). An MQE allows IS to apply computer resources more effectively while making it easier for users to access and analyze data.

[Handwritten margin notes:]

MQE advantages.
- Queries done by users
- Provides security
- allows to control and schedule how queries are executed

4-4 DSS/EIS

DSS
supports
specific tasks

D SS components
- interface
- analytic aids
- data

Decision support systems are designed to support specific decision-making tasks, such as providing a risk analysis for a proposed capital expenditure, helping assess the impact of various marketing plans, or scheduling a month's production. A DSS provides a user with an easy-to-use interface in order to access and manipulate a set of analytic aids (i.e., models) and a database. These three components (interface, analytic aids, and data) are supported by DSS software.

Because this DSS conceptualization is broad, it is not surprising that a large variety of software can be used for DSS purposes. For example, an Excel or Lotus spreadsheet might be appropriate for certain needs. A spreadsheet interface is familiar to most users, and though the analysis and database capabilities are modest, they may be sufficient for the application. OLAP applications and managed query environments can also be thought of as providing DSS capabilities. In these cases, the interface and database capabilities are strong, but the analysis tools are limited.

When DSS software first appeared in the 1970s, the modeling capabilities were especially strong. This was due in part to the belief that mathematical modeling (e.g., linear programming, simulation) would become increasingly popular in organizations. It was also because many of the founders of these companies (e.g., Comshare, IRI, SAS) had backgrounds in management science/operations research and statistics. The vendors from that era have broadened the scope of their products to cover more of the data warehousing software domain (e.g., multidimensional databases, data mining), but they still include powerful analysis capabilities in their product offerings. Examples include various types of mathematical programming, forecasting methods, probabilistic analysis, and multivariate statistical methods. If a company's planned DSS applications require sophisticated mathematical models, there are appropriate tools available in the marketplace. They are also designed to work especially well with data warehouses and marts.

Some of the more recent vendors of DSS software put less emphasis on mathematical modeling capabilities. They see a larger market for products that provide, for example, OLAP, spreadsheet-type capabilities, and Web-based solutions.

DSS and EIS are different, yet interrelated applications. A DSS focuses on a particular decision, whereas an EIS provides a much wider range of information (e.g., key performance indicators, financials, news). They are interrelated, however, in that most EIS software has DSS capabilities embedded in it. For example, some of the information provided by an EIS might be generated by a forecasting model, or a user may be able to perform an OLAP analysis. Vendors recognize the need for this integrated capability. Consequently, their software allows both DSS and EIS applications to be developed. Common tools and capabilities of this software include:

- *Support for multiple interfaces:* The keyboard and mouse are required; the touchscreen has faded away for DSS/EIS use; voice is still in the future.

- *On-line, context-dependent help screens:* Context dependent help is important; wizards are likely to emerge, such as those found in the Microsoft office products.

- *Multiple methods for accessing information:* A good menuing system, keyword search capabilities, and indexes are useful.

- *Access to external news databases:* After creating user-defined profiles, news stories of interest are delivered automatically to the users' desktops from sources such as Dow Jones News Retrieval; these systems are becoming increasingly intelligent in terms of presenting the information (the most important information is placed at the top of the list or on the front page of the newspaper) and learning what news is really important to the user.

- *Integrated with other software*: Works seamlessly with other products, such as Lotus Notes and Excel.

- *Integrated decision support*: Provided by the OLAP, DSS, or application engine or server (the term used depends on the vendor).

- *Easy screen design and maintenance:* Supports rapid prototyping.

- *Object-oriented development tools*: Allows developers to develop applications and to reuse work quickly and easily.

- *Screen design templates*: Some screens are used by most organizations, such as comparing actuals to budget; templates for these screens speed up application development.

- *Packaged applications*: To differentiate their products and services, decision support vendors now offer turnkey applications, some for vertical markets.

- *Data extraction software*: Provides easy access to a data warehouse or mart, or to any of the most popular DBMS; sometimes referred to as *pipeline software*.

- *Graphical, tabular, and textual information on the same screen*: Windows are created on the screen for each kind of presentation; it is easy to toggle between a tabular display of the same information.

- *Multitier security*: Multiple levels of security, all the way down to specific data elements.

- *System usage monitoring*: An especially important capability; provides information about who the users are, how frequently they use the system, and what information is and isn't used.

- *System administration tools*: Especially important for applications with large user basis.

- *Software agents*: Frees users from searching for exceptions and other needed information; there are many kinds of agents, some search through numerical data, others through documents and news stories; they can be event or time triggered.

- *Open architectures*: Once proprietary, now vendor software is largely open; vendors publish their APIs so that other vendors' products can be used with an application.

- *Web enabled*: Allows users to access information through a Web browser; all of the vendors are moving as quickly as they can to integrate Web technology (e.g., Java, Active X) into their product offerings.

- *Support for multiple kinds of users*: The same software can be used by different kinds of users, such as executives (point-and-click accessing of information), analysts and power users (spreadsheet-type analysis capabilities), and remote and casual users (accessing information through a Web browser).

4-5 INTERNET /INTRANET AND DATA WAREHOUSING

web browser → primary interface

With the Web browser becoming an almost universal interface, both in-house and vendor-built data warehouse systems are using the browser as a primary vehicle for end-user access. Data warehouses are being integrated with organizational intranets and extranets, as well as with the Internet. In addition, the thin client approach is being seen by more and more firms as a way of reducing cost and gaining control over their PC's. The thin client typically has a browser interface. These interfaces, either Netscape or Microsoft Explorer, are low cost or free. The ubiquity of the browser interface, together with the rapid expansion of the Internet, intranets, and extranets, led vendors to introduce these capabilities into their data warehouse offerings. Not just data warehouses, but old and new applications alike, are moving to the browser interface. It is increasingly becoming the favored application environment and the single interface for client/server applications.

THIN CLIENTS

A *thin client*, is also known as a *network computer* or NC. The idea is a reaction to *fat clients*, that is, personal computers used on networks which also have stand-alone capabilities that allow them to execute many programs independent of the local area network. Personal computers require large hard-disk storage for programs and data and, because of their capabilities, are relatively expensive to purchase and maintain. They also require extensive support from the information systems department. The thin client, on the other hand, is a stripped-down version of the personal computer, with minimal storage, which uses the server in the client/server arrangement to download both programs and data. As a result, proponents of thin clients believe they will be cheaper to purchase and operate even with the extra information systems department support.

For example:

- The Internet is being used by some data warehousing companies to distribute software directly.

- The Environmental Protection Agency is running an extranet that allows the public to access environmental data though a browser.

Security, privacy, and consumer risk are major interrelated issues on the Internet. Although encryption can be expected to become routine, major technical questions (e.g., 40 bit versus 140 bit) remain to be resolved: similarly, server security is an issue.

In the rest of this section, we concentrate on intranets, the private networks that overcome many of the difficulties of the Internet. Be aware, however, that many of the discussions apply to the Internet and to extranets as well.

Advantages and Disadvantages

Advantages [handwritten]

In addition to the reduction in cost anticipated with the Web and with thin clients, the following advantages are anticipated (Eckerson, 1997):

- *Universal interface.* As the interface for the client in a client/server data warehouse, the Web browser provides an intuitive method for accessing files and applications. Because they are easy to use, training time and cost are also reduced.

- *Lower administrative overhead.* The Web browser reduces administrative overhead costs by reducing software distribution and support costs, particularly for companies that are large and scattered in many locations. Distributing software via the intranet also ensures that end users are working with the latest software release.

- *Portable code.* The Web provides a true cross-platform development environment. By using intranet standards, an application can be deployed on any platform on which a browser is running.

Of course, wherever there are advantages, there are disadvantages. First, the Web was designed for document and file exchange, not to support mission-critical applications. In addition, the following disadvantages must be considered (Eckerson, 1997):

Disadvantages [handwritten]

- Need to program to solve technical constrains imposed by the Internet. [handwritten]

- *The HTTP protocol.* The standard protocol used on the Web is HTTP (Hypertext Transfer Protocol). This protocol maintains connections only long enough for a Web client to submit a request to a Web server and receive the results before a session is terminated. The server doesn't know who submitted a request or what the client requested.

- *Long-running transactions and complex queries.* Web servers are not set up to handle long-running transactions or complex queries that require a continuing, knowledgeable client/server connection. Developers have to build gateways and programs to circumvent these shortcomings.

- *Immature Technology.* The Web, wonderful as it is, is built on immature technology and standards. Both are evolving rapidly. Many firms are waiting for a stable Web environment before committing to it.

- *Security.* Firms are using private intranets and creating firewalls as a way of overcoming the security problems associated with the public Internet.

Intranet Economics

Using thin clients in a client/server architecture appears to offer cost advantages over conventional PC-based systems. Thin clients are currently believed to offer not only lower purchasing costs compared to PCs (fat clients), but also lower operating expense. The trade-off between keeping copies of applications on each PC and distributing applications from a server on an as-needed basis seems to be in favor of the thin client approach. Advocates also argue that software licensing costs will go down as the pricing shifts from a per seat to a per server basis. Thus, an intranet is expected to lower communications cost, client hardware costs, and applications software costs. However, an intranet requires more robust (and hence more expensive) servers.

↓ Costs in
· hardware
· software
· communication

↑ costs in
· servers

Integrated, Multiple Data Format Environment

weblinks
to integrate
multiple data
format

Decision makers need to integrate information available in multiple formats. With browser technology, they can obtain both typical column and row reports and unstructured information, tied together by hypertext capabilities. For example, an apparel manufacturer can find both the image of an advertisement and the sales reports on the dresses and accessories shown in the ad.

INTERNET, INTRANETS, EXTRANETS

The technology of the Internet is being applied by companies in three ways:

Conventional *Internet* servers allow anyone who knows how to access the company through its Universal Resource Locator (URL) to obtain data made available to the public at large on its Internet server. For example, the publisher of this volume, Prentice Hall, can be reached at http://www.prenhall.com

The Internet itself is an organization that provides the needed connections. The Internet is also referred to as the World Wide Web, or the Web, for short. However, it is not necessary to use the World Wide Web for Internet access.

Intranets use the technology of the Internet but can be accessed only by people within the organization. An intranet is, in essence, a private corporate version of the Internet. An organization has to create the local and wide area networks required and has to run the intranet using its own resources. The major advantage of using an intranet is that it provides privacy and better information security. A "firewall" prevents access by unauthorized users.

Extranets are a step between the Internet and an intranet. They allow multiple organizations to share access to (some of) a company's data. They are used both for marketing and sales and for sharing information with trading partners. Companies are using extranets to allow external parties to access their data warehouses (e.g., customers can reach into a company's parts database).

[margin notes:] Definition intranet

Definition extranet.

Group Support

Because an intranet contains information from multiple sources and has e-mail capabilities, it is a way that groups in the organization can communicate. The intranet allows sharing among workgroups. Although these capabilities are independent of the warehouse, with the warehouse users can create dynamic reports and manipulate the information they receive. They can drill up or down, in any dimension, perform additional calculations, pivot or rotate results, and then forward the results to others. The result is a higher level of interactive analysis and knowledge sharing.

sharing information [handwritten annotation]

SQL and HYPERTEXT

The conventional approach to data warehouse retrieval is through SQL queries, either independently or embedded in other applications. However, intranets use HTML (Hypertext Markup Language). A key technical problem is to make these approaches compatible with one another. The SQL and HTML approaches are compared in Figure 4-1 .

In the conventional three-tier client/server model, a fat client sends queries to a server. The server provides

With web an extra step is needed: -translate html into SQL [handwritten annotation]

1. SQL processing
2. A scheduler for sending the query
3. A report generator

The SQL query is sent to the data warehouse. In the intranet model, the browser sends HTML requests to a Web server, which uses a Common Gateway Interface (CGI) to forward the request to a query engine, which generates the SQL. The recipient may be either a data warehouse or a data mart. (SQL was is discussed further in Section 4-3.)

Other Desirable Features

In addition to providing good query response, an intranet system should provide the following capabilities:

- Support *data warehouse access* from an HTML browser request, that is, get the intranet to talk to the corporate database. To do so, the Web server must have a robust analytic layer that can generate SQL dynamically, perform computations, and format reports based on user requests. Without these capabilities, the user can only list stored data elements.

- A server-based *file management system* to support knowledge sharing among users.

Figure 4-1: Conventional and Web Processing Models

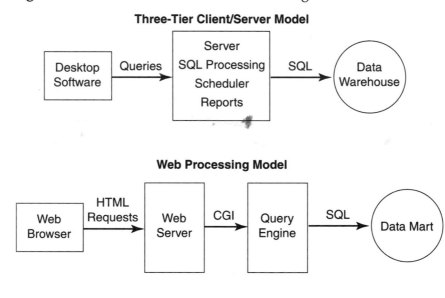

Three-Tier Client/Server Model

Source: Adapted from Eckerson (1996).

- A *security system* that makes sure people have access only to information for which they have a need to know.

- Filters and agents that guard against information overload, yet provide alerts to users about important new information. For example, an agent may notify the appropriate managers when the data warehouse indicates that the average forecasting error for inventory has exceeded some preset level.

Interactivity

Web-based query and analysis tools can have four levels of interactivity. They range from static to dynamic viewing and from local to dynamic querying (Eckerson, 1997).

1. *Static viewing* implies that the tool provides static reports. That is, the report cannot be updated or changed in format.
2. *Dynamic viewing* adds interaction to HTML reports. Users can get the latest report and can also schedule when the report is run. However, once the report is downloaded to the user's computer, it becomes static.
3. *Local querying* allows users to interact with a chunk of data that was downloaded to their desktop. Using plug-ins, help applications, or applets, the user can manipulate the data and the report structure.
4. *Dynamic querying* allows users to query databases directly. Queries are made in the form of HTML forms or applets. Queries range from user-selected variables within an existing report to ad hoc queries against the database.

Generations of Web Sites

The ability to use a Web site interactively is related to the level of sophistication of the Web site. Eckerson (1997) identifies four generations of Web sites:

- First-generation   file distribution
- Second-generation   dynamic HTML publication
- Third-generation   Java-assisted publishing
- Fourth-generation   dynamic Java publishing

First-generation servers support a file server in which users can retrieve HTML files stored on the server. Second-

and third-generation servers use a four-tier architectures, where the tiers are Web browsers, Web servers, application servers, and databases. Fourth generation sites work entirely using Java code. The server is used primarily to download Java applets to the client. The client interacts directly with the database. Which specific generation will win out in the marketplace is still uncertain.

Limitations

The commercial availability of Web-enabled data warehousing software, particularly software for complex OLAP applications, is quite new. Applications that center on straightforward information retrieval, as distinguished from analysis, migrate well to the intranet. They have a low level of functionality but are able to present information in a multiplicity of formats to broad audiences. Functionally intensive applications with a small number of users, typical of the requirements of analysts, are more difficult. OLAP developers are still working on several issues:

- The browser's procedural environment to make it closer to Windows than to DOS.
- Improving delivery of information and user friendliness in the browser, including how best to use new technologies, such as Java, CORBA, and ActiveX and how to provide plug-ins and helper applications.
- Handling the volume of data that potentially can be needed on the client.

Requirements For Web-based Query Tools

Table 4-2 is a list of requirements for Web-based analysis and query tools required for decision support and some of the questions you need to ask about how the tool meets these requirements. The requirements were proposed by Eckerson (1997). Eckerson also provides a long table of specific Web-based tools available in the marketplace in early 1997.

Conclusions: The Browser, the Intranet and the Data Warehouse

The bottom line is that user companies view intranets and browsers as an easy-to-manage, relatively low cost medium for providing knowledge sharing and decision support capabilities on a global basis. Intranets can handle most of the conventional queries to data warehouses. However, for complex analyses, the browser interface may need to be supplemented.

Table 4-2: Requirements for Web Browser Tools

REQUIREMENT	QUESTIONS TO ASK
1. Interactivity	What level of interactivity (see interactivity discussion above) does the tool support?
2. Functionality	Does the tool have more functionality than the client/server version?
3. Architecture	Does the tool support your present and anticipated architecture?
4. Performance	How quickly can users access the data they need? What is the trade-off between interactivity and performance?
5. Design	Do you have to be able to code in HTML or write CGI scripts to use the tool?
6. Administration	Is the tool able to control access to reports by user, by group, and by role? Are access menus individualized?
7. Output	Can the tool provide outputs in a variety of formats and languages?
8. Scalability	What platforms does the tool's execution engine run on? Does it support load balancing?
9. Databases	Does the tool support your databases? Does it support text?
10. Pricing	Does the tool support a Web pricing model, that is a number of concurrent users and server size?

4-6 DATA MINING

Data mining refers to finding answers about an organization from the information in the data warehouse that the executive or the analyst had not thought to ask. Data mining is made possible by the very presence of the large databases in the data warehouse. It provides the techniques that allow managers to obtain managerial information from their legacy systems beyond that which can be obtained from reports and queries. Its objective is to identify valid, novel, potentially useful, and understandable patterns in data.

Data mining is also known as *knowledge data discovery* (KDD). Those seeking to make a distinction between the terms data mining and KDD generally use KDD to refer to the process of discovering useful knowledge from data, while using data mining to refer to the application of algorithms for extracting patterns from data. The difference lies in KDD's use of appropriate prior knowledge and proper interpretation of results rather than blind application of the data mining techniques.[2] Thus, KDD is closer to an R&D process, and data mining to an operational process.

Some Successes in Business

Every new field has its initial successes which intrigue others to investigate it further. The following are some examples of early successful results with KDD:

- People who buy scuba gear take Australian vacations
- Men who buy diapers at convenience stores buy beer
- Children who take aspirin are at risk for the deadly Reyes disease
- Fraud detection and consumer loan analysis
- Optimizing production lines

---

[2] Applying statistical techniques blindly, called data dredging, it can lead to finding patterns that are meaningless.

Handwritten margin notes:

Data mining:
New information
not thought
before

Objective:
identify patterns

Dmining and Data
discovery are
equivalent.
People making the
distinction:
Data discovery = use
of previous
knowledge.

- Database marketing (called *mailshot response* in Europe) to find future customers
- Play selection in the National Basketball Association

These results are the extreme cases. Usually, data mining leads to steady incremental changes rather than major transformations. It leads to small advantages with each customer, each project, each year. Over time, these changes accumulate like compound interest. Occasionally, of course, a major breakthrough is found. However, firms should not count on such happenings. In its present state of development, data mining is relatively unsophisticated. The methods cannot substitute for domain knowledge or for experience in model building or analysis.

In the case of loan analysis, plots of data on repayment versus income and debt (as well as other variables) provide rules as to whether or not a requested loan should be granted. Although companies treat successful fraud detection techniques as proprietary, successes have been reported in such areas as detecting health care provider fraud in electronically submitted claims and in using neural network tools to detect credit card fraud.

In the National Basketball Association, a large number of teams use a system developed by IBM called Advanced Scout. The system searches for patterns in the data and then links that data to a video of the game. Thus, a coach need only look at the game video which comes from the pattern. The coaches use Advanced Scout in developing strategy for the game. Strategy includes play selection, the association of individual player performance with the players who are on the floor simultaneously, and how a player performs when guarded by a particular opponent.

The Data Mining Process

As shown in Figure 4-2, the following are the basic steps in the KDD process:

1. Develop an understanding of the application, relevant prior knowledge, and the end user's goals.
2. Create a target data set to be used for discovery.
3. Clean and preprocess data (including handling missing data fields, noise in the data, accounting for time series, and known changes).
4. Reduce the number of variables and find invariant representations of data if possible.
5. Choose the data mining task (classification, regression, clustering, etc.).
6. Choose the data mining algorithm.
7. Search for patterns of interest (this is the actual data mining).
8. Interpret the pattern mined. If necessary, iterate through any of steps 1 through 7.
9. Consolidate knowledge discovered and prepare a report.

Figure 4-2: Steps in the Data Mining Process

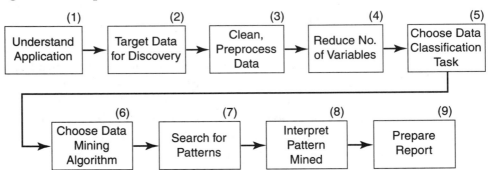

The first two steps, understanding the application and determining the target data to be used for discovery, are common to all forms of data analysis. This step includes knowing what relevant prior knowledge exists, the goals of the project, and what data exists. In the case of data warehouses, the metadata helps in pinpointing what data exists.

The third step, cleaning and preprocessing the data, is the usual one used in preparing data for warehousing. Organizational data are cleaned and validated before being put in the warehouse. For knowledge discovery, further preprocessing is used to remove outliers and noise in the data.

The fourth and fifth steps involve reducing the number of variables and choosing the data classification task. With too many variables, it becomes difficult to make sense out of the results. Therefore, the analyst applies dimensionality reduction or transformation techniques and also tries to find representations of the data that are invariant.

KDD involves looking in the data for the following factors to solve the problem:

- *Associations*: things done together (buy groceries)
- *Sequences*: events over time (house, refrigerator)
- *Classifications*: pattern recognition (rules)
- *Clusters*: define new groups
- *Forecasting*: predictions from time series

The algorithm selected depends on the task to be performed.

The sixth and seventh steps (choosing the data mining algorithm and searching for patterns) are the heart of the KDD process, where the actual mining is done. It involves fitting models or determining patterns from the warehouse data.

Patterns are represented according to classification rules or trees, regression models, clustering, sequences, and dependencies. Data mining can be:

- Bottom up (explore raw facts to find connections)
- Top down (search to test hypotheses)

Therefore, the specific models come from a variety of fields, including:

- Statistical analysis of data
- Neural networks and expert systems
- Fuzzy logic

- Intelligent agents
- Multidimensional analysis
- Data visualization
- Decision trees

Siftware – software associated with Dmining process (margin handwriting)

Gonna?? ?? (handwriting)

The software associated with these steps is called *siftware*. As used in siftware, data mining algorithms consists of three components:

- The model
- The preference criterion
- The search algorithm

The parameters of the model are determined from the data. The preference for a particular model depends on the data available. Usually, some form of goodness-of-fit criterion is used. Care has to be taken to make sure that the model does not try to infer too much (overfitting) or too little (too many degrees of freedom) from the data. The search algorithm is selected based on the model and the preference criterion being used. The selection of these three components is still an art.

The eighth step reintroduces the human being to the picture. The results of the data mining operation of step 7 are examined by an analyst who judges whether the outcomes are

- possible,
- internally consistent, or
- plausible.

Possible implies that the result is physically possible (e.g., doesn't exceed the speed of light); internally consistent implies that the result does not contradict itself; and plausible means that the association found is believable, that is, could happen.

If the analyst is dissatisfied with the outcome, he or she can rerun the case with revised or refined queries and conditions. That is, the process is iterative, with the analyst asking questions after each new set of computer results. Once the analyst is satisfied with the output, the results are interpreted (step 8) and the findings are reported (step 9). These steps involve presenting the results in a form that is more understandable to decision makers. Such approaches as representing patterns graphically, structuring rules based on the patterns, resolving redundancy and conflicts with previous patterns and explaining findings in natural language are all involved here.

Finally, actions are taken based on the findings.

Helpful Hints

The following helpful hints are based on Small (1997). First, the relation between the people who have domain knowledge and those who are data mining experts is a critical success factor. A data mining expert without domain knowledge or a business expert who knows nothing about models and data are both useless. The data mining expert and the people who understand the business must work closely together.

Second, data mining cannot find patterns of interest unless the tool is told what to look for. For example, to find ways of improving mailing list impact, the search would be directed to customers who have bought large amounts previously or who have responded frequently to previous offers.

Third, data mining can be useful in many areas, not just those in which it has previously been successful. However, cost/benefit analysis needs to be done. If the cost of mining is larger than the anticipated return, it should not be undertaken.

Fourth, the techniques being applied in data mining are generally not new. They have been used for many years but not in a business context. With the large amounts of data now available in data warehouses and with new user-friendly software and interfaces, they have become accessible. Data mining no longer needs to be an extremely complex process.

5. Datamining can be used with small databases Large databases should be sampled.

Fifth, data mining can be undertaken with relatively small databases. Large databases can (and should) be sampled. It is possible to have too much data and lose sight of the information it contains. For example, using both age and date of birth results in both factors being judged equally relevant and each will be assigned a lower weight.

Current Limits to Data Mining

- New field
- Few vendors
- Skill personnel through consultants

Data mining is a relatively new field. The vendors developing commercial products tend to be small. Their products are being bought by larger vendors (e.g., Pilot, Seagate HOLOS) who incorporate them into their systems. Usually, only a few of the many data mining techniques are being incorporated into these large packages.

Organizations should recognize that data mining requires:

• Subject area expertise
• Experience with large databases
• Data mining skills

Data mining skills are often provided by consultants because they are usually not available in-house. Few IS personnel have the statistics and artificial intelligence background needed to understand the various data mining methods, nor do they understand how and when to apply them. Data mining product vendors are quite willing to sell consulting services, but also see the market for products that require little external help to use. The difficulty they face is how to sell packaged solutions for specific problems in specific industries, such as credit card theft. By targeting a particular application, it is possible to preselect the best data mining algorithm(s) and to provide the application with an appropriate user interface.

Limits

Among the limits to data mining are:

• Dealing with very large (e.g., terabyte) databases

- Dealing with high dimensionality, which increases the size of the search space and may also create spurious patterns
- Overfitting available data
- Rapid changes in data (nonstationarity) that make previously discovered patterns invalid
- Missing and noisy data
- Reducing the emphasis on fully automated, rapid-response environments and increasing the human/computer interaction
- Lack of full understanding of the patterns observed
- Managing changes in data and knowledge as available information is updated
- Dealing with nonnumerical data, such as objects, text, and multimedia, more and more of which is being stored in databases
- Lack of integration with other systems

All of these problems are areas of current research, but they are not yet fully solved. Nonetheless, despite these difficulties, data mining offers an important approach to achieving value from the data warehouse for use in decision support.

4-7 DATABASE MARKETING[3]

One of the major applications of data warehouses and data mining is database marketing. The basic idea is to use the information in the large, clean databases available in the warehouse to market products and services which are customized to the individual. Database marketing has come to the forefront because of a number of trends and opportunities,

---

[3] We are indebted to David Petrie for much of this section.

[handwritten margin note: From To Product → customer push pull]

described in Table 4-3. These changes resulted in a shift from a "product push" mass marketing to "customer pull" target marketing. Target marketing reduces the emphasis on the broad middle market and on competition based on price and selection.

Table 4-3: Trends and Opportunities in Marketing

TRENDS	IMPLICATIONS
Slowing growth	Fewer customers
Increased diversity	Development of multiple markets
Education and income gaps	Creation of multitier markets
Aging population	Changes in disposable income
Increased work time	Fewer hours available for shopping
Changing families	Increased numbers of singles and single parents
Increased competition	Focused search for market niches

During the twentieth century, to achieve economies of scale, marketing shifted from the neighborhood storekeeper who knew the individual customer to large, impersonal retail chains. Toward the end of the century it became clear that the limits of the retail chainapproach were being reached. As a result, marketers tried a new approach: using information technology to sell customized products and services to large populations. This return to personalized service while maintaining economies of scale was made possible by three factors:

[handwritten margin note: Forces pushing database marketing]

1. The necessary data became available.
2. Advances were made in the cost and capabilities of data storage and indexing.
3. Data mining and knowledge discovery techniques began to be applied to data warehouses.

Database marketing is being used in two ways: marketing to existing customers and marketing to prospects (people who are potential customers). In both cases the objective is to lower both marketing and direct-mail costs. The database

[handwritten margin notes: Objectives — Keep customers — ↑ sales — ↑ referrals — ↑ new customers]

makes it possible to maintain a closer relationship with the customer in the hope of keeping more existing customers, increasing the sales to them, and obtaining more referrals from them. For prospects, the database is used to match the profiles of potential customers to those of existing profitable customers. The hope is to add new customers and sales and bring previous customers back.

Database Marketing Issues

Database marketing creates three issues that marketers must resolve:

1. Too much data is available, but not enough information.
2. A choice has to be made as to whether the focus is on the product or the customer.
3. Reliance on the computer (and the concomitant investment of large amounts of time and money) reduces the efforts placed on human creativity, analysis, and innovation.

Relationship Marketing

One way of resolving these issues is to apply the concepts of relationship marketing, shown in Table 4-4. Figure 4-3 shows how the data warehouse fits into this process. Note that in database marketing it is important to keep detailed transaction data to be able to run the needed analyses. Also, among the tools used are geographic information systems (GISs) to visualize the spatial implications of the data.

Relationship marketing has been applied successfully when one or more of the following conditions apply:

- Periodic, repeat purchases of products or services make it possible to capture names at the point of sale (e.g., auto service, medical care, home services).

[handwritten margin notes: When to establish relationship marketing. - Periodic data]

Table 4-4:   Concepts of Relationship Marketing

Gather data about customers.	Include current and prospective customers. Note that this data is generally not summarized.
Identify "best" customers.	Calculate profitability and customer lifetime value.
Find underlying characteristics of "best customers."	Use analytic tools (multiple regression, CHAID, etc.) to find the important variables.
Identify customers that have these characteristics.	Select individuals from data in warehouse.
Test the marketing plan and forecast results.	Use about 10% of customer list selected and run market tests. Use results to forecast effectiveness.
Track results.	Analyze results with OLAP and, if needed, iterate through steps and refine process.

Figure 4-3:   Use of Data Warehousing in Relationship Marketing

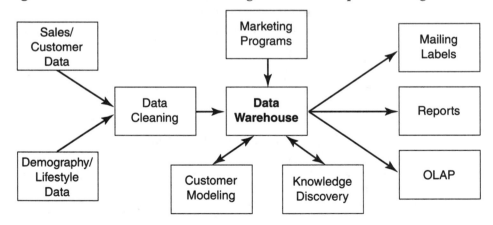

2: Affinity groups

3: Reward systems

- Affinity groups with common interests can be constructed (e.g., new babies, gardening supplies, sports, music).

- Frequent buyer reward systems can be developed (frequent flyers, department stores, supermarkets).

It does not work well when the product is a commodity with a markup too small to finance building the relationship

Database
marketing
not suitable
for:
- commodity
products
- Seldom and
unpredictable
purchases.

DECISION SUPPORT TOOLS **155**

(e.g., grocery items) or where the purchases are seldom and unpredictable (e.g., furniture). Among companies that have established relationship marketing systems are Merrill Lynch, General Motors, Blockbuster Entertainment, American Express, Vons supermarkets, Federal Express, and Lands' End.

Conventional Retail Marketing

Database
marketing
for retail
objectives.
- Look for
causes of
high and
low
performance

The database marketing arrangements are somewhat different when the marketing and analysis activity is focused on the retail outlet and on general advertising rather than the individual customer. Here the marketing database captures price/sales, display/promotion, and competitor data. External information is also used. The data is used to look for "causes" of high and low performance and to generate a variety of decision support analyses. The warehouse arrangement in this case is shown in Figure 4-4.

Figure 4-4: Use of Data Warehouse in Retail Marketing

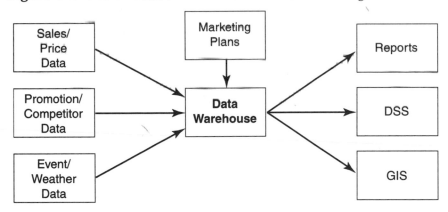

Many of these systems rely on OLTP data gathered by using the bar codes from each item sold. The results are huge, dynamic databases that require summarization and analysis over time if they are to be used for decision making. Companies with such conventional systems include Benneton, Coca-Cola, Frito-Lay, Ocean Spray, Quaker Oats, and Wal-Mart Stores.

Social Issues to Be Resolved

Database marketing also creates social issues, particularly in terms of the environment, privacy, and confidentiality.

- Direct mail results in large environmental waste. Targeting individuals helps reduce the waste, but it is still quite large.

- Database marketing is the result of having very large amounts of information available about individuals. Many people feel that using the data about them invades their right to privacy. This feeling of wanting to be left alone is even more marked in Europe than in the United States. European countries such as Sweden have quite strict laws governing what information can be used.

- In addition to privacy, there is concern about confidentiality of the information. People believe that information about themselves should not be traded.

Chapter

5

BUILDING DECISION SUPPORT APPLICATIONS

5-1 INTRODUCTION

In previous chapters we discussed the data warehouse from a decision support systems (DSS) point of view. In this chapter we reverse the process to discuss decision support applications from a data warehousing point of view. The discussion is intended to teach people who are not decision support experts about the major DSS issues and to indicate how the data warehouse (and the data mart) affect DSS. Readers who already know a lot about DSS will find much that is familiar to them but will learn about the changes that the warehouse creates in how decision support systems are created.

A variety of applications support decision making: queries, managed query environments, decision support systems, executive information systems, and data mining. Each has been discussed in previous chapters. Each has similarities and differences from the others. For example, each requires a prototyping development methodology because of the difficulty of initially determining information requirements. It is only through trial and error and experimentation that requirements can be fully understood. However, the applications typically serve different user groups. For example, data mining is normally performed by analysts with backgrounds in statistics or artificial intelligence, while for executive information systems, the user base is a firm's senior executives. Because these applications have strong similarities as well as differences, it is not surprising that their development has many, but not all things, in common.

5-2 OLAP IN DECISION SUPPORT

OLAP was discussed both in Chapter 1 and in Section 4-3. From the point of view of building decision support applications, OLAP can be thought of as either a separate application, or a capability within other decision support applications.

OLAP
1: Independent,
2: within other
D.SS

The first perspective is to emphasize the ability to query, analyze, and present multidimensional data. The ability to do this is important to many knowledge workers and virtually all business units and companies. In response, database and end-user access tool vendors have developed a variety of products to meet this need.

The other perspective is that OLAP is an important capability in a variety of decision support applications, such as those discussed in this chapter. For example, an executive information system typically supplies a wide variety of information, and one type might be provided through OLAP.

Both of these perspectives are valid. They refer to a set of capabilities, discussed either separately or in the context of an application.

5-3 DECISION SUPPORT NEEDS OF EXECUTIVES, MANAGERS, AND ANALYSTS

People in organizations perform very different jobs. Consider, for example, the responsibilities of an executive such as a CEO. Research into the nature of executive work has found that:

> *Executives have a large work load, work continuously and rapidly, and endure frequent interruptions throughout the day. Executive work is very complex, demanding, unstructured, unspecialized, unfocused, unpredictable, disorderly, and long-range. Executive work activities are typically brief, diverse, and fragmented, and demonstrate high degrees of uncertainty* (Watson, Houdeshel, and Rainer, 1997).

A typical morning in the life of an executive is described on the next two pages.

Middle-and-lower level managers also have busy workdays, but their focus is on the organizational units that they manage, which typically results in a narrower range of activities. Analysts investigate specific topics, such as the impact of a new product promotion, and report their findings to management.

Because executives, managers, and analysts perform different jobs, their information needs differ. A CEO might want information about the external economic and technological environment, actions of competitors, performance relative to key indicators, product rollouts, and the like. The information needs are broad and diverse, but include the ability to drill down into detailed data as part of investigations into problems and opportunities. A lower-level manager, such as a department head, needs such information as how actual performance compares to plans and whether expenditures are within budget. Analysts are typically more information producers than information consumers because their job is to create information for others.

Work differences also affect how decision support applications are developed. To illustrate, because of the many demands on their time, it is usually difficult to obtain much face-to-face time with executives. This complicates determining the information requirements for a DSS. On the other hand, analysts are usually more available to work with sys-

An Executive's Morning

As Mr. M. enters his office at 8:30 am. and greets Janice, his secretary, the telephone rings. It is the manager of the local manufacturing operation and the call is put through. "We had a fire in the plan last night," Mr. M. is told, "and the damage amounted to $30,000; we should be back in operation by next Wednesday."

As he hangs up, Janice enters and reminds him of an 11 am appointment and of his intention to call the company lawyer. "Joe dropped by and would like to see you, and, oh yes, that flight to Paris is booked, so I put you on the 4 pm leaving on the fifth. Nothing much in the mail except for that letter from Antwerp." The seven pieces of mail are processed immediately:

The invitation to speak to a trade organization is declined, with a note to Janice to reply that Mr. M. will be abroad.

The advertisement for a magazine on mergers and acquisitions is thrown away.

A notice informs Mr. M. of the data of the board meeting, and the data is noted on the calendar.

Fortune magazine is skimmed, and an advertisement for certain production equipment is clipped.

The head of the organization's Antwerp office has written to complain that the treasurer will not release funds for his tenth anniversary celebration. Mr. M. calls to Janice to ask the treasurer to drop by today.

The internal financial statement for the month is glanced at and put in the "out" basket for filing.

Without reading it, Mr. M. signs a document received from his vice-president of research and development. It is a request for funds under a federally supported program, and Mr. M. must sign it before it goes to Washington.

The time is 8:40 and Mr. M.'s assistant looks in: "It looks like there will be trouble at the meeting--they think Mike was forced out, and they are prepared to make a stink about it." They proceed to discuss the situation.

At 8:55, Mr. M. calls the chairman of the board. "There'll be trouble at the meeting, George," and Mr. M. goes on to repeat the information he has just received.

The conversation ends precisely at 9:00, and a Mr. Jamison is ushered in with a member of the personnel department. Mr. Jamison is introduced to Mr. M. who asks, "Well, what will you do when you leave us?" After some discussion about Mr. Jamison's camp in New Hampshire, he is presented with a plaque commemorating 30 years of service to the organization.

An Executive's Morning (Continued)

At 9:30, the treasurer, who has been waiting at the door, enters. "John, look at this," says Mr. M. as he hands him the Antwerp letter. "What's the story?" The treasurer explains his side to Mr. M.'s satisfaction; when the treasurer leaves at 10 am., Mr. M. immediately writes a letter to Antwerp explaining that he cannot interfere with the treasurer's deicsion.

Ten minutes later, Janice is called in: "Now who are therse people coming at 11?" Once told, he asks Janice to arrange for his assistnat to be present at the meeting.

At 10:10, Mr. M. walks through the executive offices toward the plant.

On the way, he passes the medical center and appears to note something. Once in the plant, he stops by various machines to watch the operations and chat with the workers. He stops at the office of the production superintendent, who is not there. He hands the assistant superintendent the advertisement clipped from *Fortune* magazine, commenting, "Jerry may find this useful for production scheduling."

Back in his office at 10:40, Mr. M. finds a message to call the executive vice president, who is in Los Angeles. "They are asking $13 million? Tell them we won't go a penny over $10 million, but, Joe let's be prepared to settle for $12 million."

This telephone call is followed by one to the controller. "Have you been-through the medical department lately? They don't need that new wing--they are not using the space they have now."

The 11 am meeting in the board room is with Mr. M., his assistant, and two members of a consulting firm. These meetings are held monthly for the duration of a consulting contract. After brief pleasantries, it becomes clear that there is friction here. The consultants are trying to justify their fees, while the assistant questions them. Mr. M., who has been silent, suddently asks, "What about the charge for reprogramming? I don't think it should be borne by us." After some negotiation, a settlement is reached at lunch.

Source: Mintzberg, Henry. *The Nature of Managerial Work*. New York, NY: Harper and Row, 1973.

tem developers. Taking another example, most executives have limited computer skills and experience and are unwilling to learn complex interfaces. Analysts are often power users and are willing to trade off simplicity of use for power and flexibility in interface design if it enhances their job performance.

When thinking about the jobs that people perform, do not generalize or oversimplify. Most people function in multiple modes of computer use. For some information, they want the easy point-and-click access associated with an EIS; at other times, they may need a more complex OLAP capability. Fortunately, it is possible to provide multiple capabilities in a single decision support system. For example, managed query environment software in a data warehouse (see Section 4-3) supports both ad hoc queries and preestablished queries that can be executed by clicking an executive button.

Provide multiple capabilities

5-4 DEVELOPMENT METHODOLOGY

Traditional SDLC is ok for transactional because requirements are known.

For transaction processing applications, the systems development life cycle (SDLC) is used to manage the development of applications. It breaks the development process into a set of interrelated steps. Most companies have manuals that specify that company's version of the SDLC. The number and specific steps vary, but they typically include establish the business need, identifing information requirements, logical systems design, physical system design, programming, testing, and implementation.

The purpose of the SDLC is to bring structure and order to the development process. Each step is required and feeds later steps. Each step and the entire process can be planned, organized, executed, and controlled. It allows different groups of people to work on the same project by using the specifications that are created. The SDLC requires that information requirements be determined early on. Because poorly specified requirements can lead to costly and time-consuming redevelopment efforts, it is common practice to have users "sign off" on the requirements. This approach forces users to think carefully about their requirements and discourages changes.

*DSS require
Prototyping
to determine
requirements*

Although the SDLC is well ingrained in IS practice for transaction systems, unfortunately it does not work well with decision support applications. It implicitly assumes that users know what they want. Typically, users have some idea about their information requirements but only really find them out through a trial-and-error process. They need to see and use an initial version of the system and then specify the changes that need to be made. This approach goes by a variety of names, including prototyping, evolutionary design, and iterative design. They all emphasize the rapid development of an initial version of the system, use of the system, and rapid revisions. The "start small, but think big" adage is often heard. Start with a small version of the system but have plans for how it will evolve into a more complete, comprehensive system.

*Prototyping:
Developers
- skilled
- comfortable
working/users
- able to cope
with uncertain
and shifting
requirements
Users
- willing to spend time
Development tools available.*

The prototyping methodology has several important requirements. Developers must be skilled and comfortable working with users over an extended period of time. They must be able to cope with uncertain and shifting requirements. Users must be willing to spend time discussing requirements, work with early versions of the system, and provide suggestions for improvement. Development tools must be available to support rapid application development and change.

5-5 DETERMINING INFORMATION REQUIREMENTS FOR DECISION SUPPORT

A critical step in developing any computer application is determining its information requirements. When these are known, the processing and data requirements can be determined. Many of the data requirements can be met through the development of a well-planned data warehouse. Planning the warehouse and determining information requirements are intertwined.

Four generic strategies for identifying information requirements are (Davis, 1982):

1. Asking
2. Deriving from an existing information system
3. Synthesizing from characteristics of the utilizing system
4. Discovering from experimentation with an evolving information system

The first strategy is to obtain information requirements by asking people about their information needs (Telem, 1988a, 1988b). The second strategy is to derive information requirements from an existing information system (Byrd et al., 1992). The third is to develop information requirements based on the characteristics of the system being served (i.e., the object system). The requirements for information stem from the activities of the object system. A variety of methods are based on this strategy: normative analysis (Davis, 1982), strategy set formulation (Davis, 1982; King, 1978), critical success factor analysis (Rockart, 1979; Zahedi, 1987), process analysis (Davis, 1982), decision analysis (Ackoff, 1967; Jenkins et al., 1984), sociotechnical analysis (Bostrom, 1989; Bostrom and Heinen, 1977), and input process output analysis (Davis, 1982). The final strategy is to establish an initial system, then refine it as information requirements become better understood. Prototyping (Naumann and Jenkins, 1982), iterative design (Sprague, 1980), and heuristic development (Berresford and Wetherbe, 1979) are based on this approach.

Determining the information requirements for decision support applications is usually a more challenging undertaking than for transaction processing systems, especially where the decision-making task is new, unique, and poorly understood. When asked, users may have a difficult time saying what information they need, because they don't know for certain. Often, there is no existing system upon which to base the application. The application developers may not have a good initial understanding of the decision-making task to be supported. It is only through a prototyping, evolutionary development approach that the information requirements can be fully understood.

Prototyping to understand requirements

Many organizations choose initially to build a data mart rather than a comprehensive warehouse. A data mart can be built quickly and at relatively little cost. It provides a learning experience and a proof of concept. There is also a clear business need that drives its development; consequently, the information requirements are narrower, better understood, and more manageable than for a data warehouse. However, as pointed out in Section 3-4, scaling a data mart to an enterprise system or making sure that the data mart is compatible with later data warehouses can be difficult to accomplish.

Queries

Analysts and managers who perform queries have information requirements that are relatively easy to determine. Interviews can be conducted to identify what queries are currently being made and what queries users would like to make once the data warehouse is built (or an existing warehouse is expanded). In some cases, particularly with users with limited computer skills and knowledge, it may be necessary to describe what data can be made available in the warehouse. After examples are given of data that might be included in the warehouse it is not unusual to hear, "I didn't know that I could get that".

On the other hand, users may request data that is not available. For example, in one company, the vice president for human resources wanted data on employee job skills. He was concerned that certain skills would be in short supply in a few years because of company-mandated requirement policies. Unfortunately, there was no reliable data source to meet this information need and it could not be obtained from the initial implementation of the warehouse. Approval was given, however, to begin a project to collect and maintain job skills data and ultimately include it in the warehouse.

Individual interviews should be used when the number of users is small. Group interviews like those employed in joint application design sessions (JAD) or in group decision support system (GDSS) sessions are appropriate with larger groups and cross-functional applications. Surveys can be used with very large groups to augment individual interviews.

Decision Support Systems

Interviews

For DSS, interviews are the most common way to determine information requirements. It is unlikely, however, that the initial set of interviews will fully disclose the requirements. These will emerge only after the users have experience with the system. Expect to hear, "Can you add ...?", "I don't need...", "Can you change...?"

Executive Information Systems

Most challenging information broad & diverse.

The most challenging information requirements to determine are those for an EIS. Because of their busy schedules, executives have little time to spend with system developers. Even when they can meet, executives have a difficult time specifying what information they want. Their information needs are broad and diverse. Some of the needs are beyond what is typically supplied by computer-based systems and includes information that is external (e.g., news stories, competitive), soft (e.g., rumors), and nonmachine resident (e.g., assessments of situations; see Figure 5-1). Most developers have limited exposure to executives and a limited understanding of what executives do; consequently, developers have a little background and knowledge to draw upon. Also, developers typically have little experience in developing systems like an EIS. The EIS is quite likely the first system of its kind in the organization; consequently, there is no existing system to analyze.

Portfolio of methods

Although there is no single method (i.e., "silver bullet") for determining EIS information requirements, research has uncovered a portfolio of methods that have been used by companies (Watson and Frolick, 1993). These methods are briefly described and commented on in Table 5-1. The methods are not mutually exclusive and often overlap. Each method builds upon, reinforces, and refines what is learned from the other methods. It is unlikely that a a warehouse design team will use all of the methods; rather, a set should be selected that is appropriate for the company's practices, policies, culture, and executives' support for and willingness to use. Some of the methods are best (or can only be used) with the initial version of the system (e.g., examinations of other organizations' EIS) or with the evolving system (e.g., software tracking of system usage).

Executive interviews are always important and need to be carefully scripted and conducted. Simply asking, "What information do you want?" seldom results in a comprehensive set of requirements. The executive typically describes information that is currently received, with an addition or two. Table 5-2 presents a set of questions that have been used effectively. They are organized to start with questions about information that is currently available and used, and to move to questions that are strategic in nature and cover information that may not be currently available.

Table 5-1: Methods for Determining EIS Information Requirements

Method	Comment
Discussions with executives. The analyst probes for information needs by asking about job responsibilities, problems currently being experienced, and commonly used information. These discussions vary from formally scheduled, heavily scripted interviews to informal, ad hoc conversations.	Executive input is critical to having a successful system. Make sure that a commitment to identify information requirements is made; otherwise, don't proceed with the development effort.
EIS planning meetings. Meetings are used to plot the course of an organization's EIS. The individuals involved in these meetings include the EIS staff, IS personnel, and functional area personnel, including, on occasion, executives. These meetings are used to evaluate the EIS and to decide and prioritize changes to the system.	This method is important when developing cross-functional applications. It also enhances feelings of system ownership.

(margin handwriting: choose appropriate methods.)

Table 5-1: Methods for Determining EIS Information Requirements

Examinations of computer-generated information. Analysts study what computer-generated information executives currently receive that should be included in the EIS. Missing information and how information should be presented are also identified.	Start with the most important reports the executives actually read. You are likely to never get to the others.
Discussions with support personnel. The EIS support staff meets with secretaries, administrative assistants, and other executive support staff personnel who have a good understanding of what information is important to the executives. Support personnel can often help identify what information was requested recently and who the executive talks with to gain information.	Although this method is important, it must never substitute for discussions with executives.
Volunteered information. Executives make recommendations concerning information that they would like to see included in the EIS.	Although helpful, make sure that the suggestions are not self-serving and do serve an organization-wide need.
Examinations of other organizations' EISs. The EIS support staff looks at other organizations' EISs to obtain ideas about what information to include in their own EIS. They also gain a better understanding of how useful different kinds of information might be.	This method is especially useful with the initial version of the system. It can also generate excitement and support for the EIS. ("If they do it, we should do it.") It will also generate ideas for interface design.
Examinations of non-computer-generated information. Analysts study the non-computer-related materials that executives refer to or need on a regular basis. Possible sources of information include newspapers, books, articles, government publications, newsletters, correspondence, and documents.	Once identified, this information can be scanned in, pulled from electronic news databases, or located on the Web. By providing such information in the data warehouse, the warehouse adds value.
Critical success factor (CSF) sessions. Sessions are held in which organizational goals are identified, the CSFs that underlie the goals are discussed, measures of the CSFs are explored, and methods for providing information relevant to the CSFs are discussed.	This method requires a good facilitator. It also requires strong executive commitment to the project because it involves group meetings that can last several days.
Participation in strategic planning sessions. Strategic planning sessions are used to develop long-range plans for the organization. When analysts sit in on these sessions, they are better able to supply information that supports the accomplishment of the strategic plans.	Some organizations do not allow analysts to use this method because of the sensitive nature of these meetings. If this is the case, it may be possible to meet with a representative of the strategic planning group to discuss the organization's strategic plans and the types of information needed to support their accomplishment.

Table 5-1: Methods for Determining EIS Information Requirements

Strategic business objectives (SBO) method. The EIS is designed to focus attention on and to provide support for the organization's strategic business objectives. Once strategic business objectives are established, the business processes required to accomplish them are identified. Information related to monitoring the strategic business objectives and to supporting the execution of the business processes is provided. This method provides an organization-wide approach to EIS design.	While the CSF method identifies important performance indicators, this method goes a step further and looks at the information needed by various people if the organization's strategic objectives are to be met. Speaking metaphorically, performance indicators are like a car's dashboard, while SBO-related information is the gas pedal.
Attendance at meetings. EIS staff members attend meetings that they think might enhance their understanding of what information executives need. Project status reviews, public relations briefings to the media, and customer review sessions are examples of such meetings.	The EIS staff member also serves as a resource at these meetings because of the person's familiarity with organizational information.
Examination of the strategic plan. The EIS staff examines the strategic plan to identify information needed to carry out and monitor the execution of the plan.	A few organizations place the strategic plan in the EIS.
Tracking executive activity. Executive activities are tracked to gain a better understanding of how they work and the information they use. Tracking involves either accompanying executives throughout the day or having the executive or executive support staff maintain logs of the executives' activities.	This method is appropriate for creating the initial version of the system. It is sometimes perceived as being too obtrusive.
Software tracking of EIS use. The EIS maintains a log of executives' use of the system. This information helps identify how the system might be changed to make it more useful.	This method can only be used with operational systems. Information that is infrequently viewed is a candidate for modifications or deletion from the warehouse.
Formal change requests. Executives indicate any changes they want made to the EIS in either paper or electronic form. The EIS support staff reviews, prioritizes, and schedules the changes to the system.	It is common for a user simply to place a call to the EIS manager to suggest a change.

Table 5-2: Questions for the Executive Interviews

What is the scope of your job responsibilities?
What computer-based information is important to you?
What other information (e.g., newspapers, industry reports) is important to you?
If you could enhance the information that you now receive to improve its value to you, what would you want to change?
What issues or problems are currently important to you?
Assume that you have been on vacation for the past two weeks. When you arrive back, what are the first things that you want to know?
What must be done right for you to be successful? What might cause you to fail?
Imagine that you pick up a copy of the Harvard Business Review three years from now. You read about your organization, and about yourself in particular. It talks about how well things are going. What does it say?
You pick up the same HBR article, also three years from today. Now it discusses why things are not going well. What does it say?

Data Mining

Defined relatively easy.

Data mining is performed to discover important patterns in the data. The analyst typically knows the kind of relationship to look for, such as the demographic characteristics of the type of people who are likely to respond favorably to a special promotion. The information requirements are defined relatively easy, but what is found can be surprising (Section 4-4).

5-6 SELECTING THE SOFTWARE

1) SS existed before DW but now DW provides better data

Decision support applications existed before there were data warehouses. These applications do not change appreciably because of the warehouse except that the warehouse provides a better source of data. The application software used is likely to remain the same. The software just accesses almost all its data needs through the warehouse rather than the many separate sources required previously.

DW is the data source for different applications

A data warehouse is typically built to support new applications or extensions to current ones. There is seldom a single software solution suitable for all applications because of the range of user requirements. This requirement normally results in the selection of additional decision support software. Some of it may be packaged with the data extraction/cleaning software that is chosen. Most data warehousing vendors offer a relatively complete product line, either through their own offerings or partnerships with other vendors. Other software may be selected at a later date, typically driven by end-user needs and preferences. The range of offerings is seen in Chapters 7 through 13 in the book where vendor products are described.

DW accessed by different software due to open architecture

Most mature data warehouses are accessed by multiple applications that employ different software. This situation exists for a variety of reasons: open architectures that make it possible, applications with different requirements, and business units that have considerable say over what software is used (since they are often paying for it). It is IS's challenge either to lead or facilitate the selection process so that the products meet the users' needs, provides a cost-effective solution, and fits within the existing computing environment.

IS to facilitate DSS selection process - meet needs. Cost effective compatible

Multiple software options are available to obtain solutions for any given application, and some of the options are dramatically different. For example, consider an EIS. Vendors offer special-purpose software, such as Comshare's Commander Decision, Oracle's Express, and Seagate Softare's Holos. Then there is general-purpose software such as PowerBuilder or Visual Basic which require programming. Web-based technology is another option. These options are not mutually exclusive, since they can often be used together, such as being able to access a warehouse either through a browser or a vendor's client software. Even when a general direction is decided (e.g., special-rather than general-purpose software), choices have to be made within that framework (e.g., selecting a particular product from a class of products).

A software selection process is shown in Figure 5-1. In many ways, selecting decision support software is similar to selecting any software (e.g., researching the alternatives, checking with other users of the software), including selecting data warehouse software. Consequently, the emphasis here is on unique characteristics.

[handwritten margin note: Selection process similar to selecting any software]

Figure 5-1: Decision Support Software Selection Process

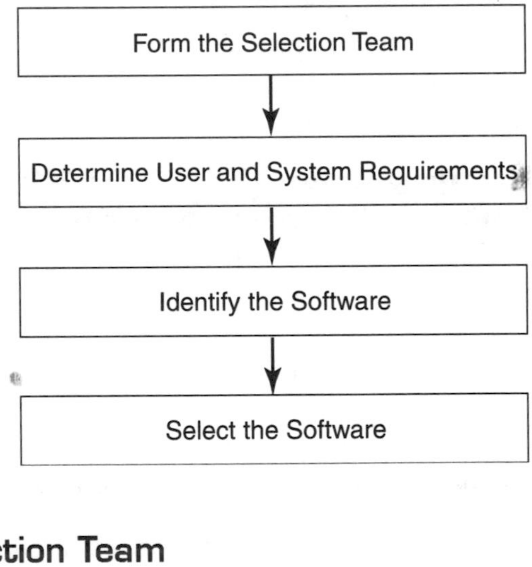

```
┌─────────────────────────────────────┐
│       Form the Selection Team        │
└─────────────────────────────────────┘
                  │
                  ▼
┌─────────────────────────────────────┐
│ Determine User and System Requirements │
└─────────────────────────────────────┘
                  │
                  ▼
┌─────────────────────────────────────┐
│        Identify the Software         │
└─────────────────────────────────────┘
                  │
                  ▼
┌─────────────────────────────────────┐
│         Select the Software          │
└─────────────────────────────────────┘
```

Form the Selection Team

A variety of organizational personnel should be on the selection team: the executive sponsor, business users and managers, decision support software specialists, information systems specialists, and members of the data warehouse

[handwritten margin note: team: People from different perspectives]

participation varies

team. The extent and nature of the involvement of the team members varies considerably. The executive sponsor provides overall direction, facilitates the process, and handles management issues. Business users and managers best understand how the software will be used and have a large stake in what software is selected. The decision support specialists may come from within the firm or a consultant may be brought in to help provide this expertise. IS personnel knowledgeable about the organization's computing infrastructure ensure that compatible products are selected. The data warehouse team member examine the software's compatibility with the warehouse.

Determine User and System Requirements

By this point in a data warehousing initiative, there should be a good general understanding of the applications that will use the data warehouse. This information should have surfaced when approval was sought for building the data warehouse and when the information requirements for the applications were developed. Most of the effort will be in getting a more detailed understanding of what the users expect to be able to do. Keep in mind that different types of users will have different expectations. An executive may want color-coded variances highlighted, while an analyst may want to be able to manipulate the same data in an Excel spreadsheet for further analysis.

different users
ferent expectation

The system or technical requirements are also important. Must the software run on both Wintel and Macintosh platforms? What networking protocols must be supported? What database and data warehouse connectivity is required? Answers to questions such as these will help ensure that the software selected will fit into the organization's computing environment.

Identify the Software Alternatives

There is no shortage of data access software for use with a data warehouse; the number of products exceeds 100. Products such as Access and Excel are well known, whereas others are recent offerings from startup companies with little name recognition. There are many ways to learn about the available products: trade journals such as *Information Week* and *Computerworld*; consultants; conferences those sponsored by the Data Warehousing Institute; organizations such as the Patricia Seybold Group, META Group, and Gartner Group; and friends in the industry. The Internet is also a valuable source of information. Vendors' Web sites provide company and product information and often include a trial version of the software that can be downloaded and used for a short period of time. The information collected begins to allow specific software to be matched to user and system requirements.

As mentioned previously, data warehousing vendors offer comprehensive product lines, either through their own products or through business partnerships with other vendors. It makes sense to seriously consider a vendor's full complement of products, since they should work together. One caveat, however: Some partnerships are more for marketing purposes than anything else; there is little real integration. In this case it is better to go with "best of breed" products.

Some of the user and system requirements are deemed so critical that they must be met. Any vendors' products that do not satisfy them are not considered further. For the other requirements, some companies prepare a checklist to compare the vendors' products. A step beyond this relatively simple approach is to do a weighting and rating analysis where a weight is given to each of the requirements (often, the weights sum to 1 or 100) and the vendors' products are rated (possibly on a 1 to 5 scale) as to how well they fulfill each requirement. Multiplying each weight by its rating and then adding all these numbers together gives an overall score for each vendor's product. This method can be used to help identify the final software candidates.

Information about the vendors is also important to the selection process: pricing, strength of technical support, long-term viability, training, future product direction, references, and maintenance. These factors can be included in the ratings used for selecting the finalists or applied just before the final selection decision.

Select the Software

After the finalists are selected, it is common practice to send a request for proposal (RFP) to the vendors whose products are still under consideration. Commonly included are requests for vendor, product, and pricing information; specifications for the prototype application that the vendor is expected to develop as a demonstration of their product; a request for the names and phone numbers of customers who can be contacted as references; and the criteria that will be used in the final selection decision.

A good practice is to require the vendors to participate in what they refer to as a *vendor shootout*. In a shootout, all of the vendors are expected to come on site (probably not on the same day) to build a specified application using the company's data. Normally, they are given a day to complete the application. Vendors will generally do this without a fee or at a day's consulting price. While the vendor's representative builds the application, decision support specialists should observe and ask questions in order to better assess a product's capabilities and how easy the application development tools are to use. The vendors' completed applications may look essentially the same, but the ease of developing them can differ significantly. Future application users should come in at the end of the day to add their assessment of what was developed. Their focus will be on the quality of the interface.

The final step is negotiating the contract with the vendor selected. Depending on the vendor, such issues as the number of users, number of concurrent users (i.e., those on the system at the same time), number of developers and run-time copies (e.g., for use but not for application development) of the client software, and number of copies of the server software may be negotiated. Vendors usually offer a "starter" package that includes a specified amount of software, plus several training and consulting days, for a set price. When negotiating a price, remember that many of the decision support vendors are small companies and are willing to deal to obtain a sale.

consultant & training

It takes a while to learn how to use most decision support software effectively and efficiently. Most companies benefit from buying several weeks of vendor consultant time or hiring a contractor to speed up the initial application development process and to help train in-house personnel. Users typically expect decision support applications to be delivered quickly.

5-7 MANAGING THE DATA

The fundamental reason for building a data warehouse is to facilitate decision support applications. In the early chapters of this book we provided useful information about how to make needed data available. Several additional issues merit discussion, however.

Not All Data Are in the Warehouse

DW contains numerical data other types of data are stored outside.

Even though a warehouse provides a large supply of decision support data, some applications require data that is not typically stored in a warehouse. Even though universal databases (e.g., multimedia, object oriented, document) are emerging, most data warehouses contain only numerical data. Consequently, applications such as EIS that provide image (e.g., employee photographs) and text (e.g., news stories) require additional data sources. Even some numerical data, such as that generated by an analyst using a spreadsheet, may be fed directly to the application instead of being stored in a warehouse.

Data Ownership Problems

resistance to share information

People and groups often feel that they "own" organizational data if either it pertains to them; they create, maintain, and are responsible for it; and/or it is used in doing their jobs. They may initially resist making it available to a warehouse, and later may be concerned about its use in specific applications, especially if it exposes them or their department to new, careful scrutiny. For example, a warehouse application may make it possible to monitor closely what is taking place within the firm, even at an operational level. This speed of information flow is potentially threatening to lower-level managers because problems that might have been kept from senior management in the past are now easily seen. Many middle managers want to convey the impression that they run a problem-free operation. They are concerned about senior managers spotting operational problems and calling to ask, "What the blazes is happening?"

Security

Data access restrictions

Some applications contain data that should not be accessible by all users (e.g., management succession planning information). Most vendor-supplied database and decision support software include security measures, such as password-protection. Security measures are not as well developed for Web software. In addition to password-protecting information, several other options are available. One is to have a menuing system that does not show that the information is available unless the user has authorized access to the information. Another alternative is to have a double security system: by user password and by PC. A user's password provides access to a set of screens, but some screens may not be accessible from all PCs. This helps reduce the unintentional sharing of restricted data and can be especially valuable in those organizations where applications are accessible in conference rooms. Access information becomes part of the metadata in a warehouse.

Data Definitions

Normally, definitions for the data elements in operational systems are recorded in a data dictionary. These definitions also become part of the metadata in the data warehouse. A problem occurs, however, when the same term has meanings in different systems or is used differently in the organization. While the problem sometimes occurs with different databases and needs to be resolved in the warehouse, it is more likely to occur with terms that are not precisely defined anywhere.

How the term, *sign up*, was used at Lockheed-Martin Aeronautical Systems prior to the implementation of its EIS illustrates the point. A sign up occurs when a customer wants to buy a plane. With a typical price tag of $20 to 30 million, it is easy to see why a sign up is a cause for celebration. Prior to the EIS, people in marketing recognized a sign up whenever a customer indicated intent to buy a plane. In the legal department, the sign up was not recognized until there was a signed contract; finance waited until there was a down payment. These differences in the use of the term had ramifications in terms of the time when a sale was recognized and the certainty of whether the sale would actually take place.

In a decision support application, terms must be clearly defined and applications must access the "approved" data source. It is good practice to include the definitions for terms used within an application, either on the screen where a term is used, in the "help," or in a dictionary. Data that comes from the warehouse should be defined as being part of the metadata.

Where Data Are Stored

Data warehouse architectures range from standalone data marts to enterprise-wide systems (see Section 2-2). If data marts are used, applications access the data mart(s) that contains the needed data. Another alternative is to have a single warehouse or to have marts "retailed" (i.e., created from) from the warehouse. This approach leads to a single view of the data while providing the simplicity and fast response time associated with marts. A multidimensional database fits well into this scheme.

OLAP tools differ considerably in where the data is located. In one approach, the data remains on the server and is analyzed there. Alternatively, data are downloaded from a *data cube* to the PC, where the analysis is performed.

Update Frequency

Decision support applications need to provide timely information. Even though timeliness is expected, experience shows that users want the data to be more up to date over time. To illustrate, a major beverage company's application initially provided daily updates on the gallons of syrup sold. A year later it was providing updates five times a day, with plans to update even more frequently. The "snapshots" of events important to the organization can be expected to be taken ever closer together. The implication is that data warehouse loading operations (Section 2-3) will become more frequent over time.

Combining Data from Different Sources

A data warehouse integrates data from multiple sources and makes it easier for applications to access data. The problem with different data definitions was discussed both in Chapter 1 and in Section 2-4, but another potential problem involves the timing and frequency of updates. Data always contain an updating cycle (e.g., daily, weekly, or monthly), so combining data updated today with data that was updated a week ago can result in a distorted picture. Other than changing updating cycles (which may not be logical or feasible) the solution lies in either not combining data if it can result in distortions, presenting the data as is but with an annotation about the timing differences, or timing the updating of the screens so that the combined data are all from the same time period.

5-8 INTERFACE DESIGN

input

To the typical user, the interface is the system. Users have little interest or understanding of issues such as the database technology used, the number of tiers in the architecture, or the communications protocols employed. The interface has three major components (Bennett, 1977):

output

user experience
system support

- The *action language* is used to tell the system what to do. The action language typically involves a mouse and a keyboard.

- *The presentation language* provides the user with output. The presentation language is typically a rich combination of numbers, text, images, and graphics.

- The *knowledge base* is what the user knows about how to use the system and how much assistance the system provides. It combines experience with previous systems, training, and on-line assistance such as keywords.

Simplicity/Flexibility Trade-off

Trade-off between
flexibility and simplicity

→ understand needs
and characteristics
of the system

The design of any interface involves trade-offs between flexibility and simplicity. Flexible systems are more difficult to use than simple systems and vice versa. The key is to understand the needs and characteristics of users. For example, if all the users are analysts with good computer skills and a need for a powerful, flexible system, simplicity can be sacrificed a bit. If, on the other hand, the users are executives with limited computer skills and experience and little time or interest in training, the system has to be especially easy to use.

→ design an interface
for diverse users

The biggest challenge lies in the design of an interface that must support diverse users. Here the interface should allow users with modest skills and needs to retrieve information through intuitive point-and-click while providing advanced capabilities for those users who need them.

User Involvement

User involvement builds commitment and feeling of ownership

User involvement in information systems design is always important because it builds commitment and develops a feeling of ownership. It is especially important for decision support applications because of the difficulty that users have in knowing and articulating what they want. They are much more successful in reacting to an initial design than specifying it.

One of the authors was involved recently in the design of an EIS. After using several methods to determine information requirements, a main menu with seven categories of information was developed. It was then taken to the executive sponsor for his review. A half hour later the main menu had 14 categories. He had a mental model, (which he perhaps did not even know initially) of how he wanted the information organized in the system. Because the review was conducted early on, with a paper mockup, it was easily changed.

Standards

Standards facilitate learning

The software selected usually gives a certain look and feel to the interface. For example, Web- and Windows-based interfaces have distinctive features and capabilities. Another example is Comshare's Commander Decision applications, which tend to have large buttons at the bottom of the screen. This standardized approach is normally good because it facilitates learning new applications that employ the same software.

Within the general framework provided by the software, many design options remain, and it is important to think carefully about standards. Lockheed-Martin Aeronautical Systems' EIS provides a good example. The screens place graphical presentations at the top, with the related numerical data below, and text annotations at the bottom. Historical or current data are displayed as bar charts, while projections are shown as line charts. On these charts, actuals are in yellow, while budgeted and planned values are in cyan (i.e., light blue). In tables, variances use the stoplight metaphor, with red highlights for unfavorable conditions, yellow for marginal, and green for favorable. When standard formats are used throughout a system, less cognitive effort is required to understand the presentation of information and there is less likelihood of misinterpreting the information displayed.

Decision support software offers a myriad of options for presenting information, including almost every color and type of graph imaginable. It is tempting for system designers to use many of the options. This temptation should be avoided since it is the antithesis of maintaining standards.

5-9 TRAINING AND SUPPORTING USERS

User training and support are not always given the careful thought and attention that they deserve. This is unfortunate because the consequence is that a well-designed application can end up not being used. Thinking through user training and support issues requires careful consideration of the users' position in the organization, the demands of their jobs, their computer skills, and experience. Training is further complicated in the case of a DSS associated with a warehouse because users now have to be trained in both the warehouse and the DSS. In this section we discuss the problems associated with DSS training. Warehouse training is discussed in Section 3-6.

To illustrate this point, a company spent over a year building a decision support system for middle and operational managers. This Windows-based application allowed users to access and analyze information important to the performance of their jobs. The one-on-one training did not go well, however. The managers had difficulty learning the application and vented their frustrations verbally and by not using the system. After thought and discussions, it was concluded that the users were not having problems with the application but were unable to operate it in a Windows environment. The users were blaming the application; to them,

Windows was just part of the application. The solution was to break the training into two sessions: one on the use of Windows and the other on the application. After this change, acceptance and use of the system improved considerably. The computer skills of the users had not been appropriately considered in designing the training session.

Training methods vary from classes, to computer based, to one-on-one. The latter is normally most appropriate with decision support applications because of the nature of the users. Managers expect the personalized attention that goes with private one-on-one training.

Training sessions should be scripted. An effective approach is to develop a scenario that is appropriate for the user, such as sales have declined in the Northeast, and show the user how the system can be used to investigate this problem. With this approach, users see, how easily and quickly the system can help in their performance. This approach is more effective than simply showing all the system's features, independent of how important they are. Users will pick up the fine points over time if they start with a good understanding of what the system does. Another pragmatic reason for a carefully scripted approach is that training sessions are often cut short because of interruptions and emergencies, and it is important to show the system's most important capabilities first. Many training sessions scheduled for 30 minutes end up being half of that.

Special sensitivity is required for executives with limited computer skills. They typically want to maintain an aura of competence. Learning a new application can be threatening. It is wise to ask discretely about the executive's skills (from a secretary or administrative assistant) so that the training session avoids being condescending (assuming too little) or overwhelming (assuming too much).

Expect to be surprised sometimes, however. One of the authors was working with an executive who had never used a computer. His secretary regularly printed his e-mail and entered replies. Our team debated for quite a while whether we should operate the mouse for the executive until he asked to take it over or to put him in charge right away. Our conclusion was to ask him which of the two approaches he preferred. It became a moot point, however, because he grabbed the mouse right away and started clicking (fortunately, he didn't lock up the system, as the hourglass symbol had no meaning to him). The real message is to think carefully about how the training session will be conducted.

Similar care should be given to how support will be provided. The higher placed the user is, the higher are the support expectations. For most senior users, an immediate response is expected. Also make sure that users know who to contact and how. It is good practice to embed in the application, the names and telephone numbers of support personnel. . People providing support need the same sensitivities as those associated with designing training sessions.

5-10 SYSTEM SPREAD AND EVOLUTION

Most data warehouses quickly grow in size if they are successful. Much of this growth is fueled by current and potential users of the warehouse who want support for additional applications. For example, a warehouse (or mart) built for sales applications may be expanded to support finance applications. The likelihood of rapid growth in both the size and the number of applications should be included in warehouse planning.

Successful decision support applications are likely to spread in terms of the number of users and to evolve in terms of the information that is available and the capabilities of the system. This is seen in Figures 5-3 and 5-4 which show the findings from an EIS study. As Figure 5-3 shows, the average number of users at the time of introduction was 8, grew to 50 after a year, and was over 70 in two years. The number of screens in the system (Figure 5-3) grew from 56 to 300 to over 400, respectively. (The values of n in Figure 5-3, such as $n =$

Figure 5-2: EIS Spread to Additional Users

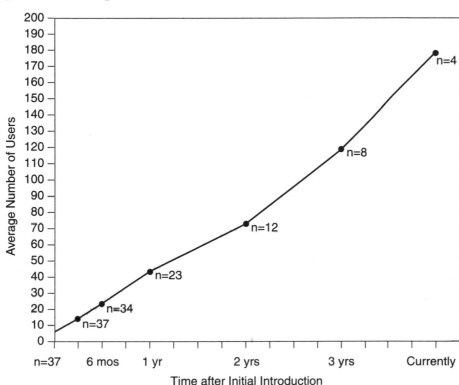

Source: Watson, Rainer, and Koh (1991)

23, indicate the number of respondents for each point on the graph.)

David Friend, an EIS pioneer and founder of Pilot Executive Software, has long claimed that an EIS that does not spread to additional users and move closer to providing real time data is a system likely to fail (Friend, 1990). Warehouse developers should anticipate and plan for system spread and evolution. Accommodating more users requires a system that is scalable. A system may be fine with 100 users but provide unacceptable response times as the numbers increase. Additional support staff time will be required to install the system for users, train them, and respond to calls for assistance. Staff

Figure 5-3: Growth in the Number of EIS Screens

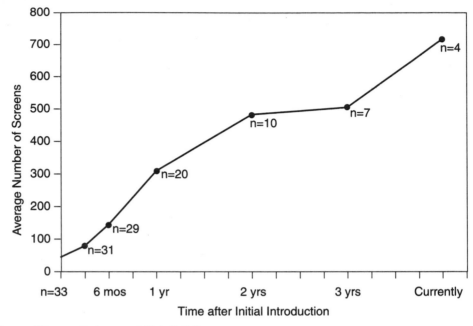

Source: Watson, Rainer, and Koh (1991)

time will also be required to identify and respond to new information and system requirements.

Because system spread and evolution require additional resources, they should be included in the project plan. A successful system facilitates getting additional resources, but it is useful to provide advance warning that they will be needed. A well-written proposal should include information about long-term resource requirements.

5-11 CONCLUDING REMARKS

The introduction of the data warehouse changed the way that decision support systems are built and used. Whereas previously DSS designers and builders needed to find where data inputs were located, had to create their own data extraction and cleaning routines from a variety of legacy sources, and often created specialized databases for each DSS application, the data warehouse now provides a single, centralized clean source for almost all DSS data. The net result is that decision support systems can now be created more quickly and can use a larger and better source of input information. Table 5-3 summarizes, in the order in which they appear in this chapter, the impacts of the data warehouse on DSS issues. These impacts are presented in the order in which they were presented in this chapter

Table 5-3: Impacts of the Data Warehouse on DSS Design

Use prototyping rather than system development life cycle.
If you use data mart for prototype DSS, make sure that it scales to full data warehouse.
DSS queries are compatible with data warehouse capabilities.
When selecting DSS software, consider its compatibility with the warehouse.
Include a member of the data warehouse team in the software selection committee.
Consider connectivity of DSS and the data warehouse.
Involve a member of the data warehouse team in evaluating vender shoot outs.
Be aware that all data may not be in warehouse and that it may not be possible to add to the warehouse data needed for a given DSS.
Put access information for DSS security in the warehouse where appropriate.
Use metadata in the warehouse for DSS data definition and DSS data management.
Consider whether warehouse data for a DSS is analyzed at a server or locally at a PC.
Make the warehouse update frequency of input data used by a DSS compatible with the update frequency required the DSS.
Consider the needs for combining data in a DSS when selecting update frequencies for the warehouse.
Standardize the data warehouse interface and the DSS interface if at all possible.
Consider the compatibility of DSS and data warehouse standards.

Table 5-3: Impacts of the Data Warehouse on DSS Design

Expand training so that both the DSS and the warehouse are covered. `
Provide support for both the DSS and the underlying warehouse.
Make sure that the warehouse can be expanded to handle the spread and evolution of DSSs.

Chapter
6

Final Thoughts Before
Building a Data Warehouse

This final chapter of Section IV presents practical information that puts data warehousing in perspective. We begin (Section 1) by considering the pitfalls that can be encountered. We then present the results of a survey of current practices that considers who has built data warehouses and what they are using them for. The Chapter concludes with a look to the developments that can be expected in the near future.

6-1 WHAT CAN GO WRONG?

This book deals with the considerations that go into the creation of a successful data warehouse for supporting decision making. We would, however, be remiss if we did not warn about the problems that can be encountered. Although companies are loath to discuss their failures, a sufficient number of them have come to light to be able to catalog some of the pitfalls that can plague a data warehouse project. After all, data warehouse projects are inherently complex. Projects run 18 to 36 months or longer and involve expenditures that can run into six digits. The simple size of the project makes it more likely to encounter difficulties.

Here are some of the hidden dangers. They are based on Foley (1996).

- Losing sight of the business problems that the warehouse is supposed to solve. As a result, the warehouse becomes unused, being rejected by the user community.

- Failure to ensure data quality. If even a little of the data is unreliable, people question the accuracy of all of the data. Data accuracy is a must.

- Failure to have systems in place that manage data as it is extracted from operational systems and transformed into meaningful information.

- Inability to coordinate data marts. If data marts are not coordinated, they propagate in an uncontrolled fashion across the enterprise. Such lack of coordination can result in dragging down operational transaction processing systems. For example, in one company, unrelated data marts were pulling data from the same data operational system, reducing its capabilities.

- Scalability can be a major problem. Both the amount of data in the warehouse and the number of users increase with time. The initial warehouse size may be adequate, but the warehouse can become too small. Adding users can create response-time problems. The design has to be capable of scaling upward because data warehouses do have breakpoints where they can no longer function.

6-2. CURRENT PRACTICES

Outdated information version 2001 in ISM

Who has built data warehouses, and what do they use them for? This section presents the findings of a survey[1] of people who attended one of The Data Warehouse Institute confer-

---

[1] The survey results are reported in detail in Watson and Haley (1997).

ences (Watson and Haley, 1997). The data are based on 121 respondents, with 44 having a data warehouse in place, 72 developing one, and 5 planning or thinking of creating one. This group consisted of 82% (99) working for U.S. firms, and 18% (22) from abroad.

In this survey, the data warehouse life cycle was divided into five stages, as shown in Figure 6-1. We discuss the responses to each stage, in turn.

Figure 6-1: Stages of Data Warehouse Life Cycle Used in Survey

DW = Data Warehouse

1. *Principal characteristics of the population.* The group represented a diverse set of industries. The largest groups represented were manufacturing (15%), banking (13%), and medical (13%). They came principally from large organizations. The modes of the categories checked were revenue in the $1 to 5 billion range, and 20,000 to 100,000 employees. The respondents were an experienced group. They consisted principally of IS managers (36%) and data warehouse project managers (36%), with a mean work experience of 16.5 years, of which 13.5 were in IS. Their data warehouse experience averaged 2.1 years.

2. *Why were the projects undertaken?* Data warehouse projects were initiated to provide decision makers with accurate, effective information that reflects the entire business. In the survey the need was stimulated more by internal than external pressures. In 79% of the cases, the need was information related.

3. *The champion.* Major projects such as data warehouses typically require an internal champion, that is, someone in the organization with sufficient influence and clout to make the project happen. The responses indicated that 41% were executive sponsored and 48% were sponsored by IS. The heavy concentration of IS sponsors may indicate that the data warehouse is considered part of the technical infrastructure and IS has responsibility for creating and maintaining the infrastructure.

4. *Approval.* A data warehouse is a large expenditure that affects many portions of an organization. As a result, many organizations require formal, explicit justification before giving approval to proceed. The data showed that in 90% of the cases, a cost/benefit analysis was run, and in 66% of the cases, a written proposal was presented. The benefits were often soft because it is difficult to assess the increases in revenue beforehand. Opposition to the warehouse was encountered in 25% of organizations. Concern was expressed by executives and functional area groups over the cost of and the need for a data warehouse. Nearly half of the opposition came from within the information systems group, who feared loss of control of data ownership and the empowerment of end users who might only then need minimal IS assistance. Also, warehouse projects can reveal inadequacies within IS in their technical skills, their understanding of corporate data, and their understanding of the methods for building a warehouse.

5. *Data warehouse construction.* Table 6-1 shows the average values found for the sample. The data show that construction of a warehouse is not an overnight

Table 6-1: Mean Values for Construction

Person-years of effort	4.5 years
Consultants used	59%
Project length	0.93 year
Architecture	typically three -tier
Cost in year 1	$1.57 million for data warehouses, $1.07 million for data marts
Source of funding	34% IS,17% functional area, 49% joint

activity. The projects lasted almost a year and averaged 4.5 person-years of efforts.

Construction of a data warehouse requires:

- Knowledge of technology and data that exists in the organization:

- The hardware and software available in the marketplace; and

- Knowing how to integrate technical components and development activities

As a result, more than half the organizations used consultants.

IS provided funding when the objective was to improve infrastructure, whereas the functional area provided funds if there was a business need. The breakdown of first-year costs are given in Table 6-2 based on the few people (*N* in table) who answered these questions. Note that these answers do not sum to the total cost values shown in Table 6-1.

6.*Use.* The extent to which the data warehouse is used suggests how well it meets organizational needs.

Table 6-2: First-Year Costs

	Mean	Median	N
Data extraction, transformation	200,000	100,000	30
DBMS software	100,000	50,000	28
Data warehouse administration	150,000	80,000	27
Hardware	600,000	150,000	30
System staff, system integration	225,000	170,000	28
EIS, DSS, and data mining	275,000	70,000	18

This sample experienced rapid growth in user populations. Initially, the average number of users was 16 people. It grew to 100 by the end of year 1. Over a two-year period, the growth was exponential (Figure 6-1). Users came from throughout the organization. The order of rank by departments was sales and marketing, finance, forecasting and planning, accounting, and production. The popularity in sales and marketing supports the perception that data warehouses are being used to obtain a better understanding of customers. Table 6-3 shows users by job responsibility. Here the numbers indicate the fraction of the responding organizations where a given type of employee used the warehouse. Overall, 67% of the respondents rated their data warehouse successful (4,5 on a 1-5 scale) and only 16% rated them unsuccessful (1,2, on a 1-5 scale).

7. *Critical success factors and obstacles to success.* The final data obtained was on the factors that led to success and the obstacles that were encountered during development. These were open-ended questions. The success factors, in rank order, were:

Table 6-3: Percent of Organizations in Which a Given Job Category Used the Warehouse

Job Category	Percentage
Analysts	75
Middle managers	64
Operational managers	61
Administrative personnel	48
Senior executives	33

- Upper management support
- User involvement
- Having a business need
- User support
- Using a methodology, modeling
- Defined, understandable goals
- Good, clean data
- Managing expectations

The success factors listed are like those described for all large projects. User involvement and support were needed to obtain buy in and to understand business needs. Other items in the list reflect the need for management input (the champion) and the ability to manage the project. The obstacles to success, in rank order, were:

- Poor data quality
- Resources, money
- Poorly defined goals
- Technical limitations
- Understanding legacy data
- Lack of user support
- Meeting deadlines
- Lack of development team training

•Managing expectations

These factors mainly involve data, management, and quality-of-data issues. The data issues reflect the complexity of data extraction, storage, and access. Management issues can delay projects, and slow delivery of tangible products which can erode the support and commitment of users.

8. *Conclusions.* The results presented here were obtained in early 1996. However, we believe that they remain true. They should provide helpful insights to both line and IS managers and their staff who have been given responsibility for warehouse projects.

6.3 DEVELOPMENTS IN DATA WAREHOUSING

In this section we examine some of the ongoing developments in data warehousing which we believe are important and/or interesting. Included are issues that we believe are important but are not receiving sufficient attention. These observations are based on attending meetings of The Data Warehousing Institute and on talking with vendors.

1. Internet/intranet/extranet capabilities for data warehouses are arriving at a fast clip. Old and new applications alike are moving to the Web[2]; it is increasingly becoming the favored application environment.
2. The Web browser is becoming a primary vehicle for end-user access. Use of browsers is being integrated with Web servers, and application servers to post reports to intranets and to support end-user queries.
3. The thin client approach is being seen more and more as Web technology comes to the fore. The Web is also

---

[2] We use the term *Web* generically. It refers to the technology used for the Internet, intranets, and extranets rather than just the World Wide Web.

being used for distributing and installing new software.

4. Companies are allowing external parties to access data warehouses via the Internet or extranets. For example, the Environmental Protection Agency allows the public to access environmental data through a browser.

5. Data mining is starting to be embedded in data warehouse and DSS/EIS products. Data mining is still in its infancy. Despite the high-profile examples reported in the press, only a handful of companies are actually doing data mining. Data mining is largely a product being developed by small vendors (companies of 100 people or less). The notable exception is IBM, which has invested heavily in this area.

6. Some vendors of DSS/EIS products (e.g., Pilot) are licensing the rights to integrate data mining capabilities developed by other vendors (e.g., Thinking Machines). The data mining products that became available initially included only a subset of the available techniques.

7. The challenge for vendors is to develop an interface that allows nontechnical people to use and understand the "rocket science" algorithms that are used in data mining. More "packaged" solutions are to be anticipated for specific data mining applications (e.g., demographics of people most likely to respond to a direct mailing).

8. Suites of products are increasingly available. Vendors recognize that individual users are not specialized. A user may be working in executive information systems mode seeking a point-and-click answer at one time, directing a complex query at another, and doing OLAP-type analysis at another. In other words, every user needs multiple tools.

9. Despite its importance in data warehousing, metadata remains an unresolved issue. The view of metadata is expanding. Rather than just being information

about the contents of the data, it now includes information about the management of the data such as when the data was entered, or when a job using particular data is scheduled.

10. Managing the warehouse is an issue that has come to the fore. Organizations are becoming aware that their data warehouse is a major resource and, like all resources, must be managed if full value is to be obtained. This understanding at the corporate level of the need to determine what the warehouse will be used for is going on in parallel with the emerging managerial role of the information systems department. Information systems wants to maintain order and data integrity within the warehouse.

11. The data warehousing vendors marketing in the United States are now international. For many years, software developed in foreign countries came to the U.S. and failed to establish any significant market share. SAP was the first real exception. Now DSS/EIS/managed query environment software products from throughout the world are doing quite well in the U.S. marketplace. Such companies as Andyne (Canada), Cognos (Canada), Lingo (Canada), Speedware (Canada), Business Objects (France), Holos (U.K.), Planning Sciences (U.K.) are all competing.

12. Parallel computing, once thought exotic, is now thought of as standard. It is being helped by quad Pentium machines and RISC computers.

13. Not much attention is being paid to security. Vendors generally do not feature security as a key element of their offerings. Talks about security are rare at trade shows.

14. There are two opposite views of the role of the information systems department with respect to data warehousing. On the one hand, data warehouses are being seen as a way of reducing the role of IS in organizations. That is, the products and concepts are being touted as suitable for direct implementation by end

users and not requiring much support from IS. On the other hand, there seems to be a trend toward recentralization of data, with IS having the responsibility for it. For example, the managed query environments require considerable IS support in order to allow users to make queries without knowing about data tables and SQL, and protecting against "the query from hell."

15. Databases are getting bigger. This finding has direct implication on the argument between relational OLAP (ROLAP) and multidimensional OLAP (MOLAP). If the database is small enough (a few gigabytes) and response time is critical, MOLAP is to be preferred. However, until a breakthrough occurs in MOLAP so that it can handle terabytes of data, only ROLAP can be used for larger databases.

16. Precalculating values is faster than ROLAP or 64-bit parallelism. The key to faster response is understanding users' information needs well enough to make precalculations and store them in the warehouse for later retrieval.

17. Data mart packages (the so-called "data mart in a box") are being offered by several vendors. These packages provide all of the software needed to build and maintain a data mart. Vendors claim that they are able to reduce development time from months to weeks.

18. Determining data requirements is still a black art. The assumption that data requirements are obtained easily is almost never true. On the other hand, there is general consensus that enterprise data models are essential for a successful warehouse project.

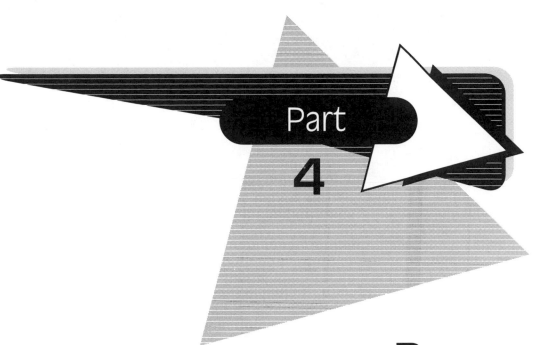

Part
4

Data Warehousing Products for Decision Support

Foreword to Part 4

This part contains chapters contributed by seven leading vendors of data warehousing and decision support software and hardware. The purpose is to show the range of offerings available in the marketplace. When these vendors were asked for their input, they were given a template to follow. Specifically, each of them was asked them to present the following information:

- A brief company profile
- A description of their products and services in the data warehousing marketplace
- Customer success stories.

We asked that their responses be limited to factual presentations, without marketing overtones, of what their products did and how the products have been used by clients to achieve the clients' goals. We believe that the chapters that follow are responsive to these specifications. The chapters are copyrighted by the vendors and represent their viewpoints. We are grateful to each of them for their contribution.

The companies represented in the following chapters and their World Wide Web addresses are:

CHAPTER	COMPANY	INTERNET ADDRESS
7	NCRCorporation	http://www.ncr.com
8	Oracle Corproation	http://www.oracle.com
9	Red Brick Systems, Inc.	http://www.redbrick.com
10	Platinumtechnology, inc.	http://www.platinum.com
11	Brio Technology	http://www.brio.com
12	Comshare, Inc.	http://www.comshare.com
13	SeagateSoftware	http://www.seagatesoftware.com

The authors of the contributed chapters are:

NCR Corporation: Ron Swift

Oracle Corporation: MichaelAult

Red Brick Systems, Inc.: Fred Wee

Platinum technology, inc.:David Gleason

Brio Technology: Will Hansen

Comshare, Inc.: Dr. David King and Doug Hockstad

Seagate Software: James Lucy

NCR Corporation:

Scalable Data Warehouse Solutions

7-1 INTRODUCTION[1]

NCR is different than most other data warehousing providers. NCR, through it's Teradata experiences, was one of the original inventors of the data warehouse concept and built computers and sophisticated software during the early 1980's. Similar to such notables as Bill Inmon, NCR Teradata challenged the thought of how to provide data management for decision support. This new process and totally new technology were combined for organizations to maintain and use large amounts of information about their customers. Other providers relied upon older transaction processing technologies to define and develop decision support environments. Many of those operational mainframe approaches continue to have much difficulty in providing scalability in the operating system, database management system, and the data storage

---

[1] This chapter was contributed by NCR Corporation and is copyright by them. It was written by Ron Swift of NCR Corporation.

compatibilities required for high-performance query processing.

7-2 NCR Company Background

Founded in 1884 by John Patterson, NCR Corp. is probably the oldest computing company in the world. Success with customer service machines led NCR to enter the computer business in 1960, with the introduction of a payroll processing system. In 1990, NCR was acquired by AT&T, while NCR was in the process of purchasing Teradata Corporation.

The acquisition of Teradata Corp. was a turning point in the long history of NCR. NCR had evolved from supplying cash registers to an array of customer service machines and then, with Teradata, to providing a highly-automated capability for processing simple and complex queries in constantly changing environments.

Teradata provided the first platform for what is commonly known today as data warehousing. The key to that development was the first commercially available massively parallel processing (MPP) hardware system, called The Teradata DataBase Computer.

The acquisition of Teradata expanded NCR's capabilities in the high-end MPP systems. However, in 1991, NCR began designing and delivering an entire hardware family based on Intel Corp's microprocessors chips. Today, the enhanced platform, known as NCR WorldMark series, provides symmetrical processors (SMP), clustered systems processors, and the scalable open systems MPP solutions available with Intel technology.

From 1991 through 1995, NCR was known as AT&T Global Information Solutions. However, in January 1997, NCR divested from AT&T and re-listed on the New York Stock Exchange (Symbol: NCR). In 1997, NCR Corporation reported worldwide revenues of $7 billion annually and had 36,000 employee/associates in 130 countries.

7-3 NCR's SCALABLE DATA WAREHOUSE FRAMEWORK

Through 1997, NCR had implemented over 700 scalable data warehouses. To solve the business problems, NCR has developed a "Scalable Data Warehouse (SDW) Framework" which encompasses the practical and strategic approaches to data warehousing. This is a non-technical, visualization and layering approach to planning for a data warehouse. As shown in Figure 7-1, it involves I/T resources, technologies, processes, and business usage.

The SDW Framework facilitates either independent data marts (which eventually grow into the enterprise data warehouse that NCR believes is the correct approach for the long run) or in directly building a scalable data warehouse with dependent data marts. These data marts can be either included inside the Teradata enterprise data warehouse (as logical data marts), or be distributed to additional platforms through a network (which then makes these dependent physical data marts). This approach is designed for easier management of the total environment, the ability to expand the business model and the data model, and to maintain a single version of the truth.

Defining a SDW Framework and Building a Data Warehouse

The NCR Scalable Data Warehouse Framework includes a series of steps to transform existing operational data into informational data, thereby making a company's data more organized, consistent and valuable. Informational data can be the source of strategic perspectives about how a business ought to be run to achieve maximum advantage in its market. To achieve informational data, it is necessary to perform data transformation on raw transactional or operational data.

Figure 7-1: The NCR Scalable Data Warehouse Framework

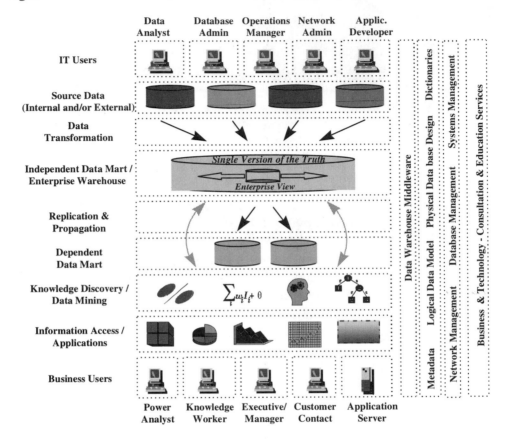

The goal of a data warehouse is to co-exist with operational systems, extracting significant operational data from those systems for use in a centralized, relational database. Significant operational data is defined according to the customer's line of business. Generally, though, it is mission-critical information generated by the business from such day-to-day operations as sales, orders, request for payments, shipping, or activities that start or complete a cycle (such as manufacturing, delivery, production, or customer contacts or requests).

Managing Operational Data into the Warehouse

The SDW Framework solves a number of common information systems problems. Inconsistent data formats make it difficult and sometimes impossible to use increasingly common decision support systems to analyze raw operational data for changes in customer behavior, market trends and changes, or product/market cause-and-effect relationships. DSS technology requires consistent data that cuts across functional departments. A company can be at a distinct disadvantage against its competitors without the ability to use DSS tools effectively to understand cross functional aspects of the business.

Operational data applications frequently are the result of customization based on individual user or departmental requirements. Customized applications were designed in isolation, without taking into account how other applications use and store the same data. The way operational data has been stored and organized depends on how it has been used: for instance, on whether it undergoes high or low volume transactions. Plus, the manner of updating data may differ. It may be updated on a field-by-field or block basis. Then there is often data that has accumulated over years without being maintained. All of these circumstances make it difficult to apply operational data to DSS technologies that were built to add value to a business.

One of the greatest challenges in building a SDW Framework is in the process of transforming operational data into the informational data that is needed to create business value. Despite the challenge, however, the process is crucial. It creates a consistent format, which paves the way for the use of the kind of advanced decision making rendered possible by applications such as DSS and data mining.

Transforming Data into Information

Data transformation is the logical and physical movement and transforming of data from operational systems into informational systems. Depending on existing conditions, data transformation activities can include accessing, reconciling, extracting, conditioning, condensing, filtering, scrubbing, merging and loading. The value of a warehouse is realized when companies use it to ask cross-functional complex questions of detailed data.

Architectural Strategies - Centralized versus Distributed

The key business decision, at the outset, is in the architectural approach to data warehousing. Whether to build a small or single focused data warehouse, sometimes called a data mart, is a critical decision.

There are two classifications of data marts: independent and dependent. Independent data marts are unconnected and non-integrated. Very few of these grow up into real data warehouses, unless they are designed from the beginning for expansion of both the business model and the data model.

A dependent data mart is a logical and/or physical subset of data from the enterprise warehouse that is selected and organized for a particular set of usage requirements. Performance and cost are often the key reasons why dependent data marts are implemented.

The dependent data mart provides an enterprise view, as it resides closer to power users in specific areas such as financial and marketing departments. Dependent data marts can be organized by user group, in which case they are physically located in users' departments, or by subject area, for which information is organized logically in a separate partition within the data warehouse. Data replication and propagation synchronizes data between the enterprise data warehouse and dependent data marts.

Independent Data Marts versus Enterprise Data Warehouse

The goal of the NCR data warehouse approach is to provide a centerpiece of collected and transformed information in a single data store of clean, accurate detail, and summary data for the enterprise. This foundation alleviates many of the problems associated with "stovepipe" or non-integrated operational or decision support systems. Independent data marts do not provide a single version of the truth, thereby continuing the frustrating and limited-ROI reporting environment of the past.

When building a scalable data warehouse, NCR recommends starting with a small or manageable enterprise data warehouse which is focused on one or two particular subject areas. Within this context, NCR also recommends that a dependent data mart be a part of the planning and architecture of an enterprise strategy. Although NCR has built many data marts, it has become clear that multiple, unconnected, non-integrated, un-modeled data marts are not acceptable for high return on investment and successful growth of the data warehouse.

As a smaller version of the data warehouse, the dependent data mart, provides power users instantly with the most current information possible. Users don't have to wait for a database administrator or a consultant to get access to queries or the data needed to query. They can use the dependent data mart independently; consequently, they can react more quickly to market changes. Sometimes these data marts are physically located within the data warehouse database: Teradata. The business user believes that they have a special data warehouse (e.g., data mart) prepared for them, when actually it is part of an integrated environment within the enterprise data warehouse. These are known as logical data marts.

Data Replication and Propagation

Data replication and propagation synchronizes data between the enterprise warehouse and the dependent data marts. Independent data marts do not really utilize replication and propagation, but merely use copy utilities (in most cases) to move data from the originating source (operational) files and databases.

Middleware Requirements

A scalable data warehouse does not stand alone. Instead, it must fit into an existing systems environment, which may include a diverse collection of legacy and client/server applications, logical data sources, external data sources, etc. For maximum effectiveness, all systems components must work together as a single "virtual" system, accessible to end users through a consistent graphical user interface.

The glue that dynamically connects the disparate components into an integrated system is called middleware. Middleware can connect the databases in the operational environments to the data warehouse and also connect the business users to the data warehouse database(s) for access and use of information access and analytical tools.

The data access layer of middleware refers to the industry standard interfaces or APIs such as ODS and ODBC which allow access to both data managers and legacy operational data sources. Middleware is the essential connector for a successful and complete data warehouse solution.

Data Modeling and Design of the NCR Data Warehouse

The data modeling and design layer of the NCR SDW Framework is a logical data model to support the business information needs, and the physical design of the database supports the logical model. This layer also includes the data dictionary for consistent data definitions, and metadata for establishing an efficient directory to support usage of the data. This is one of the most crucial aspects of creating a sustainable data warehouse.

7-3 NCR PRODUCTS AND SERVICES

NCR Terabyte Relational Database Management System

The NCR Teradata RDBMS serves in-production data warehouses ranging from 10 Gigabytes to 24 Terabytes. With the seventh generation of the NCR Teradata RDBMS for UNIX, Teradata is able to handle large data loads and complex queries through the use of highly automated database functions.

NCR Teradata uses massively parallel-processing technology to split the work among dozens, hundreds or thousands of Intel microprocessors, depending on the scalability requirements of the user. The NCR Teradata RDBMS is available on NCR WorldMark UNIX. NCR Teradata for Windows NT is scheduled to be available on SMP systems and on MPP systems during 1998.

NCR Teradata supports the current SQL standard as well as the ODBC and X/Open XA standards through third party gateways to Oracle, IBM DB2, and many other databases. It works with other UNIX systems, IBM mainframe systems, Macintosh, and Windows servers and clients.

Teradata was designed to scale simultaneously in multiple dimensions; for example, from the amount of data loaded, the number of users submitting queries concurrently, the number of complex queries, and the number of business entities being accessed by queries.

The NCR Teradata database uses the rules and relationships of business in a data model. It looks at the basic functions in a business without making assumptions that would ultimately restrict the kinds of queries that could be run against the database engine with decision support or data mining tools.

Highly automated database functions make it possible to run a 10 TeraByte data warehouse supported by one or two database administrators. Several NCR Teradata technological advances contribute to reducing the database administrators (DBA) workload. These include high-speed parallel utilities (load, update and export), mainframe connectivity, and a hashing algorithms for data storage and retrieval, which provides a random distribution of data for parallel database performance that eliminates the need to re-balance the system. NCR Teradata's hashing facilities also act as an index reorganization utility.

NCR Teradata's database utilities and tools -- such as Fast Load, MultiLoad, FastExport, Dump/Restore/Recovery Utility, and Basic Teradata Query Tool -- support execution on both network-connected clients and channel-connected mainframes from IBM, Amdahl and Unisys.

Database Queries

NCR Teradata handles complex database queries by using a process called Automatic Query Optimization. Designed in 1979 expressly for executive decision support and parallel processing, Teradata processes queries by utilizing a technology it calls an Optimizer to choose an access method, regardless of how large the data set, how many users are executing queries simultaneously, or how often the queries change. The Optimizer does not require a DBA to tune queries. If an Optimizer is given a poorly constructed query, it automatically rewrites the query as an equivalent but better performing one.

Third Normal Form (Teradata) Versus Star Schema (Other DBMS's)

Structured Query Language runs against any kind of data model, but the two most common ones are the star schema and third normal form. While some database companies are just now beginning to add third normal form versions to their star schema-based products, NCR Teradata has been fine-tuning third normal form products since 1983.

Third normal form is a flexible data modeling methodology that does not make assumptions about the basic functions of a business. Deployed as an accurate yet adaptable model of the business, third normal form shows how and why patterns as well as anomalies in a business are occurring. Having knowledge of these patterns is particularly valuable when the business leverages that knowledge through data mining activities.

NCR (and a growing number of other DBMS providers) believe that data models based on star schema limit business intelligence. This can be illustrated when a company misses an opportunity by organizing its sales information based on the assumptions inherent in star schema. If the company looks at sales data only by how sales have done in the past week, the assumption is that there is no variation in days or hours of the day and that customers' behavior is even and predictable throughout the week.

For example, retailers during the Christmas season know which store has sold what merchandise and when. If they discover in time that they have overstocked inventory of product X in one geographic area, but under-stocked it in another region, then they can move product X to the needed location where it is selling well. But if retailers only look at sales data by the week, then Christmas day will come and go by the time they discover where merchandise is needed in order to sell the most. If retailers gain knowledge of this a day or two in advance, they can act quickly to move the leftover merchandise from low-selling regions to the high-selling areas in time to realize profits from this information.

The star schema approach makes certain assumptions about data, presuming to know relationships among data in advance. One of the ways in which assumptions are made is through denormalizing, which reduces the complexity of information so that a DBMS can handle it better. Denormalizing two or more pieces of data by combining them into one may make the DBMS job easier, but it decreases the quality of the information. In the process of denormalizing, assumptions about relationships are set in stone to relate in ways where they often don't relate at all. When internal business or external market circumstances change, the process and the model must be completely redone.

A typical example of denormalizing is in the health insurance industry when a claim is filed for a doctor's visit. The doctor may have taken ten separate actions during the visit and reported each one separately. Yet in denomalizing the data, by combining health actions in a claim, the real circumstances are not reflected.

Utilizing third normal form for both the logical and physical aspects of a computer model minimizes the need to denormalize data. It avoids the data integrity compromises that can lead to business problems. However, NCR Teradata has developed a process for working with existing star schema data by allowing the requisite joins resulting from a star schema model to be viewed within a third normal form model. The process will accept star schema data without letting the data compromise the faster, more accurate third normal form model. Still, NCR Teradata encourages customers to build enterprise data with third normal form models that require minimal denormalization of data.

Scalability

The goal of a scalable system is four dimensional: to allow the maximum number of users the ability to input extract data while running complex queries against complex data models with minimal support.

The first of the four dimensions of scalability is the ability to input and extract data with consistent response times. The second dimension is the number of users or queries that run simultaneously. The third is environmental complexity, represented by the complexity of the data model and the queries run against the model. The fourth is the degree of support needed to maintain scalability.

NCR Teradata achieves a high degree of scalability through a combination of software automation and hardware parallelism. Through intelligent use of algorithms, the NCR Teradata Optimizer Technologies use a hybrid of the two basic kinds of Optimizers, rules-based and cost-based. With rules-based, a DBA knows the rules and sets up queries to take advantage of those rules. Using cost-based, an Optimizer tries to find the least costly way to handle an SQL query.

Another factor contributing to the optimization of queries is the intelligence in the way data is loaded and placed in the warehouse. Through the use of Automated Data Placement, which is based on a NCR Teradata's hash algorithm (a division algorithm), data is divided in a way that permits scalability and accuracy. A repeatable randomizing routine places data in a random, balanced way that does not make assumptions based on time.

Availability

NCR Teradata defines high availability in business terms. If a business user can't use the system, then it is regarded as completely unavailable. Downtime is divided into scheduled and unscheduled. Scheduled downtime represents routine maintenance, such as the need to reorganize data and perform data loads. Unscheduled downtime results from power outages or from either software or hardware failures. Three things can break and they are handled in the following ways:

1. Disk drives, backed up by a RAID 5 system to cover any type of disk drive breakage;
2. Computer node (or a symmetric multiprocessing computer system), in which case NCR Teradata redistributes the process that was occurring when the component went down and evenly redistributes the processes on the remaining SMP systems; and
3. Node connections, where the RDBMS automatically reroutes all messages.

Mainframe Integration, Automated Data Loading, and Automated Data Conversion

Many mainframe integration systems require that users specify loads, telling the system exactly where to load the data. Whenever they add new hardware, users must change all of their load routines to accommodate the new hardware. However, NCR Teradata's hash algorithm automatically recognizes how much hardware it has to work with and adjusts for it.

The use of Automated Data Loading (ADL) eliminates the seven steps of data loading that a DBA ordinarily must perform. The software sets itself up to look like a peripheral device on the mainframe. Once the user tells the system where the data load is coming from and which table it is going to, then the system selects multiple parallel channels and sends the data through them automatically. NCR Teradata users do not have to split files, load them, or convert data. Automated Data Conversion performs those functions by converting automatically to the format of the requesting platform when users run a query. It automatically collates according to the collating sequence of the requesting platform as well. Data conversion occurs automatically as part of the process when users pull data back out from the query.

As a result of the extensive use of automated processes, NCR Teradata systems need only one DBA for support. Most of the routines that must be performed manually by other systems are done automatically by the NCR Teradata software.

NCR Teradata Manager, Query Manager, and Archiving and Backup

The NCR Teradata Manager is a PC-based command center, available for 70 languages specified by the International Standards Organization (ISO), which allows the DBA to centrally monitor and control all aspects of the Teradata warehouse across multiple platforms. This administration hub includes a single database view combined with performance tracking, problem resolution, database management, operational control, query execution, security application scheduling and other tools. Likewise, the NCR Teradata Database Query Manager automatically manages complex queries to insure that parallel processing and thus optimal performance is consistently maintained. The automatic archiving and backup of warehouse data is managed by NCR's Archive Storage Facility, which provides the centralized backup and storage for parallel databases and the ArcMain Backup and Restore utilities, which allows firms to use existing mainframe backup facilities in conjunction with the Teradata warehouse.

Middleware for Administration and Connectivity - NCR'S *TOP END*

Top End is a suite of NCR middleware products that balances workloads across available systems, both day-to-day and when a failed system's work must be redistributed to other systems. The software's message-oriented, 3-tier architecture minimizes the number of permanent connections between systems, reducing traffic below that of 2-tier database schemes. Top End performs load balancing, message and workflow management, data transformation, authentication and encryption, and inter-system communications: all of which are transparent to the end user. It provides a platform independent interface through which users can access integrated applications and data. If a system fails, Top End queues transactions for future application to the database, so work can progress even though a system is down for repairs.

Warehousing High Availability System Management - NCR's *LifeKeeper* and Computer Associates' *Uni-Center*

Within an integrated systems environment, each hardware and software component contributes to the successful and timely completion of multi-step mission critical processes. System faults, if they are not caught in time, can lead to processing delays or even a total systems failure that negatively impacts a firm's core business activities -- sometimes to a serious extent. To ensure that key processes are not disrupted and to protect a firm's assets, enterprise systems environments must contain some form of "high availability"" software that is capable of, first, monitoring system components for faults and second, dynamically re-allocating system processes in response to faults (usually caused by external conditions such as power failures) so that system access is not interrupted. NCR's Lifekeeper system performs all of these functions on both Unix and Windows NT platforms.

NCR supports implementation of Computer Associates International's UNI-CENTER for managing the systems and operational environments. NCR and CA maintain a software alliance partnership.

NCR WorldMark Servers

Data warehousing technology should be capable of growing at the same rate as a firm's core business activities grow. Otherwise, processing slows down and failures resulting from a system's inability to handle increasing volumes of data and related query requests can make it difficult for the firm to respond quickly to market changes and new customer demands. To obtain broad scalability,large corporations have turned to massively parallel processing systems.

NCR's WorldMark family of scalable servers provides a powerful platform for MPP and DSS. NCR WorldMark srevers are available as high-powered clients as well as small, medium and large-scale enterprise servers. Based entirely on industry-standard Intel processors, WorldMark systems can be upgraded on an as-needed basis.

NCR's WorldMark family scales from high performance desktop client machines to entry level servers with 1-4 CPU's, to small scale enterprise servers with 1-8 CPU's, medium scale enterprise servers with 2-16 CPU's, up large scale enterprise servers with up to 4096 CPU's. All machines are based on Intel Corp.processors and run NCR Unix SVR4. Generally, the hardware supports Teradata, Informix, Oracle, Sybase and others.

As a result of NCR's clustering technology for Windows NT, customers can operate their Web sites 24 hours a day when they run their sites with NCR WorldMark servers and Windows NT. In 1997, NCR released all WorldMark servers for Windows NT and Unix MP-RAS with pre-loaded Internet software as well as a dormant bundle of Check Point Firewall-1 security software. All WorldMark servers can be delivered to customers with Netscape FastTrack Server and Netscape Navigator (Unix or Windows NT) or with Microsoft's Internet Information Server (IIS) software for Windows NT.

Enterprise Security

Through strong integration with its partners' offerings, NCR offers secure network transactions with Check Point Firewall-1 software and Cisco router-based security, system and application level security, and services to identify, develop and implement security policies for protecting business assets. Based on Computer Associates Unicenter TNG enterprise manager, NCR also provides remote monitoring and management of Web servers, including security and storage management.

Java Interfaces

NCR offers an enhanced gateway for the Java language that gives application developers a way to use Call-Level Interfaces to NCR Teradata from the Internet, intranets or extranets. Java can access any SQL database supported by a Windows NT ODBC driver and it can support concurrent access to different databases.

Data Warehouse Multimedia Functionality

NCR provides complex object support to the NCR Teradata RDBMS in a multimedia option that lets users store, retrieve, manipulate and analyze complex objects such as video, audio, graphics, animation, text and other user-defined data types. Users can also link to multimedia to traditional alphanumeric relational data. A "deep content analysis" function lets users go beyond the data and use images in the database to get answers. There is also a mapping or geo-coding capability for using demographics and charting to determine, for example, where a branch office or store should be located. A Multimedia Object Server that stores, retrieves and computes on complex objects is based on a user defined function that searches for a key word in an audio track or finds the closest supplier to a dealer.

7-4 CONSULTING SERVICES

NCR spent more than a decade refining its consulting methodology and practice to the point where the Professional Services division now covers the full spectrum of data warehouse tasks. It has over 500 consultants around the world who specialize in the planning, design, building, implementation and support of data warehouses. There are also industry solutions consultants whose skills are industry-specific, in such areas as retail, financial services, communications, transportation, government, insurance, and electronic commerce.

The NCR *RightSTART* program sets up the architecture for and delivers a Scalable Data Warehouse or data mart within a guaranteed 90 day period. NCR RightSTART consultants design the SDW or data mart so that it can grow into a full production data warehouse when the business is ready. RightSTART includes a customized configuration of an NCR WorldMark server running either UNIX or NT, a choice of relational database (NCR Teradata, Informix, or Oracle), industry standard data access and transformation tools and a suite of NCR professional services.

The suite of professional services includes the following seven steps:

1. Interactive information discovery and logical data modeling sessions with NCR business and technology consultants, resulting in a data model that supports the business needs of the department or function.
2. Physical database design, for which the logical data model is translated into a physical database design, then the physical database design is constructed, loaded, optimized, and tested.
3. Data transformation of up to 50GB of data.
4. Query development typically addressing five business questions in the form of report queries that are designed to provide answers identified through information discovery.
5. A technology assessment to identify any potential technology barriers to a successful implementation, as well as recommendations for corrective action.
6. An education assessment plan which suggests a curriculum to ensure the solution is successfully implemented and utilized. The plan can be the basis for knowledge transfer, which should follow the initial implementation.
7. Project management, including system installation and software staging.

Industry-Specific RightSTART

RightSTART provides industry-specific logical data models along with application roadmaps for future growth. For example, RightSTART sales analysis for the retail industry lets retailers access detailed data on-line to better track, analyze and understand the lifecycle of merchandise by store in order to make sound purchasing decisions, as well as better serve customers.

RightSTART in the financial industry provides analytical models and applications to help small, medium and large banks gain insight into their current and potential customers. The results include propensity to buy, marketing analysis, and channel analysis.

In the communications industry, RightSTART includes yield management, which helps customers address business problems such as customer churn and product-line profitability. There are also customer retention models which are jointly provided with Sabre Decision Technologies as well as network infrastructure models which leverage NCR's data warehouse and methodologies to support communications service providers in their network planning and analytical processes.

7-5 THE NCR DATA WAREHOUSE METHODOLOGY

NCR Professional Services group uses the following methodology:

1. Planning;
2. Design and Implementation and
3. Usage, Support, and Enhancement.

Each phase provides a series of clearly defined processes (Figure 7-2).

This methodology also provides a logical data model design process. Activities include the confirmation of requirements, creation of a project plan, and the generation of the logical data model showing relationships and attributes. The logical data model is not specific to any platform or database and is separate from any physical dependencies. Instead, it represents a metadata layer which describes data about data.

A Data Warehouse Methodology With Multiple Entry Points

NCR's Data Warehouse Methodology has multiple entry points. Most methodologies, developed for project management or information processing applications development, usually have one starting point and a specific finishing point- NCR's methodology is able to segment the sections and prov-

Figure 7-2: The NCR Data Warehouse Methodology

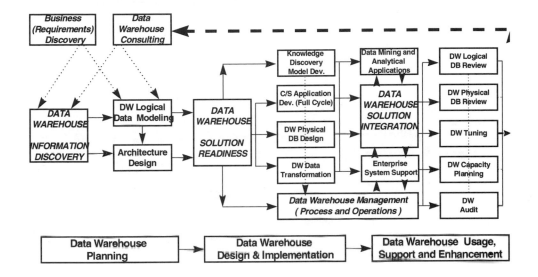

vide services for customers and prospects which allow for entry at any point (Figure 7-3).

The most important contribution of NCR's Data Warehouse Methodology is the iterative nature of the process. The small organization, or newly formed data warehouse team, can begin small and grow their data warehouse using this methodology. For example, Wal*Mart Stores started with 30 Gigabytes in their initial data warehouse and today has the largest commercial data warehouse in the world with 24 Terabytes of storage available on multiple NCR WorldMark and Teradata RDBMS data warehouses.

NCR's VERTICAL INDUSTRY APPLICATIONS

NCR provides vertical industry applications to a spectrum of business sectors such as financial services. These applications include a comprehensive data model designed to optimize financial organizations' ability to perform complex analyses in the following areas: sales and marketing, profitability, risk

Figure 7-3: NCR's Data Warehouse Methodology with Multiple Entry Points

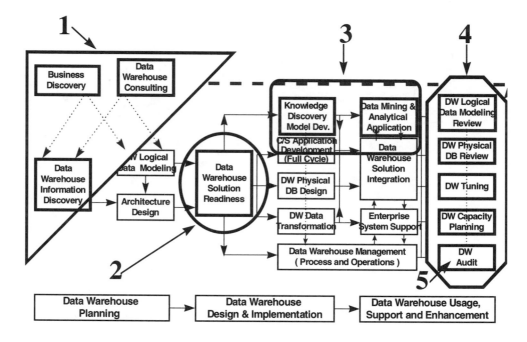

management and channel management. Other models, which can be customized to suit the requirements of specific industries, include:

- *Customer Retention Models* -- developed in conjunction with Sabre Decision Technologies, they predict the long term worth of current and future customers, describe the trade-offs which customers make when choosing products, and anticipate the likelihood that customers will end a business relationship. These include :

1.Current and future value models

2.Behavioral market segmentation models

3.Attrition models

- *Product Line Profitability Modeling* - matches specific customer populations with an appropriate menu of products and/or services. Analyses may include price sensitivity, and market saturation densities by product and the size and depth of user-defined market segments.

  1.Market share models

  2.Product usage and affinity analysis

  3.Acquisition and market targeting models

  4.Product profitability scoring models

- *Financial Services* - For the banking and financial services industries, implementations of data warehousing have been specialized for each organization. They include :

  1.Risk assessment

  2.Lending risk assessment

  3.Prediction of customer profitability

  4.Targeting direct marketing

  5.Predicting market rates

  6.Fraud detection

  7.Customer profiling

  8.Market research

  9.Increasing response rates to marketing or surveys

  10.Estimating missing values in data

- *Customer Relationship Management - Logical Data Model (RM-LDM)* - The RM-LDM is a customer-centric logical data model for financial institutions. It addresses the business questions that manage relationships with consumers across four areas: sales and marketing, profitability, risk management and channel management. The RM-LDM is designed to be used

  •as a data foundation during RM logical data modeling.

  •as a template when developing a relationship

management logical data model for a specific financial institution.

•as a guide for developing a strategic information roadmap and long-term perspective for future business needs.

The RM-LDM provides direction and a model to reduce the risk in building a data warehouse for relationship management and also to accelerate the benefits of the investment in the warehouse. This process and model :

- captures years of financial and cross-industry expertise.

- avoids the blank sheet or false start syndrome and accelerates model creation.

- provides a mechanism for recognizing data redundancy and controlling it.

7-5 NCR AND THE WEB

Most corporations seek to take advantage of secure intranets and extranets for more effective delivery of information, products, and services to both internal and external constituencies. For internal customers, Web-based networks can give decision makers quick, remote access to key company-wide data stored within a data warehouse or a data mart. For external customers, the Internet provides another gateway to product information such as availability and price and value-added client services. In 1997, NCR released a suite of "Internet Electronic Commerce" (IEC) products that, in conjunction with NCR WorldMark servers, can help businesses build high performance Internet, intranet and extranets. NCR's IEC can help companies optimize performance in secure Web environments which must run 24 hours a day without interruption and make information stored in corporate warehouses easily accessible to internal staff, external customers, partners and suppliers.

NCR Electronic Messaging System

The NCR IEC products, integrated with NCR WorldMark servers, include:

Intranet Access Server is for entry-level intranet deployment and for high performance delivery and management of Web site information.

High Availability Web Cluster Servers for NT is for businesses running critical applications that can't undergo any down time. It is based on clustered Web servers with fail-over and recovery software, centralized management and unique load-leveling capabilities for clusters of NCR and non-NCR Web servers.

Web Data Warehouse Solutions make information in corporate warehouses accessible to more people within a company and to a company's customers, suppliers and business partners. Using Java or CGI, users can gain high-performance access across intranets and Internets to business-critical information that resides in NCR's Teradata relational database or merchant databases. Two subsets of this service are:

WebTrack provides information on customer preferences based on Web transactions

WebMining provides mining tools to spot trends, analyze promotions and other decision-support analyses from information in the data warehouse that includes user transactions and transactions on the Internet.

Web Transaction Broker extends customers' current transaction systems to secure transactions via the Internet. Central to this solution is NCR's Top End middleware, which automatically manages and distributes service requests over the enterprise in a secure manner for quick response times.

Web-Enabled Financial Solutions includes supply chain electronic commerce solutions and, for the retail industry, Internet access for self-service kiosks, Web-enabled automatic teller machines for the financial services industry, and many other applications.

The various modules help customers align their use of Internet technology to achieve business goals.

NCR's consultants provide four types of electronic markets services :

Internet Discovery – NCR Internet consultants examine key business objectives, business processes required to achieve the objectives, and Internet technologies that can best support these processes.

Internet Solutions Design – This module extends the reach of high availability transaction processing or data warehousing or builds a cohesive intranet infrastructure. It includes a comprehensive solution requirements specification, a customized integrated solution design, and a transition strategy for implementing the solution.

Internet Implementation – This module, provided to customers who have purchased NCR Web server and client software, provides Web server installation, configuration, and testing.

Internet Audit and Refresh – NCR consultants audit a customer's existing Web server infrastructure to identify problem areas or help to prepare for changes by looking at performance, functionality, usability/content, usage profiles and security. Subsequent to this, NCR consultants provide recommendations for improving the existing site based on the results of the audit.

7-6 NCR'S DATA WAREHOUSE ALLIANCE PARTNERS

NCR maintains numerous alliances with industry leaders. For example, the company has agreements with Microsoft Corp. and Sun Microsystems Inc. to provide the Windows NT and Sun Solaris operating environments, respectively, on NCR's WorldMark servers. The Microsoft consortium selected Teradata as it's only additional database solution within the original eight companies selected (Fig. 7-4).

Some of the alliances serve vertical industries in one or more of NCR's successful data warehousing markets: financial services (including banking and brokerage), telecommunications, retail, manufacturing, insurance, online information subscription systems, insurance, federal government, state and local government, and transportation.

Figure 7-4: NCR's SDW Tools and Partnerships

NCR's SDW Tools and Partnerships

Operational Data		**Tools for Managing Data Warehouse**	
Data Transformation		• NCR's *FastLoad & Multi-Load*	• SAS - *Management Tools*
		• Evoluntary Tech. Inc (ETI) *-Extract*	• Synectics
		• Prism *-Warehouse Executive*	• Trillium
Enterprise Warehouse Tools		• Carleton *-Passport*	• Apertus - *Enterprise Integrator*
		• BEZ *-BEZ Plus*	• Pine Cone Systems - *Mgmt Tools*
Dependent Data Mart		• NCR - *Teradata RDBMS*	
		• Microsoft - *SQL Server*	
Knowledge Discovery/ Data Mining		• Angoss - *Knowledge SEEKER*	• KD1 - *Analysis Tools*
		• SABRE Decision Technologies	• Quadstone - *Decisionhouse*
		• HyperParallel - *//Discovery*	• SAS - *Explortation Tools*

Tools for Information Access & Analysis

Information Access Server OLAP		_Server OLAP_	_Client OLAP / Query & Reporting_	_Multi-Dimensional DB_
Client OLAP/ Query & Reporting		• Platinum - *InfoBeacon*	• Platinum- *Forest & Trees*	• SAS
		• Information Advantage - *DecisionSuite*	• Cognos - *Impromptu / PowerPlay*	• Broadbase
			• Andyne - *GQL / Pablo*	• Pilot - *Decision Support Suite*
MDDB		• MicroStrategy - *DSS Agent/Server*	• Brio Tech. - *BrioQuery*	
			• Information Builders *-Focus*	
Applications			• SAS - *Explortation Tools*	

As of October 1, 1997 - Check www.ncr.com for Updatess

In addition, some partnerships are advancing with joint experiences. For example, NCR and Sabre Decision Technologies have an arrangement whereby NCR tailors Sabre's data analysis software as part of a customer retention solution for data warehousing customers in the telecommunications industry. Other alliances fall in the category of Internet electronic commerce partners, such as NCR's agreement with Cisco Systems, Inc. for internetworking with routers, local area networks or asynchronous transfer mode switches.

NCR also partners with SAS, Information Advantage, Platinum Technologies, Microsoft, Computer Associates, Cognos, and MicroStrategy.

7-7 NCR'S DATA WAREHOUSE CASE STUDIES

NCR Case Study Profile: Sears

Faced with growing competition during the 1980's, Sears Roebuck and Co. had to defend its position vigorously as the third largest retailer in the United States. But by the early 1990's, Sears still operated with 10- to 20-year old sales information systems, each running off 18 major databases that were overflowing with redundant, conflicting and sometimes obsolete data.

Sears finance, marketing and merchandising departments each had its own systems, which meant a buyer might come up with a different sales figure than the accounting department for the same region. Even within departments, information was scattered among numerous databases, forcing users to query multiple systems even for relatively simple questions.

Sears executives decided that the solution was a single data source for key performance indicators -- sales, inventory and margin -- and a huge system, which it dubbed the Strategic Performance Reporting System (SPRS), that would let users generate consistent, reliable reporting of sales and other results.

Sears chose NCR and subsequently installed a 1.7 terabyte WorldMark solution, the third-largest NCR system in existence. Its configuration: 10 application processors, 44 parsing engines, 216 AMPS and 864 disk storage units. The system utilizes NCR's Teradata database, NCR Top End middleware, and TCP/IP as its network protocol. Front end applications are written in Powersoft Corp.'s PowerBuilder. Sears IS staffers consolidated 18 separate sales, inventory and other systems. They delivered the sales system in mid-1995. Then they rolled out store, distribution center, inventory, and ad hoc reporting systems in 1996 and a consolidated financial system in 1997.

Based on NCR's Teradata and NCR's WorldMark technologies, the warehouse lets users view each day's sales nationally, by region, district, individual store, line and stock-keeping unit via a graphical user interface. Sears staffers monitor the impact of advertising, weather and other factors on sales of specific items.

NCR Case Study Profile: Travel Unie

This Netherlands tour operator and travel agency uses the NCR Teradata Data Warehouse to profile their customers and provide new or enhanced products and services to succeed in a highly competitive marketplace. Travel Unie offers tour packages to travelers through 400 branch offices, as well as providing travel package services to more than 1,400 independent travel agents throughout Europe.

The Challenge

Travel Unie must provide "on demand" services to each office and agent, or risk losing business to competitors. The travel agency also must be able to capture and use customer data to more easily tailor tour packages to customer needs.

The Goal

Develop an open, highly-available enterprise-wide information and analytical system capable of supporting hundreds of concurrent users for both online transaction processing and decision support. Define an environment for scalability and growth of both the business and also the technology, which will provide effective information and responsiveness for a long period of time through incremental growth.

The Results

The key to the marketing and resource planning is in the data warehouse elements of the total systems approach that NCR provided. Executives can access detailed information about their customers, their financials, their plans and tours, while also understanding the profiles and behaviors of their customer. They are able to retain and re-sell them with successfully planned and executed travel tours and vacations.

The agents and managers analyze trends and create customized tour packages, plus join with appropriate outside resources to fulfill market and sales opportunities. The customer retention rate is very high because of the use of the data warehouse, historical analysis, and customer follow-up communication are all tied together.

The strategies of using the NCR Teradata Data Warehouse in conjunction with it's customer contact people and systems, provided Travel Unie sales growth in excess of 40 percent in one five-year period and reduced total operating costs per passenger booked by more than 60 percent over a period of approximately 12 years.

NCR Case Study Profile: Army And Air Force Exchange Service (AAFES)

The Army and Air Force Exchange Service (AAFES) is a $7 billion per year retailer serving 12 million U.S. military and government personnel worldwide. The chain includes 230 general merchandise stores; 600 specialty stores such as sporting goods, liquor, and furniture; 125 food courts; 120 Burger Kings™; and dozens of movie theaters and bowling alleys.

AAFES also operates hundreds of gas stations, barber shops, beauty parlors, and coffee shops.

The Challenge

AAFES needed to manage merchandise with precision and accuracy knowing hundreds of individual products shipping to stores throughout the world, including locations as remote as Guam and Bosnia.

The Goal

AAFES' goal is to deliver the right merchandise, to the right place, at the right price. AAFES needs logistical and distribution information to ensure their success in providing products and services. In addition, AAFES strives to be very price competitive, plus customer service-oriented in a world of high competition from other providers in the communities surrounding many of the military and civilian locations.

The Solution

AAFES is using NCR's Teradata RDBMS running on NCR WorldMark 5100 and 3600 massively parallel processing servers, as the platform for a 700 Gigabyte data warehouse. The solution also includes highly available disk arrays from EMC Corporation.

One of the applications, NCR's retail access module, allows hundreds of buyers and merchandisers to mine detailed point-of-sale data. This is done via an easy-to-use graphical user interface with drilldown decision-support capabilities. AAFES is a strong proponent of NCR's concept of maintaining transaction detail data from all appropriate sources throughout the enterprise.

The Results

The Retail Access Module, along with many other recently implemented applications and query decision support processes, helps AAFES accurately purchase and allocate products. The NCR Teradata RDBMS system enables accurate forecasting of future sales activity through analysis of two year's worth of past sales data. By uncovering trends that were previously difficult to identify, the system takes the guesswork out of proper stocking at the store level, resulting in a 98 percent service-level accuracy.

AAFES is working with NCR to create market basket analysis applications that will help AAFES better understand its customers and its potential profitability. By knowing what products customers buy, and in what combinations, AAFES will target specific customers to market directly to them with frequent shopper programs and other loyalty incentives.

Oracle Corporation:

Enabling Informed Business Decisions

8-1 COMPANY BACKGROUND[1]

Oracle Corporation is the world's largest vendor of information management software. Oracle software runs on almost every computer in the world, from personal digital assistants to supercomputers, managing everything from personal information to global information networks.

Oracle is the world's largest independent provider of software and services for managing information, with more than 20,000 dedicated software professionals, and operations in more than 90 countries. The company headquarters are in Redwood Shores, California.

8-2 ORACLE'S DECISION SUPPORT PRODUCTS

Oracle's suite of decision support products combines a data model optimized for analysis with query and analytical tools.

---

[1] This chapter was contributed by Oracle Corporation and is copyright by them. It was written by Michael Ault of Oracle Corporation.

Two classes of users benefit from these tools: "analyis providers" and "analysis consumers."

Analysis providers may be financial or marketing analysts. Analysis providers uncover trends and exceptions. They build "what-if" models that reveal, in precise and measurable terms, the impact of alternatives in pricing, policies, or budgets.

In most enterprises, only a few users provide analyses but many users are analysis consumers. They use the interactive reports, graphs, and multimedia briefings that answer analytical queries: "What will sales be in Asia next quarter if we raise prices relative to competition?" "How much will orders increase this quarter if customers forward-buy to beat an announced price increase, and will the overall effect be positive or negative to the bottom line?"

Ideally, both classes of users receive the benefits of decision support with intuitive, easy-to-use tools. Oracle's suite of query, reporting, and analysis tools is designed to meet this ideal. Comprised of Oracle Express® OLAP (on-line analytical processing) technology and Oracle Discoverer©, this suite of products addresses end-user needs from ad hoc query and reporting to sophisticated multidimensional analysis and analytical applications. Together, this range of analytical functions is called *enterprise decision support*.

Enterprise decision support integrates cross-departmental data into a coherent whole, enabling users to work from a common information base. It gives users the ability to work with all of the information in a data warehouse or with a subset in a data mart. Enterprise DSS can also integrate data from disparate systems—relational, legacy, or external. This integration enables new applications that transcend departmental boundaries, such as fact-based selling, activity-based costing, and product profitability analysis.

Oracle Express: Dynamic Multidimensional Analysis

Oracle Express is the family of OLAP technology products from Oracle. The OLAP Council, a consortium of vendors, published the following definition of OLAP:

Figure 8-1: Oracle's Suite of Decision Support Tools. Includes the web-enabled express server, an advanced calculation engine and data cache which integrates data from disparate systems—relational, legacy, or external.

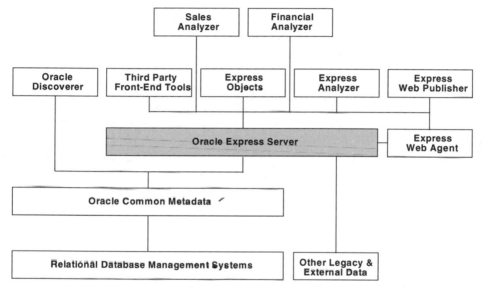

"On-Line Analytical Processing is a category of software technology that enables analysts, managers and executives to gain insight into data through fast, consistent, interactive access to a wide variety of possible views of information that has been transformed from raw data to reflect the real dimensionality of the enterprise as understood by the user.

"OLAP functionality is characterized by dynamic multidimensional analysis of consolidated enterprise data supporting end user analytical and navigational activities including:

- Calculations and modeling applied across dimensions, through hierarchies and/or across members

- Trend analysis over sequential time periods

- Slicing subsets for on-screen viewing

- Drilldown to deeper levels of consolidation
- Reach-through to underlying detail data
- Rotation to new dimensional comparisons in the viewing area"[2]

OLAP solutions are typically implemented as a set of multi-user, client/server applications and tools, offering consistently fast access to any item in a database without regard to the size or complexity of the data. OLAP helps users synthesize enterprise information through comparative, personalized viewing, as well as through analysis of historical and projected data in various "what-if" scenarios.

OLAP enables professionals to access the data describing their enterprise and its markets, to analyze that data for insight into the workings of the enterprise, and to take action based on the new insight. Companies use OLAP to market their products effectively, control costs, and identify important internal and external trends.

Express provides a single, integrated software architecture for OLAP. Oracle Express has the following components for building enterprise systems:

OLAP Server

Oracle Express Server structures data for analysis and provides the calculation engine for creating derived data values. The server can either store data permanently or cache it temporarily. Oracle Express Server and Express-based applications operate in a range of client/server and Web-based configurations on a variety of platforms.

Pre-built Analytical Applications

With Oracle Express applications (e.g., Oracle Sales Analyzer and Oracle Financial Analyzer), users can access, calculate,

---

[2] The OLAP Council, *OLAP Glossary.*

and share information modeled after their businesses' products, markets, distribution channels, time periods, and scenarios (including budget, actual, and forecast). Oracle Express analytical tools are often used as front-ends for data warehouses.

Application Development Environment

Oracle Express offers object-oriented tools for modeling, graphing, forecasting, statistics, communications, database management, and data acquisition—especially the acquisition of relational data. A visual, point-and-click environment supports the creation and maintenance of custom OLAP applications, as well as OLAP Web sites that may be published via the Internet or a corporate intranet.

Open Interfaces that Support Applications Built with Third-party Tools

Users can access the power of Oracle Express through a variety of interfaces, including off-the-shelf spreadsheets, customized front-ends, and Web browsers. Oracle Express products are supported by over 150 third parties including independent software vendors, consultants, system integrators, and value added resellers.

How Organizations Use Oracle Express

Suppose an organization needs a production forecasting system. This need may be identified by an executive or by a functional department tasked with providing forecasts. Frequently, the historical data necessary to support a forecasting application is inaccessible, or is buried in a transaction processing system that decision support users cannot access without adversely impacting operational systems. Once IS understands the end user requirements and the business issues to be addressed, the following steps typically occur:

1. The professional IS developer accesses the data from a data warehouse or directly from the OLTP system and stages it in Express Server.
2. IS distributes an OLAP application or OLAP query tool to an enterprise-wide community of end users. This application can be based on Oracle's Express client tools, third party tools, the Web, or it can be a custom application leveraging Express' open interface. The users run the application, which accesses Express Server.

Oracle Express Server

The power of Express tools and applications comes from Express Server, Oracle's calculation engine and data cache.

Figure 8- 2: OLAP Application Architecture Using Express.

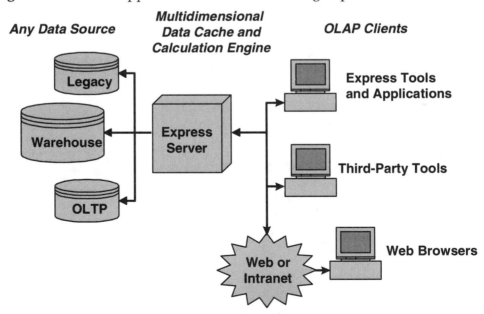

Express Server uses a multidimensional model that reflects the way users think about their business. This data model is often physically represented as a cube, where each unique data value (or "fact") exists at the intersection of multiple dimensions (see Figure 8-3). Dimensions such as time, product, and geography categorize and summarize facts, like unit sales. Although it is easy to visualize a three-dimensional cube, it is more difficult to illustrate the four, five, or more dimensions that Express supports.

Express uses a *multicube* implementation of the multidimensional model, which breaks data into separate logical entities. This approach is analogous to having multiple tables within a single relational database. Each of these data cubes can be individually dimensioned. In contrast, many other OLAP vendors use a single-structure (or *hypercube*) implementation that stores all of the data in one, uniformly-dimensioned array.

Figure 8-3: Users Can Look at Their Data the Way They Look at Their Business. In this example, unit sales can be viewed by product and by market over time.

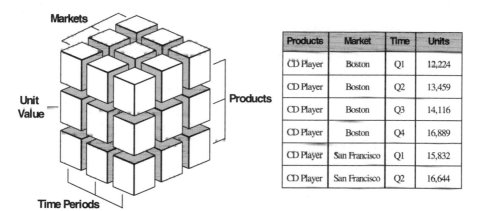

Products	Market	Time	Units
CD Player	Boston	Q1	12,224
CD Player	Boston	Q2	13,459
CD Player	Boston	Q3	14,116
CD Player	Boston	Q4	16,889
CD Player	San Francisco	Q1	15,832
CD Player	San Francisco	Q2	16,644

To understand the differences between these two approaches, consider a simple DSS system that contains both sales and manufacturing data. Sales figures are organized (or "dimensioned") by product, month and retail site. Manufacturing data is dimensioned by month and factory location. A single-structure database must organize *all* the information by *every* dimension—product, month, retail site, and factory location—even when some of those dimensions do not make sense for particular data (e.g., retail sites for manufacturing data).

A multicube database like Express, however, can store different kinds of data in separate structures with appropriate dimensions. Sales data would include product, month, and retail site dimensions, while manufacturing costs would be kept in another "cube" dimensioned by month and factory. The software matches the natural structure of the data when performing analysis.

Even with the separate data structures, Express ensures that all dimension maintenance occurs in one place. Differently-dimensioned objects (such as sales figures and manufacturing data) automatically share the same values for common dimensions such as month. This approach reduces maintenance, enforces data consistency, supports referential integrity, and makes it automatically combines or joins differently dimensioned objects.

Oracle believes that the multicube model used by Express is consistent with many of the fundamental concepts of data management and manipulation that have evolved in recent years. The single-structure approach, on the other hand, is logically equivalent to building a relational database where all the data is contained in a single table with one set of keys. Such an approach would obviously negate many of the benefits of relational data management.

Elements of the Express Data Model

The primary elements of the Express data model are *dimensions*, *variables*, *formulas*, and *relations*. Each of these is introduced below.

Dimensions

Dimensions are the keys associated with individual attributes in the data model. Each combination of dimension values uniquely identifies an occurrence of data values within the database. For example, in a sales and marketing system the dimensions might include product, market, time, and distribution channel. In the multidimensional world of Express Server, dimensions are typically "recursive," or hierarchical, in nature: individual products may be grouped into product families, product families may be organized into brands, and brands may be associated with specific divisions.

Variables

Variables contain stored data values. In a relational database star schema they are frequently referred to as *facts*. Examples of variables might include number of units sold, the selling price of the item, and the cost of the goods or services. One variable value can be stored for each combination of dimension values.

Formulas

Formulas are derived or virtual data items that are calculated dynamically. The resulting value is never stored in Express Server; only the definition of the formula is stored. Formulas can reference variables, as well as other formulas. For example, gross margin (selling price minus cost of goods sold) might be defined as a formula. In addition, total margin might be defined as gross margin times the number of units sold. Variables and formulas are collectively described as *measures*.

Relations

A relation captures a one-to-one or one-to-many relationship between dimensions. It is analogous to primary key/foreign key relationships in relational database systems. For example, production facilities may be related to particular product lines. Express Server can use these relations to perform aggregate functions dynamically, or to narrow the scope of an operation. Relations are also used to capture hierarchies. A hierarchy consists of a self relation within a dimension.

Multidimensional queries execute rapidly. Array arithmetic is used to access cells and slices of the cube. As a result, Express supports the largest, most complex OLAP queries and applications. Accompanying the multidimensional data model of Express Server are functions that analyze, forecast, model, and answer "what-if" questions about the data. The server has built-in functions for mathematical, financial, statistical, and time-series manipulation. The Oracle Express data model ensures that end users can analyze data in a structured or ad hoc fashion without requesting special programs from IS personnel.

Express Server Architecture

The heart of Oracle Express Server is an advanced calculation engine and a shared, multidimensional data cache. Query and analysis commands are issued via the Express SPL (Stored Procedure Language), a 4GL which includes both procedural and non-procedural data manipulation.

Express Server can store and manage data itself or provide direct analysis of relational data with a sophisticated multidimensional caching scheme. Drawing data from a relational database eliminates the need to store data twice—once in a multidimensional format and once in a relational format. Alternatively, a persistent cache can be created and refreshed on a periodic basis, offering significant performance advantages. Express offers both a persistent cache and a temporary cache.

"Entry points" to Express Server include a published application program interface (API) for client-server communication; a scalable, high-performance interface that allows Web browsers to access the full capabilities of Express; and the Express Communications Architecture (XCA), which provides peer-to-peer communications between two or more servers.

Oracle's open strategy provides maximum flexibility, allowing companies to choose among relational databases, development tools, and user interfaces—including customized Windows front ends, spreadsheets, and the World Wide Web.

Figure 8-4: Express Server Architecture

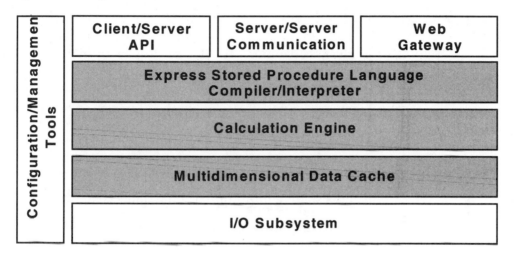

Using Express Server with the World Wide Web

The Web-enabling component of Express Server, the Oracle Express Web Agent, empowers end users to perform business-critical ad hoc analysis of multidimensional data over corporate intranets and the World Wide Web. The Express Web Agent makes it possible to use any HTML authoring tool to embed dynamic, data-aware views into Web pages. A Developer's Toolkit allows Express users to create sophisticated OLAP Web sites. This toolkit encapsulates both low-level HTML functions and higher-level building blocks for OLAP application development. Because Web browsers are available on any client machine and provide a familiar user interface, these applications are simple to deploy and use.

The Oracle Express Web Publisher is used to build live, interactive, data-driven OLAP Web sites. These Web sites, which can be defined for a given functional area or group of users, are presented as a series of briefings that logically classify information—for example, key performance indicators in an organization. For end users, the Oracle Express Web Publisher combines the of Web browsing with the analytical power of Express Server.

Oracle Express Objects

Most analysis consumers are not professional analysts, but must perform analyses to support their job function. These users require OLAP applications where the business rules have been predefined. Oracle Express Objects is a visual, object-oriented development environment for creating custom OLAP applications.

Express Objects has data-aware controls for viewing and manipulating Express data, controls for analyzing relational data stores, and is open to third-party controls. Express Objects supports both visual development and event-driven programming. This environment fully supports true object orientation: encapsulation, inheritance, and polymorphism. Applications developed with Express Objects are easily distributed and shared with end users, who can both run the applications and extend them without additional programming.

Oracle Express Analyzer

Oracle Express Analyzer is a general-purpose, object-oriented tool for end-user reporting and analysis. In conjunction with Express Objects and the Express Web Publisher, Express Analyzer provides an end-user environment with three major benefits. First, Express Analyzer can extend and publish applications developed in Express Objects. Second, it allows end users to analyze and report data by providing access to data stored in, or accessible through, Express Server. Finally, Express Analyzer allows views of Express data to be published to an OLAP Web site, extending the reach of OLAP throughout the enterprise.

Express Analyzer organizes analyses into briefings—pages of subject-oriented analyses built with reusable objects. These briefings are interactive: users can rotate, drilldown, and query data in any table or graph on a briefing page to perform their own ad hoc analysis.

Briefings are created with point-and-click tools. Casual users, who usually just read briefings, page through them with pulldown menus or navigation buttons. Power users, who can create briefings on their own or with objects they receive from IS, do not need to program. Briefings may be shared via LANs and e-mail, or published to an OLAP Web site and accessed through a Web browser.

Oracle Financial Analyzer

Oracle Financial Analyzer is a distributed OLAP application for financial planning, analysis, budgeting, and reporting. By integrating a central source of management data with powerful analytical tools, the system enables organizations to meet their critical financial objectives—to control costs, analyze performance, evaluate opportunities, submit and roll up budgets, and formulate future direction.

Oracle Financial Analyzer can access financial data from spreadsheets, general ledgers, relational databases, and legacy systems. The product integrates with Oracle General Ledger,™ to simplify data acquisition and maintenance.

Oracle Sales Analyzer

Oracle Sales Analyzer is a general-purpose application for analyzing sales, marketing, or similar data. With Sales Analyzer, users can evaluate sales trends, marketing campaigns, product or customer profitability, product life cycles, and promotional effectiveness. When evaluations are complete, the system helps users to adjust their strategies through custom analysis.

Sales Analyzer makes it possible to do market share calculations, ranking reports, and 80/20 analysis so that users can determine the answers to question such as:

- Who is likely to buy which products next, and when?

- Why is market share falling in some markets but not others?

- Which are the most profitable accounts or customers to call?

- How will a new product launch affect existing products?

- How effective was the last promotion compared to plan and compared to last year?

- What is the best pricing strategy—to maximize margin or match a competitor's price?

Sales Analyzer provides users with direct analytical access to the data warehouse and to data stored in Oracle Applications.

Oracle Discoverer: RDBMS Query and Reporting

Oracle Discoverer is an intuitive ad hoc query and reporting tool which complements the sophisticated computational engine and multidimensional analysis capabilities of Oracle Express. For non-technical, business-oriented analysts, usability of access tools is often the most important consideration. Oracle Discoverer enables users at all levels of the organization to gain immediate access to information from relational data warehouses, data marts, and online transactional processing (OLTP) systems.

Discoverer is comprised of three elements: the User Edition©, the End User Layer©, and the Administration Edition©. The User Edition enables users to query the warehouse, graph results, create reports, and perform drill-and-pivot analyses. Discoverer's End User Layer is the translation mechanism that provides end users with the ability to create queries and reports and perform analyses without understanding SQL or database structures. The Administration Edition is used for the setup and maintenance of the End User Layer. The administrator performs a variety of tasks including maintaining business areas and folders, creating summary tables, and managing end user access.

Via the End User Layer, Discoverer is able to group related sets of information logically into *Business Areas*. For example, a particular Business Area may contain personal data, data for a specific department (e.g., Sales, Marketing, Finance), or data relating to a specific topic such as customer purchasing. While the underlying technical definition of a Business Area may contain many references to complex database objects, users interact with terminology and business groupings that they understand.

Discoverer User Interface

Discoverer provides a single, consistent interface for querying, reporting, and drilldown/pivot functionality. Discoverer blurs the distinction between these tasks, enabling inexperienced users to retrieve and analyze data without understanding the technological and conceptual underpinnings of the information discovery process. A step-by-step approach leads users through the query-building process, and task-oriented assistance in the form of cue cards and computer based training ensures a minimal learning curve.

In a relational database, users often summarize detail data "on the fly" to find aggregate values. This can result in time-consuming and resource-intensive queries that seriously affect performance, especially on systems with large numbers of users. To enhance the performance of information retrieval in a large-volume data warehouse, Oracle Discoverer can create and maintain summary tables. When a user asks for detail-level information, Discoverer automatically (and transparently) redirects the request to the pre-summarized table. Discoverer does not require query requests to exactly match the available summary tables; a sophisticated algorithm uses the closest match and seamlessly aggregates within the hierarchy.

Discoverer automates the normally daunting task of summary table administration. As users issue requests to the warehouse, an ongoing audit gathers performance statistics.

Figure 8-5: Oracle Discover Product Architecture

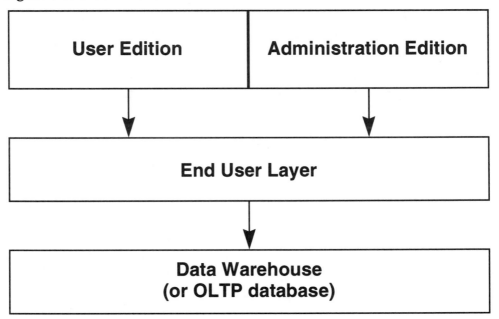

An internal algorithm monitors these statistics, determines inefficient access paths to the warehouse, and recommends to the administrator appropriate summary tables—along with estimated sizes. The tables the administrator chooses to create are automatically populated at a specified time. Discoverer becomes immediately aware of the new summary tables, and redirects subsequent user requests for that data.

Like other tools, Discoverer provides a reactive query governor to stop long-running queries. In addition, Discoverer provides a unique prediction capability that indicates in advance how long a query will take. This feedback enables users to make sensible decisions about whether to run a query immediately or refer it to a batch process for later calculation. Valuable system resources are conserved, overall load is reduced, and end users spend less time waiting.

Client Side Cubic Cache

Discoverer employs a client-side cubic cache that enables analysis without re-querying the database. Query results fetched from the server are compressed and indexed in a memory-efficient "data cube" on the client PC. This local caching, which is transparent to both users and administrators, allows end users to ask subsequent questions about the data without having to re-execute the query. When a user changes the way data is displayed, all processing is handled locally to provide exceptional performance. As additional data is requested, Discoverer fetches only this new data and incorporates it into the existing cache. The cache supports any number of dimensions or measures, and users may specify its physical size and location.

Leveraging the Web

Disseminating information quickly and easily throughout the enterprise is critical to the success of any business. The World Wide Web and corporate intranets offer a mechanism to achieve this. Reports from Discoverer may be exported as HTML documents, allowing any user who has access to the server to display data with a Web browser.

Together, Oracle Discoverer and Oracle Express address the full spectrum of user needs—from simple query and analysis of data contained in a warehouse to sophisticated analysis, forecasting and modeling, to object-oriented OLAP application development for the enterprise. Oracle's DSS products support decisions in governments throughout the world and in industries as varied as pharmaceuticals, retail, financial services, entertainment, utilities, telecommunications, transportation, and consumer packaged goods.

8-3 ORACLE DSS CASE STUDY: TAPESTRY COMPUTING

Tapestry Computing, Inc., of St. Louis provides information technology solutions to over 150 commercial accounts in the Midwest. It's targeted, aggressive strategy has positioned the company for approximately 100 percent growth since its formation in 1993.

With today's business trend of outsourcing technical and creative business solutions, competition among consulting firms is fierce. Competitive pressures require fast response at an attractive price. The key reason for Tapestry's success as one of Oracle's largest integrators is that it uses Oracle products internally.

"We're kind of unique, Not only do we use the products, we sell the products. We offer products and services that help our commercial accounts leverage their business needs through client/server applications for financials, manufacturing, and data warehousing." explains Jim Eberlin, Tapestry's vice president, sales and marketing

Tapestry has been an Oracle user since its formation. The company runs several Oracle databases on Sun Solaris and Windows NT platforms, with approximately 30 developers accessing each type of platform. The data warehouse and general office automation tools reside on the NT servers, and the financial, billing, and training applications are on Solaris.

For internal operations, Tapestry uses Oracle Discoverer against its Oracle database. Users can drilldown to the level of detail needed to support their analyses, save those results, and then access them through a spreadsheet application. The company's executives also use Oracle's Express tools and applications extensively for strategic business decision support.

Survival of the Fittest

Tapestry equipped itself with the OLAP tools necessary to be competitive and fit for survival. Within its first two years of operation, it uncovered an alarming trend by asking "what-if" questions with Oracle Financial Analyzer and Oracle Express Server. This discovery prompted a decision that literally saved the company.

"We were using the Oracle business analysis tools to help us determine exactly how profitable our business units were, through this method, we spotted a problem within one of our business units. We then determined that this unit was not profitable, and ultimately decided to spin off the unit. As a result of that decision, our company returned to profitability and became more focused."

"The new company had a happy ending as well. It was able to put the marketing and technical infrastructure in place to make it successful since it did not have to compete for resources any more." Jim Eberlin

Using Oracle Express Server's multidimensional data model, Eberlin could remove any emotion, politics, and bias from the decision-making process. The ability to drilldown to expose the hidden costs associated with unprofitable products was invaluable.

"The Express products are simple to use." "I'm not technical, but as a business owner, I can now access any part of my business." Jim Eberlin Through the use of Oracle's decision support tools, Eberlin's strategic decisions are supported with facts. He can easily identify the company's most profitable services and concentrate on them. This capability greatly enhances Tapestry's business focus, enabling the company to provide higher-quality services than those offered by its competition.

Migrating into the Future

The fact that Oracle places such a high value on streamlined product integration helps Tapestry stay ahead of its competition. *"Because Oracle's client/server applications are so modular, we've been able to compete against some of the bigger players out there. This is because we can often implement the Oracle client/ server applications much faster than the competition can. Internally, we can access information faster because of the integration of the products. For virtually every situation, Oracle has a complete solution."* Jim Eberlin

8-4 ORACLE DSS CASE STUDY: SOURCE INFORMATICS

With the onset of health care reform, Source Informatics America, Inc./PMSI—a provider of marketing information to pharmaceutical manufacturers and the health care industry— saw an opportunity to expand its role in helping clients formulate more competitive marketing tactics. By integrating Oracle Sales Analyzer with the prescription transaction data that Source collects from pharmacies nationwide, the company offers an integrated marketing support solution that puts data to more timely and effective use.

Before Oracle Sales Analyzer, Source clients simply received paper reports and data tapes. *"Because raw marketing data was difficult to leverage, pharmaceutical companies spent up to 90 percent of their time just trying to get at the data,"* Larry McAferty, CIO for Source. With Oracle Sales Analyzer, clients can quickly and easily rotate and drilldown into data, look for anomalies, and make corrections in sales/promotion strategies to optimize performance.

Measuring the Influence of Managed Care

Pharmaceutical sales forces market their wares directly to practitioners. The sales force consults on the efficacy and side effects of pharmaceuticals, and leaves samples of its products with doctors and managed-care providers. Manufacturers use Oracle Sales Analyzer to draw correlations between these marketing activities and prescription transactions at the drugstore.

Oracle Sales Analyzer also allows pharmaceutical companies to analyze prescription data by an assortment of payment methods: third-party (HMO or insurance card), cash, and Medicaid. With trend analyses, manufacturers can track the influence that managed care has in a territory over characteristics such as: who pays, what comparable products are being prescribed, and the amount being charged. Ranking reports allow manufacturers to target their marketing strategies toward the third-party plans or managed-care organizations that exhibit the most influence.

"The goal is two-fold. First, identify those plans with which the manufacturers need to establish contracts, then determine which prescribers are heavily associated with those plans." Alan Hirshman, senior product development manager for Source

Once the product is put on the approved list by the HMO, the sales representatives can begin recommending that affiliated practitioners write prescriptions for that product. Conversely, manufacturers can avoid wasting marketing resources on prescribers who are closely affiliated with HMOs, when the manufacturer has no control over the HMO or has no contract with it.

Empowering P&L Centers with Decision Support

With the pharmaceutical industry pushing toward regionalization, Oracle Sales Analyzer is helping regional offices of Source clients to succeed as profit-and-loss centers. explains: *"Instead of depending on the home office to provide marketing and sales analyses, business units are becoming more self-sufficient in customizing central marketing's core message to coincide with the specific needs of their customers."* Frank Cali, western business unit director of Rhòne-Poulenc Rorer, a client of Source Informatics America, Inc./PMSI.

Oracle Sales Analyzer lets business units easily drill-down to district-level data to compare market-share variances, create rankings, and generate exception reports. Business units can pinpoint which territories are skewing the sales numbers, and then devise tactical plans to address those anomalies. Plans might be to revise presentation materials, or to modify the frequency of sales calls to HMO affiliates. Subsequent analyses can then track the effectiveness of these plans.

Combining Relational and Multidimensional Technology

Cause-and-effect analysis requires the integration of data from disparate sources -- such as call reporting systems, contract formulary databases, and point-of-sale prescription transactions. Storing such information in a relational repository makes it easy for clients to add tables or different models to their data warehouses.

For those reasons, Source values open databases. Oracle Sales Analyzer supports openness by allowing clients to use data stored in relational technology as if it were a virtual multidimensional database. Source therefore offers its clients an open and scalable relational database, coupled with the OLAP tools of multidimensional Oracle Sales Analyzer.

"To know whether you're getting a positive ROI from your sales force, you need to take into account all the information that affects the sale of your products. Sales Analyzer lets our clients do just that." Alan Hirshman Source currently buys prescription transactions from about 30,000 pharmacies across the country, mostly large and small chains that provide the data via Electronic Data Interchange, mainframe tapes, or PC diskettes. Data is validated and stored on an IBM mainframe running DB2. Because Oracle Sales Analyzer can manipulate data stored in a variety of formats (e.g., DB2, Oracle7), Source offers options suited to client computing environments and analytical needs.

In some cases, Source provides a turnkey solution, which aggregates and formats data to feed into a client's on-site data warehouse, and customizes analytical models for Oracle Sales Analyzer. In other cases, Source provides complete facilities management. Clients communicate via a WAN to data warehouses residing on servers housed at Source headquarters in Phoenix, Arizona.

"Integrating Oracle OLAP technology with our expertise in prescription data warehouses is helping the pharmaceutical industry react more quickly to market variances, It's also helping the industry succeed in pushing P&L responsibilities out to the business units, where territory-specific strategies and tactics can be implemented more effectively." Alan Hirshman

Chapter 9

Red Brick Systems, Inc.: The Data WarehouseCompany

9-1 RED BRICK CORPORATE BACKGROUND[1]

Since its inception in 1988, Red Brick® Systems Inc. has focused exclusively on data warehousing. Red Brick, "The Data Warehouse Company®," is dedicated to providing high performance software products specialized for the decision support/data warehouse environment.

Red Brick has grown rapidly since it first started shipping its flagship RDMS product, Red Brick Warehouse, in 1991. Red Brick now has hundreds of data warehouse customers in a wide range of industries worldwide. Red Brick is headquartered in Los Gatos, California, with offices in the U.K., Canada, Japan, and Australia.

Because of its early and sustained concentration on data warehousing, Red Brick frequently leads the relational database vendors in bringing new developments to market. Red

---

[1] This chapter was contributed by Red Brick Systems, Inc. and is copyright by them. It was written by Fred Wee.

Brick pioneered support for the star schema processing now common to data warehouses. Some of Red Brick's early innovations include special multitable join technology called STARjoin™, specialized indexing for these joins, and new algorithms for joining unindexed tables. Performance advances in decision support processing continue to be a primary focus of Red Brick's ongoing research and development.

Throughout most of its history, Red Brick focused exclusively on the relational database engine that drives the data warehouse and those components that are closely related, such as the load processes. For other parts of the data warehouse environment, Red Brick both formed strong partnerships through its PaVER^a™ partner program and acquired, then integrated, specialized technology. Its acquisitions of data transformation and query tools enabled Red Brick to provide a complete working warehouse system "out-of-the-box" for those organizations that require a fully functional, high-performance data warehouse that can be easily and quickly deployed.

Red Brick's central philosophy - driving product development and company growth - is that superior performance and functionality for data warehouse applications comes from specialization, or designing specifically for data warehousing. In the relational database world, this means disregarding the requirements of online transaction processing (OLTP), which are critical for operational systems but add significant processing overhead and complexity for the warehouse environment. This philosophy contrasts sharply to the other major movement in the database industry of providing one server that fits all needs - the "universal server" approach.

Red Brick's future focus is to provide specialized solutions that include leading-edge technology combined with application solutions based on Red Brick's platform of data warehouse products.

9-2 RED BRICK WAREHOUSE

Red Brick's core product is Red Brick Warehouse (version 5 as of 1997). Red Brick Warehouse is a relational database engine specifically designed for data warehousing. As a relational database, it supports standard SQL and fits into a distributed client/server architecture. Because it is designed specifically as a data warehouse database, it provides specialized support for decision support queries.

High Performance Queries

Decision support queries are inherently different than those performed in an online transaction processing system. A typical OLTP query might find a specific customer's record (searching only one or two tables).

There is no "typical" decision support query; data warehouses support ad hoc queries and standard reports of widely varying complexity. The key ingredient is that the more advanced the analysis, the more complex the queries are likely to become. A decision support query may interact with several different tables in the warehouse: "Find the top five customers for product X in the Northeast region over the past year."

Processing these kinds of queries quickly enough to keep up with the thought processes of the analyst performing the query requires a powerful and flexible query engine. Red Brick Warehouse achieves this level of performance by integrating a variety of technologies:

- advanced indexing
- high performance join processing
- an adaptive, cost-based optimizer
- "parallel-on-demand" parallel processing

Indexing Technologies

Red Brick supports a wide range of advanced indexing technologies, including b-tree, TARGETindex™ and STARindex™.

B-tree. This is the index type traditionally used in online transaction systems. While useful in many cases in a decision support system, a b-tree index by itself cannot deliver the performance required in the data warehouse environment by decision support queries.

TARGETindex. This proprietary Red Brick technology uses bit vector indexing as its core technique. Bit vector indexes are very efficient in terms of storage, as they frequently take much less room than traditional b-tree indexes. But the real advantage of a bit vector index is processing speed when combining constraints on a query. Comparing lists of bits is a very fast operation. Bit vector indexing is particularly fast when selecting from large and wide tables, such as the fact tables commonly found in data warehouses.

An ordinary bit-map index works best on columns with a low number of possible values (or low cardinality). So a bit-map index for gender would be very space-efficient, but one for zip code, with many possible values, would not be efficient. Red Brick's TARGETindex technology addresses this problem by implementing a family of index types, each optimized for a particular range of cardinality. Red Brick's adaptive indexing techniques automatically decide which type of index to apply based on the value. These indexes continually adapt to reflect the actual data.

STARindex. Red Brick's proprietary STARindex technology delivers fast query response when joining tables. The STARindex relates multiple tables through the foreign keys on a fact table, using highly compressed information relating the dimensions of a fact table to the rows that contain those dimensions. The STARindex provides greatly accelerated performance when joining related tables.

Consider a warehouse with PURCHASES as the fact table, linked to dimension tables for Company, Item, and Date (see Figure 9-1)

Figure 9-1. STARindex

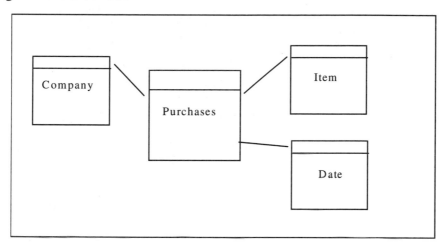

A STARindex on PURCHASES could contain any combination of the foreign key fields. (The exact index configuration should be tuned according to the types of queries most frequently performed.) For example, a single STARindex on PURCHASES that contains COMPANY, ITEM and DATE would process any query against this schema. But a query that only references the date, for example, could be better served by a STARindex on only that dimension of the PURCHASES table.

STARindexes are particularly space-efficient. As a result, they can be built and maintained quickly, which is important for warehouses that are updated frequently.

Integrated index technology. These index types are integrated into every aspect of the Red Brick product: the load system, the storage/retrieval subsystem, the optimizer, and the execution subsystem. Furthermore, they work well with each other; a single query might use a combination of b-tree and TARGETindexes, or a STARindex with one or more TAR-GETindexes. By supporting a broad range of index technology, Red Brick provides optimal performance and tuning capabilities for decision support queries.

Join Processing

Indexing is just one of the tools that the engine uses when handling queries that join multiple tables. The number of possible join configurations in a complex warehouse is very large; no single technique will provide the best performance in all situations.

Red Brick Warehouse supports three join technologies for performing multidimensional joins. These technologies are tightly integrated with Red Brick's indexing techniques.

STARjoin™. Red Brick's unique STARjoin technology uses the Red Brick STARindex to join related tables. STARjoin is a high-speed, single-pass, parallelizable multi-table join. STARjoin makes use of the STARindex to identify all of the rows required for a particular join.

TARGETjoin™. TARGETjoin is another method for joining multiple tables. TARGETjoin uses TARGETindexes on relevant foreign keys in the fact table. Using the dimension tables and TARGETindexes, it creates a list of rows for each restriction (WHERE clause) in a query, and then intersects the lists to create a list of rows from the fact table matching the query.

A TARGETjoin is less efficient than a STARjoin, but more flexible. Because it does not require the presence of a STARindex, it is a flexible solution for handling infrequent or unexpected queries quickly.

Hybrid hash join. Hash join processing joins unindexed tables. Red Brick's hybrid hash-join algorithm includes sophisticated optimizations such as full sub-join recursion (to handle very large joins), role reversals (for joining tables of different sizes), and bit filtering. The result is high performance processing for queries against complex schema.

Adaptive, Cost-based Optimizer

All of these join techniques and index structures are useless without a sophisticated optimizer that recognizes which technique to use for a query and when to change strategies.

The Red Brick Optimizer is designed for the flexible, unpredictable nature of decision support queries. While it selects algorithms based on the anticipated "costs" or processing time of the query, it remains open throughout the query processing to adapting or changing course based on intermediate results.

Using actual cost statistics: Instead of determining a strategy based on predetermined cost estimates alone, the Red Brick optimizer actually examines intermediate results to reassess its cost estimates.

Traditional cost-based estimates can be "fooled" by data skew into expecting more or less data than exists. Unfortunately, much of the data in a warehouse may be skewed; in a ski equipment database for example, more equipment will be sold in northern states than southern ones.

The Red Brick analyzer detects and adapts to skew by examining intermediate results. If it finds that an early step has returned more data than anticipated, it could revise its estimates and change course. For example, it might select another join pair ordering or another technique.

Early exits: Likewise, if an intermediate steps returns very few rows, it might be faster simply to scan those few rows for remaining constraints than to implement a complex join in the query plan. In this case, the Red Brick optimizer will "exit" from its strategy to complete the query faster.

The incremental adaptation and early exit features of the Red Brick optimizer provide fast query performance in the complex (and often highly skewed) world of data warehouse data and decision support queries.

Parallel-on-Demand Processing

No discussion of query performance is complete without a look at parallel processing support. With decreasing hardware costs, parallel processing is frequently touted as the answer to all performance problems.

While parallel processing is clearly critical for high performance in a large warehouse environment, brute-force parallel processing is not enough. Performing an inefficient operation in parallel is still inefficient - it simply uses more resources. In the data warehouse world, using the right algorithm can speed a query by a factor of 10 or 20 or more. Compensating for this kind of inefficiency with hardware alone can be expensive.

Parallel processing is a powerful and important tool for data warehouses, but requires a strong foundation for parallel operations:

- efficient algorithms that can be processed effectively in parallel
- the intelligent application of parallel processing based on the query and the system status

Red Brick's advanced optimizer selects from a wide range of sophisticated query processing algorithms. Integrated with the optimizer is Red Brick's unique parallel-on-demand technology. The optimizer examines how much parallelism can be applied to each query on a case-by-case basis and examines the current system status before assigning parallel operations.

Query-specific parallelism. Some processes are inherently more parallelizable than others. Two queries may seem almost identical, but one may make better use of parallelism.

Red Brick's optimizer examines how much each query can benefit from parallelism on an individual basis.

System resources. No query exists in a vacuum. A system that applies massive parallelism to a complex query may leave ten other important queries stalled waiting for resources. Red Brick examines the current system resource usage. On a mostly idle system, Red Brick will increase parallelism if it provides a benefit to the query. On a heavily used system, it will use less parallelism. Thus a large, complex query cannot shut down the system to other queries. This approach ensures the best overall system performance while still optimizing individual query performance.

Supporting Decision Support Functions

As important as query performance is for decision support, it is not enough to have fast processors and algorithms. The data warehouse engine must support structures and functions specifically designed for decision support applications. Traditional, transaction-based RDBMS systems are not designed with decision support queries in mind. Red Brick's emphasis on data warehousing enables it to provide specialized functionality for supporting decision support systems.

SQL Extensions for Decision Support

While Red Brick supports ANSI standard SQL, that standard alone is not sufficient to enable analytical applications without significant extra programming. Because it is designed to support decision support systems, Red Brick wrote a number of extensions to its SQL, which it calls Red Brick Intelligent SQL or RISQL.

The RISQL extensions cover functions commonly performed in business analysis. Examples include:

- rank
- tertile (splitting results into high, medium, and low rankings)

- n-tile (splitting results into n number of rankings)
- moving sum and moving average
- cumulative (running) totals
- ratio-to-report (for example, the ratio of a region's sales to total sales)

These functions support common business questions (who are my top three producers, for example). These functions would be difficult to implement writing only SQL. Red Brick's RISQL makes it easier to ask common business questions of the data warehouse for meaningful results.

Integrated Dimensional Analysis

The use of multidimensional analysis using aggregations and subtotals is common in decision support. Often called Online Analytical Processing, this kind of analysis is valuable in dealing with large amounts of data. Users can switch between different views and perspectives (product by state, revenue by month), look at summary data, and drill down to increasing levels of detail.

With either an external OLAP tool or with Red Brick Warehouse itself, the warehouse needs to support concepts of aggregation and drilldown within the basic design. Red Brick has integrated support for aggregation and OLAP within the warehouse engine itself. Red Brick supports creation and maintenance of pre-computed summaries and dynamic calculation of other summaries. The summary and detail data can all exist within one schema design.

An "Aggregate Advisor" helps the database administrator create and manage aggregates, and provides information on the space/time trade-offs for specific aggregates. An aggregate navigator system accepts base-level SQL (not aware of the existing aggregates) and rewrites them to use aggregates where appropriate. A metadata layer captures and manages information defining the aggregate tables and their relationships to the associated detail or base tables. With this support, the data warehouse engine itself is truly "aggregate-aware."

Integrated Data Mining

Data mining is the term for techniques that discover relationships in the data. This information can be used to build better business models or predict future results. A data warehouse is the logical source for data mining operations, as the warehouse data has already been gathered from operational systems in a clean and consistent form.

Red Brick integrates data mining technology in its Red Brick Warehouse with the Data Mine option. Red Brick Data Mine™ performs categorization analysis on the data and is tightly integrated into the warehouse engine itself. Because successful data mining typically leads to further analysis, this tight integration means that an analyst can work on a single system to pursue relationships discovered in the mining process.

Loading Data into the Data Warehouse

While management issues are not always considered up front in data warehouse design and implementation, manageability is critical for a successful data warehouse. If the database is unable to load the data in the time windows available each night, then users cannot access the data when they need it, or the warehouse won't be accurate. Given the massive size of many warehouses, even basic administrative tasks can become prohibitively difficult.

Because it does not have to support online transaction processing, many of the management issues that plague traditional databases are not an issue for Red Brick. Instead Red Brick focuses on the issues that are specific to data warehouses, like data loading.

Data loading is a particularly important issue for data warehouses. Red Brick measures load performance not only on how long it takes to move the bytes, but how long it takes to get the data "query-ready." This expanded load process includes:

- loading the data rows
- converting data types if necessary
- building or maintaining indexes
- checking referential integrity (RI) on new data
- handling rows that fail the RI checks

Red Brick implements data loading through its Table Management Utility (TMU). The TMU performs basic data type conversions, maps data from the source to target tables, and checks referential integrity requirements on the data being loaded. If a row fails an RI check, it is not loaded into the target table, but is loaded in a special exceptions table. The administrator can then examine the row at a later time and determine what to do; the database will be both consistent and available in the meantime.

Red Brick supports two special options for the TMU:

- PTMU or Parallel Table Management Utility, is a parallel version of the TMU that supports loading high volumes of data in parallel.
- Auto Aggregate option: With this option, the TMU automatically performs data aggregations as part of the load process.

9-3 RED BRICK PRODUCTS

The Red Brick product line as of 1997 is as follows:

- Red Brick Warehouse
- Red Brick Warehouse for Windows NT
- Red Brick Data Mine and Data Mine Builder
- Enterprise Control and Coordination

- Engage.Fusion, Engage.Discover and their object-oriented metadata repository (available in 1998)

Red Brick Warehouse, Red Brick's central product, runs on SMP and single-processor UNIX platforms. Red Brick Warehouse for Windows NT is an NT version of the same UNIX product, designed to take full advantage of the native multi-threading capabilities of the NT server. Red Brick Data Mine and Data Mine Builder are additional data mining options for the Warehouse, and the Enterprise Control and Coordination product can be used with any of the platforms. Engage.Fusion provides high-performance data transformation, and Engage.Discover provides complex analysis and staging of multi-terabyte data sets.

Red Brick Data Mine and Data Mine Builder

Red Brick Data Mine is a data mining option for the Red Brick Warehouse. The Data Mine option enables the data mining capabilities within the Red Brick Warehouse.

Because data mining is tightly integrated in the data warehouse engine itself, Red Brick Data Mine can access all of the data and discover patterns across the entire data warehouse. Data mining functions are accessed through SQL and can be combined with query-based analysis.

The Data Mine Builder is a graphical tool for Windows PCs for building and refining mining models stored in Red Brick Warehouse. Completed models can be shared among users and are accessible through standard SQL query tools.

Enterprise Control and Coordination

Managing a production data warehouse is a complex process. In addition to the basic administrative tasks common to any database, a data warehouse administrator must handle warehouse-specific tasks, such as copy management and metadata.

The Red Brick Enterprise Control and Coordination (ECC) product is a set of tools for data warehouse administration, unified by a common interface and integrated with the Red Brick Warehouse.

ECC provides four essential areas of functionality for the data warehouse administrator:

Warehouse control. ECC monitors queries dynamically so an administrator can detect and eliminate problem queries. It also provides resource utilization statistics for chargeback accounting, capacity planning, and performance tuning.

Security administration. Red Brick Warehouse uses role-based security; ECC manages roles, users and privileges, and provides password controls.

Inter-warehouse coordination/copy management. ECC automates the processes of subsetting and summarizing data from source data warehouses, transporting the data across the network, and populating the target warehouse.

Metadata management. ECC manages information about data transformation and loading, and maintains detailed systems statistics about all data loads.

ECC is available to work with both the UNIX and Windows NT versions of Red Brick Warehouse.

Engage.Fusion and Engage.Discover

Engage.Fusion and Engage.Discover provide data management for data warehouses scaling into the multi-terabyte range.

Engage.Fusion is used for data warehouse generation. Engage.Discover provides an iterative query and analysis product optimized for complex queries against very large data sets subject to frequent schema changes. Both products share a common metadata repository, and are integrated with Red Brick Warehouse.

The products, originally designed to handle the multi-terabytes of clickstream data found in the Web environment, bring scalability to data warehouse generation and analysis.

9-4 RED BRICK CONSULTING SERVICES

Red Brick provides three kinds of services: technical support, consulting, and education.

Red Brick consultants specializing in data warehousing are located in offices around the world to help with data warehouse projects. Red Brick Professional Services include:

- designing the data warehouse
- defining data extract requirements
- loading data into the data warehouse
- writing queries to meet business objectives
- managing day-to-day warehouse operation

Red Brick's consulting organization has created special, pre-defined vertical industry data warehouse templates called Fast Start Solution Templates they enable organizations to develop, test and deploy pilot data warehouses quickly. Each is designed to be deployed within 30 days instead of a typical 180 days to get a data warehouse pilot running.

Fast Start Solution Templates are available for the following industries:

Retail. Applications include Product Mix Analysis, Product Trends Analysis, Product Profitability Analysis, Competitive Analysis, Market Share Analysis, and Promotional Effectiveness.

Telecommunications. Applications include Product Trends Analysis, Product Profitability Analysis, Usage Analysis, Promotional Effectiveness, Churn Analysis, and Customer Analysis.

Healthcare. The healthcare template allows analysts to perform Provider Analysis and Member Analysis, along with other applications.

Financial Services. The financial template allows analysts to engage in Account Usage Analysis, Customer/Household Analysis, and Promotion Analysis.

Each Solution Template comes with the components needed to build a decision support system for the specific industry. Implementing the templates requires identifying source data, creating an empty data warehouse, modifying the schema, using Red Brick's RISQL Entry Tool to run the script to create the database, and loading the data. The Fast Start Solution Templates can be packaged with the consulting services needed to implement and start using the warehouses created by the template.

Partnerships

Red Brick created the PaVER (Partner and Value Extended Reseller) partnership program to foster relationships with third-party organizations whose products and services complement the Red Brick business strategy. Through the PaVER program, Red Brick has partnerships with most of the leading data warehouse tool vendors.

PaVER consultants provide a variety of services to customers implementing data warehouse applications, such as benchmarking, initial pilot implementation, discrete programming tasks, or even total data warehouse project management. PaVER consultants are selected by Red Brick based on their experience and focus on data warehousing to ensure that a supply of knowledgeable, experienced resources are available to implement Red Brick.

The PaVER Systems Integrator bundles hardware and software with Red Brick products and services to provide the basis upon which to build a data warehouse. If needed, the Systems Integrator can count on Red Brick's expertise to assist the development team. Red Brick selects PaVER Systems Integrators based on their capability and their focus on data warehousing technology and applications.

9-5 RED BRICK CASE STUDY: NASA AND THE HUBBLE SPACE TELESCOPE

Orbiting 380 miles above the earth, the Hubble Space Telescope (HST) brings us glimpses into events we can scarcely imagine: galaxies being born, the death of a star, a comet colliding with Jupiter. Its vivid images, captured outside the distortion of the earth's atmosphere, have brought new understanding to astronomers and fired the imaginations of schoolchildren and stargazers everywhere.

For all the glory of the scientific research it performs, managing the Hubble Space Telescope is a labor- and resource-intensive task. The telescope itself has 400,000 parts and 26,000 miles of wiring and depends on continual instructions from researchers on earth to find its next target. Accurate and timely trouble-shooting is critical for the staff caring for the Hubble telescope.

Consider for example the problem of power. The spacecraft is powered by solar panel wings, and by batteries which are recharged by the solar panels. If there's a problem with the batteries while the spacecraft is not in sunlight, the telescope runs out of power and all research comes to a halt. Sending someone up to fix a problem is an enormous project itself, entailing both costs and risks.

NASA's Goddard Space Flight Center monitors the basic health and safety of the spacecraft and manages the orbiting observatory. A complex computer system used to command and control the spacecraft today relies heavily on human monitoring and intervention. Engineers try to identify and resolve problems quickly based on extensive engineering data received from the HST.

The spacecraft is in constant communication with the Goddard Space Flight Center. Engineering data from every sensor on the craft is sent back once a minute. NASA receives 32 kilobits-per-second of data from the spacecraft, which includes telemetry data, temperature, switch settings, voltages from batteries and solar arrays, and other information. Telemetry data is also sent in batches from an on-board solid state recorder.

Managing this information and making intelligent decisions based on it is extremely difficult. If there is some kind of anomaly (currently detected by human operators watching color terminals for out-of-range values), engineers need to sift through stacks of printouts to try to figure out if it happened before or if it is part of a larger pattern. This kind of troubleshooting is tedious, slow, and error-prone.

Investigating problems and anomalies sometimes requires calling in experts from the European Space Agency or experts in different instruments. This delays the process of identify and solving problems and adds to the ongoing cost of maintaining the telescope.

All of this is changing, however, as part of a project called Vision 2000, whose goal is the complete reengineering of the operational and ground support systems for the telescope. The Vision 2000 effort aims to reduce the cost of HST operations and maintenance by 50% by the year 2000, while providing improved reliability and increased capabilities.

An important part of this project is a new, integrated Control Center System for the telescope. The goals of the Control Center System (CCS) now in development are to reduce the cost of operations and maintenance of the telescope, to automate as much of the regular monitoring as possible, and to provide data for timely problem diagnosis from anywhere in the world.

Red Brick Warehouse plays an important role in providing decision support capabilities for engineers managing the HST with the new CCS system. A data warehouse in the new system houses the engineering data from the telescope, from its launch up to the current moment. Data downloaded continually from the HST's on-board processors and sensors is processed and then loaded into the warehouse for access by engineering staff. Engineers can query this data to resolve problems or detect trends.

Deployment

Over one hundred people on the development team are building a complex, powerful and integrated system, of which the data warehouse is one part. The overall process started in 1996, and has seen many iterative phases and releases, including:

- business process reengineering for control center opera-

  tions

- technology evaluation and proof of concept

- system design based on business process results

- release development

- operations and maintenance

The CCS project team had to do some careful research when selecting the tools they would use for the data warehouse. After all, this is not a standard industry application. They needed to find a way to use commercially available software in combination with legacy systems to create a command and control system that is powerful and reliable. Since the new CCS application will support the next Servicing Mission for the HST, the application can be considered "mission-critical" in the strictest sense of the phrase.

The team selected Red Brick Warehouse on an eight-processor Silicon Graphics server to house the data warehouse of Hubble's engineering data. A front end processor handles the incoming telemetry data, and a plotting/graphing tool (PV-Wave) on the back end plots results of trend analysis.

One of the biggest challenges of the project is the sheer amount of data the system needs to handle. The telescope continually sends telemetry data to the Goddard Space Flight Center. In addition, data is downloaded periodically in batches from an on-board solid state recorder on the spacecraft. This telemetry data is "merged" using custom processes that correct for time and detect gaps in the telemetry data. This process then makes the data ready for the warehouse load, which loads one day's worth of data at a time. In all, pre-processing reduces the volume of data from 4-5 gigabytes per day to 500-600 megabytes per day. This edited telemetry data, along with other engineering data and spacecraft events, is what is loaded into the warehouse.

Even with this reduction in telemetry data, the warehouse is huge, gigabytes telemetry data is stored for every day since the spacecraft's launch in 1990, and the Hubble Telescope is expected to be operational well into the next century. The engineering warehouse is expected to reach one and a half terabytes in size by the year 2000.

The team selected Red Brick Warehouse because it has demonstrated that it can handle the volume of data, both in terms of the daily load requirements and the overall query response for systems that large.

One critical issue related to volume was simply loading the data as it downloaded from the telescope. Loading the data quickly reduces any impact on the users from the load; a day's data can be loaded in approximately 15 minutes with Red Brick's loader. This performance is particularly important when loading the archival data. Even loading one month at a time, a fast load performance will reduce the system impact and make the process much more manageable.

Access performance is critical as well; the CCS must support multivariable online analysis of engineering data spanning from the spacecraft's launch date. This data will be available to engineers everywhere via the Internet. Fast data access and querying will enable the ad-hoc trouble-shooting that engineers need to do.

Outcome

In late 1997, the data warehouse, along with the other aspects of the CCS system, was in "release development" mode. The development process includes design, prototyping and testing. The system is operating in a "shadow" mode to the regular operations system and will gradually be phased in before the year 2000.

The warehouse will be loaded with archival data; since the spacecraft was launched in 1990, NASA has accumulated a lot of engineering data. The team will load a month's worth of data at a time to bring it current.

Once completed, the new Command Center System and its warehouse of telemetry data will support the ongoing maintenance of the Hubble Space Telescope in many ways:

Troubleshooting: Engineers will be able to log on and perform multivariable analysis from anywhere around the world, on data dating back to the spacecraft's launch in 1990, without waiting for the right data or flying to the Goddard Space Flight Center. This will provide faster responses to problems, while making life much easier for the engineers supporting the telescope.

Trend analysis: It is not enough to fix the problems as they come; engineers must keep a close eye on the health of the spacecraft to spot problems before they become serious. Before the warehouse, engineers needed to write custom programs to extract the telemetry data from tapes, process it and analyze it. With the warehouse, engineers can construct ad-hoc SQL queries, for much faster responses that support creative problem-solving processes.

Improving the telescope's performance: when the telescope does fail to find a target or meet a goal, detailed analysis of the engineering data after the fact can help prevent the same occurrence. All of this leads to a more productive use of the telescope and, ultimately, better science.

The Command Center System will be completely operational for the Servicing Mission in 1999, but will already be supporting decision support queries on engineering data before that time. Using the Red Brick Warehouse of Hubble's engineering data, the engineers responsible for Hubble's welfare will be able to do kinds of analysis in only minutes that used to require days or even a month of work. They will be able to ask how many times a switch was thrown in a given year, or graph trends in battery power levels over temperature ranges, and get an answer in minutes. Faster response to queries leads to faster analysis and response to problems as they develop. And with luck and careful maintenance, the Hubble Space Telescope will continue to expand the boundaries of our knowledge and stretch our imaginations for years to come.

Chapter 10

PLATINUM

technology, inc.

10-1 COMPANY BACKGROUND[1]

PLATINUM technology, inc., founded in 1987, has grown from its roots as a provider of services and performance tools for DB2 to a full-service provider of IT infrastructure solutions. Headquartered in the Chicago suburb of Oakbrook Terrace, Illinois, PLATINUM became a publicly held company in April 1991. The company grew from fewer than 10 employees in 1987, to more than 4,000 employees in 1997. With $468M in revenues in 1996, PLATINUM is an independent software company. Represented in over 40 countries on six continents, PLATINUM has over 10,000 customers, including organizations such as AT&T, Sony, Lloyd's Bank, IBM, Nike, BMW, British Airways, and Federal Express. To develop and quickly bring to market the best technology possible, PLATINUM maintains development and marketing alliances with IBM, Microsoft, Oracle, Sybase, SAP, HP, and others.

---

[1] This chapter was contributed by Platinum technology inc. and is copyright by them. It was written by David Gleason of Platinum technology, inc.

PLATINUM's products include database management tools for DB2 and other relational database management systems, systems management, database management, application development, Year 2000, and data warehousing and decision support.

10-2 PRODUCTS

PLATINUM provides data warehouse and data mart tools and products.   These products can be grouped into four major categories:

3. Data transformation and movement
4. Data access and analysis
5. Metadata management
6. Warehouse management.

In each of these four areas, PLATINUM also offers consulting expertise to implement products effectively in a client's environment.

Data Transformation and Movement

Extracting, transforming, and moving data from an operational environment into the decision support environment is one of the most crucial and visible components of a data warehouse tools architecture. To construct a centralized data warehouse, distributed data marts, or a hybrid solution requires robust reliable tools to extract and transform data. PLATINUM product options fit a variety of customer architectures and address issues such as replicating large amounts of data, implementing business rule transformations while minimizing hand coding, capturing operational database changes, and loading warehouse data into the desired databases.

Depending on requirements, PLATINUM can use MVS, UNIX, or Windows NT, and provide a wide variety of data access, transformation, and movement options. To move data to a data warehouse or data mart, PLATINUM automatically refreshes and updates legacy or client/server data and integrates and synchronizes dissimilar data types. PLATINUM *InfoPump* is an application development tool that provides bi-directional replication of data between heterogeneous databases, and a data movement tool that enables running simple and complex movement tasks reliably in unattended mode. PLATINUM InfoRefiner provides a means of extracting, cleansing, merging and distributing dissimilar operational data to client/server platforms for decision support and data warehousing.

Metadata Management

Through metadata management, PLATINUM ensures consistent definitions of key data elements—such as "customer" or "revenue." Metadata can be deployed to end users so that they can discover what information is available in the decision support environment, what business rules are in effect, and how that information can be leveraged.

At the core of many of data warehousing solutions is the PLATINUM *Repository* which is the place of record for an organization's information assets. As a central shared source of metadata, a Repository provides consistent data definitions to enable information sharing and to speed development and maintenance of applications among departments and across the enterprise.

Warehouse Management

PLATINUM recognizes that the warehouse is not completed once the data warehouse is populated. As user information needs continue to evolve, the warehouse will need to grow accordingly. Data will be added, new data marts will be created, and business rules may even be modified. Performance monitoring is a major concern, as is job scheduling, data availability, security, backup/recovery, and database management. PLATINUM offers tools to build and access the warehouse as well as tools to manage and maintain the warehouse throughout its lifecycle. PLATINUM provides tools for job scheduling, financial charge back, capacity planning, security, backup and recovery, performance monitoring and analysis, change management, and application lifecycle management.

Data Access and Analysis

To improve decision support and help organizations more fully use their data, PLATINUM provides scaleable, server-centric, Internet- and intranet-enabled tools to access, analyze, and report data, including tools for OLAP, EIS/DSS development, and enterprise reporting.

In addition, PLATINUM's business applications are a new generation of online analysis and reporting tools with a data mart structure designed for query performance and quick implementation of industry- or business-specific decision support systems.

OLAP

The value of a data warehouse is directly proportional to how many people can incorporate its wealth of information into everyday decisions. Because in a typical organization relatively few workers have direct access or a complete set of client tools and the requisite skills to use those tools, data warehouses often do not achieve their potential.

PLATINUM's OLAP tool, *InfoBeacon*, delivers the functionality and performance of a 3-tier relational OLAP application via any Web browser. InfoBeacon turns a standard Web browser into a client tool capable of delivering a full range of advanced OLAP capabilities to the knowledge worker regardless of the place or platform being used.

Supporting a Subject-Oriented Multidimensional View

A multidimensional view is created in one of four ways by most OLAP tools:

- Physically restructuring the data and loading it into a proprietary multidimensional database (MOLAP cube)

- Directly reading an RDBMS which has been structured into a tool-specific schema (some ROLAP tools)

- Executing a background query which refreshes a pre-defined desktop view (Desktop OLAP tools)

- Defining the multidimensional view with metadata that maps it to an underlying relational database

The view created with InfoBeacon is defined as metadata. It does not require the physical storage of data in a proprietary format, such as with a MOLAP product. Nor does it impose strict RDBMS schema requirements on the relational database. For example, many ROLAP products require the data to be loaded into defined application tables, with space allocated for intermediate calculations, and table write privileges assigned so that the OLAP result set can be stored on the database. InfoBeacon's 3-tier architecture significantly lessens this requirement. Rather than design the data to adhere to some pre-defined tool-specific schema, users can design the database to maximize performance for their needs. This allows for data warehouse schema flexibility. It also removes the administrative burden of maintaining a large number of database tables and structures to provide OLAP functionality.

Supporting Analytical Processing

Two characteristics distinguish InfoBeacon from other OLAP tools:

- The use of a virtual analytical engine

- An object-oriented approach to analytical processing

They are key ingredients to a high performance, scaleable architecture that overcomes many of the inadequacies of using SQL for OLAP.

The virtual engine is written in an object oriented language (C++), and resides on the middle tier application server. The basic function of the virtual engine is to apply comparison objects and measures to data retrieved from the data warehouse. Although the objects are pre-defined and stored as metadata, the actual calculations are not. This is in contrast to a MOLAP tool, where practically everything is pre-calculated and physically stored.

InfoBeacon allows a comparison object or measure to be a stored fact (such as "last week's sales"), an aggregation ("last 4 week's sales"), a SQL function, or a formula which can reference other objects. Measures can contain conditional logic ("if this month's sales exceed last month's then calculate new discount") and result set math such as ratios and ranks. Measures can be quite complex, such as "average retail price per sales unit for the previous period," yet an end user can treat it as a single object among many in an analysis, and manipulate it quite easily within a Windows drag and drop environment. An end user does not have to know or care if a measure is a stored fact or derived calculation. It can be treated interchangeably. Furthermore, measures are stored in metadata for consistency and ease of maintenance.

By using an object-oriented language instead of SQL for analytical processing, InfoBeacon overcomes certain inadequacies inherent in SQL. Calculations that require row math, such as net present value, internal rate of return, and 3-month moving average do not cause unpredictable scratch table operations on the database. InfoBeacon also provides a choice of execution, where some operations can be done on the database and others on the application server. This is in contrast to some ROLAP tools that perform OLAP entirely in SQL on the database.

When combined with multithreaded computing, high speed memory and network architectures, the analytical processing strategy of InfoBeacon provides the ability to do OLAP analysis against large data sets while maintaining an interactive environment for end users. In addition, having this engine available on a dedicated server and exposed via an API provides an OLAP interface for front end tools.

Supporting Interactive Problem Solving

Where the multidimensional view of an OLAP tool provides end users with a vision of their business, and the analytical processing capability provides the tools from which to obtain insight, the interactive problem solving component provides the discovery method. InfoBeacon provides a number of problem solving components matched to the skills and preferences of end users.

InfoBeacon's Web browser delivers both static and dynamic views, formatted as HTML reports. The static reports are results of analyses run on a scheduled basis and published to a Web page. In the dynamic view, users can select specific dimensional items via drop down selection boxes, or they can drill up or down on a live HTML section of a report. Each choice triggers a new analysis against the data warehouse. By using a dynamic view, organizations can provide a path for end users to obtain the information they need without having to publish a large number of pre-defined reports.

The InfoBeacon Web environment offers three distinct advantages over other OLAP environments that are Web enabled:

Performance. InfoBeacon creates a multithreaded link between the data warehouse and a Web server using an ISAPI interface, which offers performance advantages over the more commonly implemented CGI interface.

A programming-free environment. An organization can produce an OLAP Web environment for their end users without having to know HTML, Java or Internet architecture.

Security. InfoBeacon complements an organization's Internet security layer by not requiring the transmission of database log-on information across the firewall.

As an example of how the InfoBeacon API functions with other applications, Microsoft Excel spreadsheet users can drill to obtain more detail from the data warehouse without leaving the spreadsheet. They can use an imbedded tool bar within Excel to move back and forth between the multidimensional view and the result set, and set up formatting and charting options in Excel before running an analysis. By tightly linking InfoBeacon with Excel, analysts gain direct access to a data warehouse without their having to learn a proprietary interface, and in a way which preserves the OLAP formatting features of such an interface.

Another problem solving function within InfoBeacon allows agent and workflow creation without programming. This function facilitates business rule-based information flow through an organization. With InfoBeacon, an end user can create an analysis and add business rules that trigger subsequent communications or activities. An analysis of sales for a given region can trigger a second analysis of distributor inventories and then an e-mail message to those distributors who need to place stocking orders, for example.

InfoBeacon supports over 100 of the most commonly used desktop applications, including databases, communications applications, fax, e-mail, word processors, spreadsheets and graphics presentations tools. By supporting these tools, people can use what they have already learned to use, and companies can leverage existing investments in productivity tools.

EIS/DSS Development

PLATINUM *Forest & Trees* enables the rapid development of user-specific applications that seamlessly integrate managed query, graphical desktop decision support, data navigation, and data investigation. It allows organizations to build and deploy graphical EIS/DSS applications that enable business users to collect, combine, monitor and analyze information from a variety of sources.

Built-in features allow developers to apply more than 200 functions to applications. As a result, end-users can:

- view data in specialized, multi-dimensional layouts, charts and graphs
- navigate and manipulate data through cross-tabs and drill-down capabilities
- identify and analyze business trends and historical data
- monitor key business indicators, such as stock prices, inventory levels and competitive activity
- set alarms that automatically notify individuals or groups if pre-defined business events occur
- design high-impact reports with a fully-functional, easy-to-use report writer

Forest & Trees allows integration with third-party or application-specific DLLs, and integrates with other Windows applications through OLE Automation Server/Client and Container, supporting OCX controls.

Through add-in technology, developers can even create their own functions and incorporate them into Forest & Trees applications.

With Forest & Trees, developers can embed Web browsing and data gathering capabilities directly into EIS/DSS applications. End users can leverage the Web data with graphs, alarms, triggers, and schedules. And with Forest & Trees' unique HTML interface, end users can use templates to easily convert Forest & Trees objects into Web pages.

Enterprise Reporting

PLATINUM Report Facility is an integrated suite of MVS-based tools for end user query and report generation. It gives users point-and-click access to mainframe data, while giving IT management complete control over resource consumption and security. PLATINUM Report Facility provides access to

DB2 for MVS data, as well as to non-relational data in VSAM and sequential files. It supports the TSO, CICS, IMS/DC, and batch environments.

PLATINUM *InfoReports* is an enterprise reporting tool that delivers desktop- and server-based reporting across multiple, large databases. It incorporates both ad hoc and high-volume production report writers, with wizards to simplify use. InfoReports is scaleable, server-centric, and Internet- and intranet-enabled. InfoReports can generate multiple queries, from heterogeneous databases, across multiple platforms. It provides reporting features such as extensive logic, crosstabs, variable manipulation, desktop publishing, graphing, and object orientation. Users can employ wizards to develop reports from a Windows/Motif interface. InfoReports allows both novices and experts to:

- Use wizards to create ad hoc and production reports, ranging from simple to complex

- View, publish, or run any report from a standard Web browser, and set parameters if desired

- Design a report on a client and run it on a server— retaining all formatting attributes and conversion capabilities

- Link data from multiple queries in a single report

- Link data from multiple diverse databases

Users with access to a report can enter their own runtime variables and obtain information without help from the technical staff. Executives and knowledge workers can access reports designed by power users or IT staff, then execute, browse, and convert them to the application they are most familiar with.

InforReports allows distribution of presentation-quality reports with the same rich combination of data, text, graphics and formatting throughout the enterprise. Reports can be accessed by any word processor, distributed via e-mail, and viewed with a Web browser. Inforeports does not have to be resident on the desktop.

Desktop Report Design and Server Execution

InfoReports uses both the desktop's design capabilities and the server's data processing power. All data, text, and graphics in a report become objects, which can be manipulated with drag-and-drop and cut-and-paste facilities on the desktop. Data is presented in either graph or tabular form, or included in objects such as Excel spreadsheets by using Object Linking and Embedding (OLE). A single window is used to change attributes such as fonts, borders, and colors for multiple object types, making refining reports fast and intuitive.

For efficient execution, the server can take over and perform complex calculations against large volumes of data for:

Production reporting. InfoReports Server, a companion product, allows executing reports on a UNIX or NT server instead of tying up the desktop. This approach increases speed, dependability and security, and reduces network traffic.

Web-based reporting. Reports can be designed to use HTML fonts, colors, graphics and link and to obtain a fast path through data. Instead of scrolling through long reports searching for important information, users can take advantage of automated outline reporting and jump directly to the desired section. They can drilldown from summary reports to display report details or use automatically generated input forms to access reports and pass parameters for execution.

Reports run directly from application menus by clicking an icon, or can start from Windows or Motif. Users can create special icons for reports that run on a regular basis.

InfoReports' built in scheduler allows scheduling reports for automatic execution, conversion, and distribution. Reports can be converted to RTF format, which is accepted by any word processor, MAPI, for distribution through e-mail, or HTML, for viewing with a Web browser.

Reports can also be converted for use in Excel, Lotus 1-2-3, the SAS System, Word, WordPerfect, dBase, FrameMaker, and other popular programs.

InfoReports' wizard-driven interface creates both simple tabular reports and complex cross-tabular matrices that analyze the data from different perspectives. Users can apply conditional filters, sort, group, and calculate functions. Multiple one-to-many relationships can be resolved with parent-child query relationships. Other functions include the ability to:

- Use runtime variables for report attributes, conditional expressions, and calculations to create complex reports, such as financial statements;
- Include an summary calculations involving multiple columns and user-entered values anywhere in the report
- Specify filtering and calculations to be done either locally or at the database
- Ensure that cross-tabular reports are automatically updated with the latest unique column values
- Define the order in which different parts of the report are executed
- Print the whole report or just the summary information

InfoReports allows multiple queries—including imported queries—to retrieve data from multiple database types, regardless of platform. Supported databases include Oracle, Sybase and Microsoft SQL Server, Informix and the DB2 family. Others can be accessed through ODBC and leading gateways.

Users can retrieve, combine, and manipulate data from these diverse sources, and then present it in numerous ways. The range of user reports runs from quick ad hoc information to scheduled production reporting from client/server applications. InfoReport also provides integrated support to data warehouses, including those from PLATINUM technology, HP-IW, and Red Brick.

InfoReports uses a server-centric architecture. Although the database server can be used for execution, environments with very large databases can maximize performance by distributing processing in three tiers—report design on the client, data manipulation on the database server, and execution on an application server.

Business Applications

An emerging trend in data warehousing is a move away from custom-developed warehouses to packaged warehouse applications. This parallel the recent increase in the popularity of large packaged application system solutions over totally custom-developed applications. A data warehouse "application," designed for a particular industry or type of company, can give an organization a head start in developing a warehouse. If the application delivers a significant amount of the business functionality required by the organization, it can usually be deployed more quickly and with less risk than developing a custom warehouse solution. Even where the warehouse application does not deliver all of the decision support capabilities required by the organization, the reduced risk and faster time to implementation usually make the warehouse application a valuable proposition.

A data warehouse application consists of two fundamental components: a data model and an accompanying decision support application. The decision support application is designed to offer commonly needed data analysis and decision support applications, based on a particular industry or market segment. While the application may not cover all information needs for a particular company, it is designed to support a spectrum of needs common to that industry. By deploying such a decision support application, a company will reduce the effort required to design and build their own interface for the data warehouse, and can defer some of the risky process of determining user information needs. Rather than determining every information need in the user community, a company can simply ask the business users to validate the application and assess whether it adds value. In order to implement such an application, the data to "feed" it must be procured and organized. This is where the data model component of the data warehouse application comes in. The data model provides an industry specific "template" for the design of a data warehouse or data mart, and is optimized to support the packaged decision support application. Many organizations spend considerable time developing data models to support their data warehouses. In some cases, they can readily adopt this template data model, and then spend their time customizing it and extending it to their business.

A data warehouse application is certainly not intended to replace custom warehouse development. Rather, it can be a good way to launch a warehouse effort, by implementing a pre-determined package of functionality. Then, successive increments of the warehouse can be built around this kernel.

One example of a data warehouse business application is PLATINUM *RiskAdvisor*, a Windows-based property and casualty insurance decision support system and integrated data model that provides a visual, intuitive interface to an insurance industry-specific data warehouse. A data warehouse structure designed for optimal query performance is combined with a decision support system that provides users with timely, easy access to value-added information, presented in a form everyone can understand.

From premium analysis to loss control, RiskAdvisor provides the big picture and enables users to drilldown to the level of detail required to conduct an investigation and confidently take action. The system not only finds the numbers users need, it automatically analyzes the data and presents it in highly usable forms—from simple summaries to sophisticated analysis models. RiskAdvisor helps insurance companies meet their challenges and requirements by providing a total solution for analyzing insurance data.

10-3 PROFESSIONAL SERVICES

PLATINUM believes that the key to delivering the best business solution for any organization lies in finding the right balance among three key ingredients: technology, skills, and process. In the information management and data warehouse arena, this dictates a necessity to deliver the right combination of:

- data warehouse-related tools
- consultants with the skills and experience to plan, design, and implement a data warehouse
- repeatable methods that can be used to build a sustainable process for the delivery of data warehousing

To deliver these business solutions effectively, PLATINUM relies on a combination of data warehouse consultants and product implementation specialist consultants. The data warehouse consultants bring skills in planning, designing, building, and supporting data warehouse and data mart implementations. The tool implementation specialists have expertise in deploying warehouse-related tools in a technologically heterogeneous environment. Their mission is to integrate products into whatever mix of other products, tools, and technologies a company selected for its warehouse architecture. To ensure consistent quality consulting on a worldwide basis, and to ensure that companies can sustain their warehousing efforts after the consultants have departed, PLATINUM employs a best-practices-based methodology for the delivery of data warehousing solutions.

Figure 10-1: Tools, People, Methods

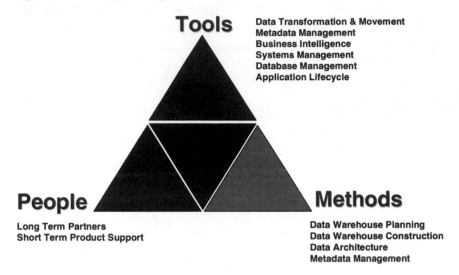

Information Management Consulting Approach

PLATINUM believes that one of the fundamental objectives of information management is to build a sustainable process for organizing and deploying the information available to an organization, in such a way that it supports the ongoing and ever-changing information needs of the organization's decision makers. Therefore, information management must be treated like a process rather than a project. This implies that an information management infrastructure must be built to allow an organization's information management capabilities to keep pace with changing business needs. If information management and data warehousing are treated like a project rather than an ongoing process, there is a serious risk of underestimating the extended commitment required to achieve successful data warehousing. Where a typical application development project has a discernable lifecycle that includes phases such as startup and design, construction, rollout, and maintenance, data warehouses do not ever go into "maintenance mode." An application system is usually designed to automate a discrete, operational business process.

As a result, we can assume that the business process is not changing continually. That is, the process remains the same until a conscious decision is made to change it. Of course, in some cases that decision is not planned very far in advance, such as when an operational process must change to allow an organization to keep pace with its competitors. But the fact remains that the organization must decide to change the process, and therefore that change comes in quantum amounts.

The data warehouse, by contrast, must respond to the constantly-changing tactical and strategic information needs of the organization. Therefore, in designing and implementing a data warehouse, emphasis must be placed on building an infrastructure and establishing a process that will allow the warehouse to adapt quickly to new information needs.

To achieve the goal of building a process to support information management, an organization must satisfy three objectives:

- extracting business value from available data
- leveraging that information to support decision making
- managing the information assets to use and maintain them efficiently and promote reuse

Extracting business value from the data available to the organization represents the traditional data warehouse challenge. As organizations have grown and matured, they have created a wealth of information. This data is used to automate a variety of operational business processes, ranging from billing and transaction processing through order entry and inventory control. However, in most cases information systems are designed around a single business process or a collection of related processes. This has led to a great deal of repetitive, dis-integrated data stored throughout the enterprise. While each system may be very good at performing the automation of the operational tasks for which it was designed, these systems have not provided much useful information to aid in making long range tactical and strategic business decisions. Data warehousing is the process of identifying this information and how it can be applied to business decisions, and then integrating it and reorganizing it to meet those needs.

Of course, it is not enough to merely create a managed storehouse of good quality data. One must also ensure that it can be delivered to business users in a fashion that makes sense to them. Different users will have different ways of interacting with the data. Some may prefer a "dashboard," or executive information system, approach, while others may want to select queries from a menu of available queries and be able to modify them. Still others may need to perform sophisticated data exploration using OLAP capabilities. Different users will have different technical constraints. Some users may work in the corporate office, using high- powered workstations with high-speed network connectivity. Others may be field- based users, with less-powerful notebook computers, limited disk space, and dial-up phone connectivity only. Obviously, the best technical solution for delivering information to the first group of users would not work at all for the second group. Countless warehousing efforts have labored to produce high quality, usable data, and then failed because they did not provide the right means for their business users to access that information.

Finally, a warehouse or data mart represents a significant investment of effort, time, and money. This newly created "information asset" must be managed and controlled. The people responsible for extending and maintaining it must have clear and accurate information about the inner workings of the warehouse, both at a logical and a physical level. The end users need to be able to find an accessible and reliable description of what kind of information is in the warehouse, and what specific business rules are represented. The vehicle for maintaining and providing this information about the data warehouse environment is metadata. For the developers and owners of the warehouse, metadata can be the "wiring diagram" that tracks the inner workings and the flow of data through the environment. For the end users, the meta-data can provide the "road map" that guides them to the data they are looking for, and helps them understand it when they find it.

PLATINUM's Information Management Consulting focuses on helping firms develop the architecture and infra-structure, as well ask the skills, that allow them to sustain their information management efforts as their business evolves.

Methodology

PLATINUM has developed a methodology for Information Management. This methodology is not a traditional, in the sense that it does not attempt to lay out a detailed "cookbook" approach to solving problems. Rather, it offers the consult-ants a place to organize their work products from previous engagements and to share ideas and innovations.

PLATINUM's Information Management Consultants firmly believe that organizations embarking on data ware-housing efforts must have this sort of methodology. PLATI-NUM shares its information management methodology with clients so that they can take this methodology and evolve and adapt it to fit their own environments.

Principles for Effective Warehousing

PLATINUM's approach to professional services to ensure a successful data warehousing effort is built around four cor-nerstones. A data warehouse effort must be:

- *Business Focused.* More data warehousing efforts col-lapse for failing to "make a difference" to the business than for failing to meet technical challenges. The tech-nical challenges of a data warehouse can indeed be daunting, but they should not be overshadowed by the essential business issues and opportunities. A data warehouse should be tuned to the changing nature of the business, and must focus on delivering precisely the data required to meet the information needs of decisions makers in the organization.

- *Incremental.* Like many large efforts, the implementation of a data warehousing environment should be broken down into smaller increments of work. However, it can be very difficult to identify these increments in such a way that each increment has business value, and that combines with previous increments to form a synergistic whole. Even more difficult can be the task of scoping and estimating these increments.

- *Sustainable.* It is not enough to roll out a successful first increment of a data warehouse, or a data mart. The business will continue to change rapidly, and the information needs identified today may change substantially by the time the warehouse components required to address those needs are built. New competitors may emerge in the market, new regulations may be proposed, and new ideas and philosophies may be developing within the company. The warehouse should be nimble and flexible enough that the it can respond appropriately to changing business conditions. This requires investment in architecture and infrastructure, so that the resulting warehouse solution is responsive to rapidly shifting business needs.

- *Supported By Metadata.* Because a data warehouse is a rapidly evolving and complex environment, it must be managed and documented with great care. The metadata which describes this environment should be collected, synchronized, integrated, and deployed to business and technical users in a useful form.

PLATINUM's Information Consulting group is dedicated to making sure that companies are well prepared to meet the challenges.

Brio Technology

11-1 COMPANY BACKGROUND[1]

Brio Technology provides business intelligence solutions for client/server and Web enabled data warehouse environments. Brio's family of products, Brio Enterprise, deliver user-centric solutions that are flexible and open in a multi-tier architecture.

Brio Technology has roots in data warehousing which go back to the early 1980's. Brio's senior management team collectively has over 60 years experience in data warehousing, including product design, company direction and overall management. Katherine Glassey, one of Brio's co-founders recently co-wrote a book titled *Managing the Data Warehouse.* with Bill Inmon (the father of data warehousing) and J.D. Welch (Inmon, Welch, Glassey 1997).

Using its implementation of dozens of custom enterprise business intelligence solutions as a consulting organization,

---

[1] This chapter was contributed by Brio Technology. and is copyright by them. It was written by Will Hansen of Brio Technology.

Brio began building products which are specifically architected to optimize existing data warehouse environments. Brio Technology pioneered both the first graphical drag and drop query tool and the first distributed OLAP product. In 1996, Brio Technology was the first to deliver interactive OLAP within the Web browser. Based in Palo Alto, California, Brio Technology sells directly in the US, Canada, United Kingdom, France and Australia and through a global network of distributors, system integrators and VARs. Brio Technology maintains technical partnerships with leading suppliers of data warehouse solutions, databases, high-performance hardware, system consultants, and Web technology. Brio Technology is a privately held, venture-based corporation whose investors include Kleiner Perkins Caufield and Byers, Integral Capital Partners, Novus Ventures, Deutsche Morgan Grenfell and EMC Corporation.

Brio Technology's approach to the data warehouse market is to deliver an integrated desktop query, OLAP, charting and reporting tool that meets the decision support needs of a broad range of knowledge workers. The solution is based on several key premises for warehousing success. The well-designed warehouse should contain a primary repository for standard queries and reports. In some cases, it is also useful to define user-acceptable logical models of the physical database schema and store them in the data warehouse. The most successful warehouses today (1997) are being designed for user readability, most typically using principles of star schema design.

A data warehouse should also deliver the right data to the right people. People are always asking new questions, so predicting what they need is an art, not a science. Users often don't know what they need until they see it. Thus, end-user access tools should enable users to follow their own paths through data. The best access tool is one that serves the needs of the widest variety of users (from IT managers who require database administrative capabilities, to those who need direct access to analyze data, to novice users who just need to view pre-built reports).

On the desktop, users need more than just reporting. They need the ability to perform complex multidimensional analysis with drilldown, drill everywhere, and trend and comparative analyses. Brio's patented desktop OLAP engine creates datacubes at the desktop from which analysis can be performed on or off-line, wherever the users work best. Brio believes that a scalable OLAP analysis engine optimizes the use of desktop computing power as well as scarce server and network resources.

The ideal desktop OLAP tool should also reduce the pro-liferation of metadata. IT staff will be burdened with trying to synchronize all occurrences of metadata across query tools, data warehouse loading tools, CASE tools, and RDBMS's. Query tools that require their own proprietary metadata only exacerbate the problem. Brio Technology products assist in reducing metadata by reading and leveraging existing meta-data.

11-2 PRODUCTS

Brio Enterprise 5.5

Like the supply and demand principle of economics, the flow of information throughout an organization is controlled by two groups: information producers and information consum-ers. Within these two groups lies a wide spectrum of users defined by need and skill set.

At the top level of both need and skill are information tech-nologists. These information producers use BrioQuery™ Designer to manage the data warehouse or data mart and the deployment of end user tools. They also administer Brio-Query.Server™ which automatically distributes queries, anal-ysis results and reports via network, email, printers or acrossthe Web. Power Users and information producers use

BrioQuery Explorer to directly access data and to perform in-depth analysis and reporting on a daily basis.

Active analysts need to perform occasional analysis but do not necessarily require direct access to the database. They are typically users on-the-go and need limited access to data to create reports anytime, anywhere. BrioQuery Navigator,

Figure 11-1: Spectrum of Users

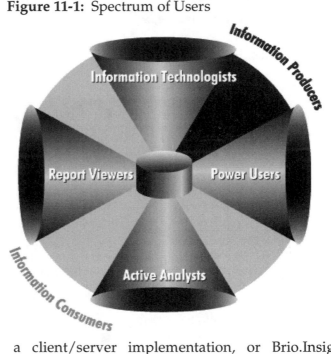

a client/server implementation, or Brio.Insight™, which offers Web-based OLAP, are designed for this type of user. Report Viewers require the least amount of interaction with data. They may be top level executives who need to view snapshot reports. Brio.Quickview™ delivers these reports to them within their familiar Web browser.

The Brio Enterprise product family can be used either separately, or together in an integrated, distributed client-server and/or Web-enabled implementation for delivering business intelligence throughout the enterprise. The diagram below illustrates the spectrum of users described and the correlating Brio Enterprise product that best fits the user's need and skill.

Brio Technology's products are designed to adhere to the fundamental principles of systems design: they are modular, interoperable across platforms, and SQL compliant. They also are designed to provide lower total cost of ownership by minimizing training and support costs; being easy to use; and providing a consistent user interface, functionality, and documentation across platforms.

Figure 11-2: Spectrum of Users and Corresponding Brio Products

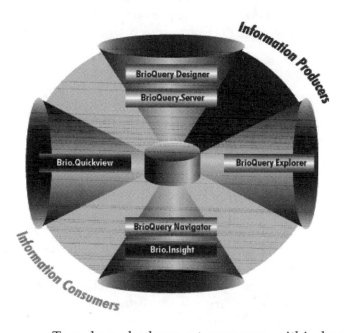

To reduce deployment resources within large organizations, business intelligence products also need to be scalable and easily distributed. Brio Technology's products are scalable across a wide variety of user query, analysis and reporting needs. They meet the need to access data from a variety of databases, ranging from transaction processing systems to data warehouses. Built in version control and automated distribution across local and wide-area networks assist in making Brio Technology's products easy for IS to maintain and deploy. They provide support to client/server and/or corporate-intranet implementations, enabling IT to provide solutions tailored to the enterprise's global needs.

Brio products incorporate a consistent user interface, common file structure and support for client/server and Web-enabled architectures. In addition, Brio Enterprise provides functionality matched to user requirements along with comprehensive administrative, installation and auditing capabilities to simplify enterprise-wide deployment and management. Brio Enterprise delivers a zero-administration technology that reduces the IT backlog by allowing centralized distribution and maintenance of Brio clients throughout the organization. Our zero-administration technology:

- reduces client-side configuration and administration
- maintains high-performance
- uses existing platforms
- optimizes network traffic bandwidth
- removes client database connection setup headaches and fees
- enables end users to update their Brio Web extensions directly from the browser

Our adaptive client technology enables organizations to deploy Brio's range of end user tools to the entire enterprise with minimal IT intervention. The client software adapts based on security and connections information centrally maintained by IT.

Brio Enterprise products are currently in use at over 3,500 customer sites worldwide, with over 60,000 end users. They are available in five languages: English, French, German, Italian, and Japanese.

11-3 PRODUCT DESCRIPTIONS

BrioQuery

BrioQuery integrates query, analysis (OLAP) and reporting capabilities in one product. Since 1994, Brio's flagship client/server product has been Brio-Query, the original desktop OLAP query tool that continues to lead the industry in ease-of-use, functionality and flexibility. Beneath its appealing user interface lies a sophisticated query engine, allowing both ad-hoc and managed queries

Figure 11-3: Reports in the Browser Combine Charts and Add Data to Reports in the Browser Window.

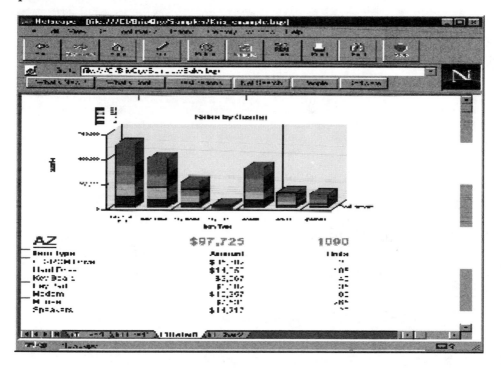

When users create a portfolio of charts and reports, Brio-Query's OLAP engine transparently creates compact, dynamic datacubes optimized for desktop analysis—on-line or off. BrioQuery simplifies complex analysis functions with one-touch pivot, drill everywhere, quick data sorts, ad hoc

custom groupings, local calculations, and weighted averages. BrioQuery offers a patented, award-winning "pivot" engine which enables users to change rows to columns and columns to rows with the swipe of the mouse. Numerical data can be presented in fully interactive 3-D charting and reports. SmartReports incorporate charts, cross-tab reports and corporate templates into presentation-quality reports.

With the Open Metadata Interpreter, BrioQuery can dynamically read existing metadata, eliminating redundant or proprietary metadata stores. While business professionals and end

Figure 11-4: Pivot Tab. Portable OLAP engine moves rows to columns and back with a simple drag(even when disconnected from the database)

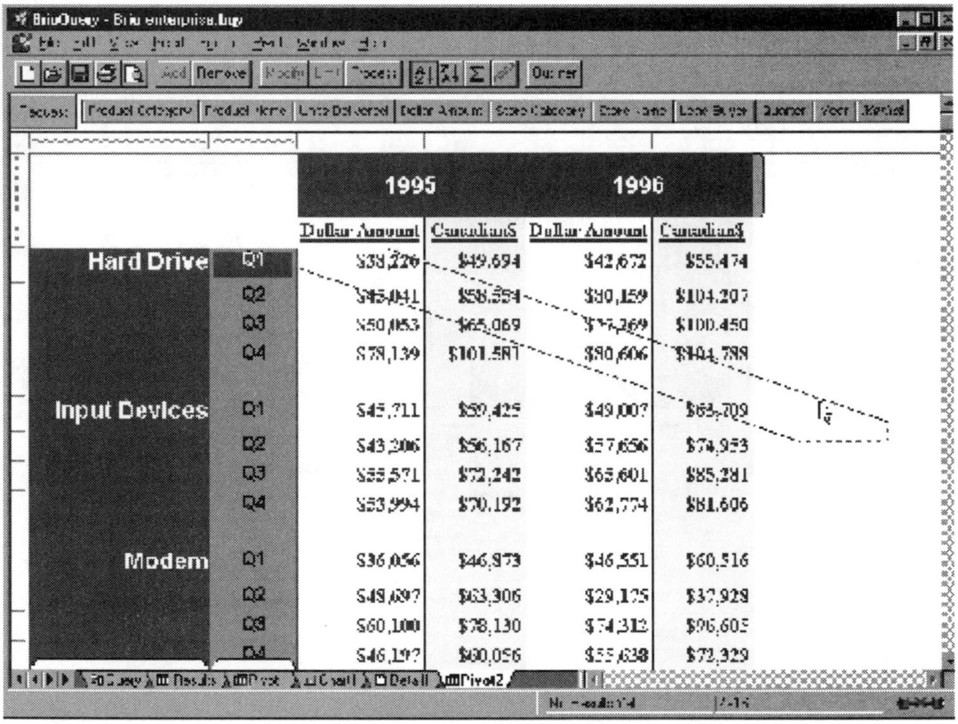

users benefit from a view of the data warehouse they understand, IT professionals and power users are assured that a single metadata source is used consistently throughout the organization. With Automatic Distributed Refresh, BrioQuery distributes changes to all users and synchronizes their views of the database.

Scalable to meet the needs of all levels of users, Brio-Query is available in three editions:

1. *Designer* is used by administrators, usually in an IT department
2. *Explorer* is preferred by power users or independent analysts with some understanding of relational databases
3. *Navigator* is used by analysts or occasional users who are managed by the Designer user.

Figure 11-5: BrioQuery. Automates the synchronization of metadata and logical database models to reduce maintenance for IT departments.

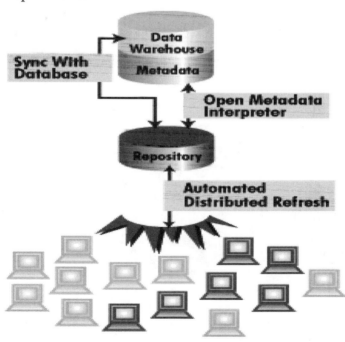

BrioQuery is available in all major client/server platforms including Windows, Macintosh and UNIX.

BrioQuery.Server^{tm}

Brio's three-tier architecture allows distributed processing between the multidimensional or relational database server, the BrioQuery.Server and the desktop. This architecture has several distinct advantages in a client/server and/or Intranet environment. First, it permits CPU-intensive data extraction and report generation to be scheduled at convenient times (such as overnight). Second, it enables users to maintain control of their desktop by off-loading processing to the BrioQuery.Server, which can notify the user of a job's completion via email. Third, queries can be run once, generating a data set which can be accessed by multiple users for analysis (with BrioQuery or their Web Browser), eliminating the need for the same query to be executed multiple times by the database server.

Figure 11-6: BrioQuery.Server, the Hub of the Brio Enterprise Distributed OLAP Solution

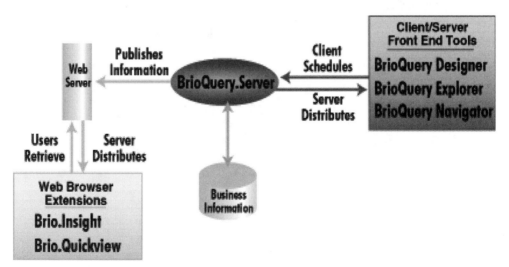

BrioQuery.Server enables BrioQuery users to schedule queries and reports to run against a data warehouse or other relational databases. BrioQuery.Server distributes reports and analyses via the Web or Intranet, or through other network resources such as email, printers, and LAN-based file servers.

Users can schedule jobs to run at regular intervals, and can take advantage of features such as custom calendars, event-based processing, and report bursting—a feature that allows one job to create many reports, each with independent results. BrioQuery.Server supports both "push" and "pull" models of information distribution across the Web.

BrioQuery.Server's security model enables IT organizations to control centrally the level of querying and analysis that users can perform, based on their established user group access security. This security model is delivered using the HTTP protocol without interfering with the existing internet infrastructure of corporations.

BrioQuery.Server is available for UNIX and Windows NT. Database administrators can control users' database privileges, set up distribution options and polling frequency, as well as manage security.

Brio.Insight ^{tm}

Brio.Insight delivers interactive OLAP and querying inside a Web browser. Brio.Insight features BrioQuery's graphical user interface and all of its significant analysis and reporting functionality including ad hoc query, drill-everywhere, pivot analysis, 3-D charts, SmartReports, data sorts, ad hoc custom groupings, local calculations and weighted averages. Brio.Insight users can update their client software on their desktops. All updates can be downloaded from within the browser window.

Brio.Quickview^{tm}

Brio.Quickview enables organizations to deliver a portfolio of reports within standard Web browsers. Users move beyond static HTML to flexible, interactive report viewing. The reports are received fully formatted with color, highlights, charts and tables. Users scroll through the reports viewing them from different perspectives and in different formats.

Most importantly, key information can be disseminated throughout the organization.

11-4 SPECIAL PRODUCT FEATURES

Web Environment Support

Brio Enterprise includes a full range of products for delivering solutions via the World Wide Web, from simple HTML to full interactive OLAP within a browser. Brio Enterprise's Web architecture enables delivery of report portfolios with or without encapsulated data sets. For maximum analytical interactivity, report portfolios are delivered with encapsulated data sets. This gives users the ability to create new reports and perform drill everywhere analysis within the browser window— even when disconnected from the network. For organizations which require more control of their data but want users to have the ability to customize reports and analyses, Brio Enterprise enables the delivery of portfolios without data sets.

Multiple Platform Support

Brio Enterprise products offer separate versions for 16- and 32-bit Windows, 68K and Power Macintosh, and UNIX Motif: Sun Solaris-SPARC, Sun Solaris Intel (x86), SunOS and IBM AIX. Any and all objects created on one platform are sharable with no loss of functionality on any other platform. Brio's small footprint executables with their optimized OLAP algorithms are engineered to take advantage of the operating system on which they are deployed.

Read Existing Metadata

BrioQuery does not require introducing additional proprietary, redundant metadata into the firm's business intelligence architecture. With its Open Metadata Interpreter, BrioQuery dynamically reads existing metadata from a variety of sources making metadata "transparent" to all. While information consumers see a view of data they understand, information producers are assured that there is consistent metadata which is shared dynamically across the organization. "Time to first query" is hours, not weeks.

Auditing

Brio allows continuous auditing of all aspects of the data warehouse. Administrators can track who is running what queries how often, and can make structural or procedural adjustments accordingly. Brio's customizable implementation allows Administrators to tailor the auditing which is performed according to their specific needs.

Support for Asynchronous Processing

Brio's suite of products support asynchronous query execution ('Background Processing') where this capability is present in the middleware. This capability allows users to switch to other applications while still processing a query from their desktop, ending the wait time present in other tools and allowing users to maintain productivity while awaiting query execution.

Index & Join Awareness

BrioQuery is capable of reading either user-defined or database-specific index and join information. In addition, BrioQuery Designers can predefine join relationships within a data model, so that any queries generated from that model will inherently be optimized.

Repository Hub

Brio allows for the storage of data models, queries and reports to be separate from the data warehouse server. By placing these objects in a database other than that used for the warehouse, the warehouse is reserved for it's primary intention, to deliver data to those who request it.

11-5 CONSULTING SERVICES

Brio's services focus on three levels:

- **Organizational** - data warehouse design and implementation, including support for activities related to the design and modeling of data warehouse databases, and the implementation of project plans for the effective roll-out of enterprise-wide business intelligence applications.

- **Project** - assistance to project teams in the design of specific applications based on Brio products.

- **User** - instruction in design and modeling of business intelligence applications and the specific use of Brio products. Brio provides technical support to users through the World Wide Web and through a customer support hot line to facilitate world-wide "follow-the-sun" support.

11-6 PARTNERSHIPS

Through the Brio Partner Enterprise program, Brio Technology has developed strategic partnerships with key players in the data warehouse market to serve customers seeking to implement business intelligence solutions. Close partnerships with database vendors are required to achieve the level of integration Brio demands. Brio Technology provides its partners with leading-edge technology and a comprehensive support program.

Brio is a member of Oracle's WTI program, Informix's Partner Solutions for Data Warehousing, Sybase Warehouse Works, Red Brick PaVER Gold (only three other vendors have this level of integration with Red Brick), Arbor, IBM CSP Business Partner, Microsoft Data Warehouse Alliance Program, and Hewlett Packard's Open Warehouse Program, to name a few.

To allow Brio products to work directly with data warehouse metadata, providing full metadata synchronization across the enterprise, Brio maintains integration with metadata management and extraction tool vendors. Brio's products are engineered to support Prism Solutions, Carleton, Informatica, D2K and V Mark. Brio is also a member of the metadata coalition committed to developing industry standards for metadata.

11-7 SUCCESS STORIES

Brussels Airport

How do you manage an airport terminal? When most of us travel by air, we simply purchase our ticket, arrive an hour before our flight, check in, board the plane, and we arrive at our destination.

Behind the scenes, airlines handle the critical issues of terminal management, competing airlines, shipping companies, security, customs, and maintenance to ensure that passengers reach their destination as quickly and easily as possible. In order to accomplish this, information must get to the right people at the right time. As an airport terminal IT manager, how would you ensure that this happens?

The Brussels Airport IT management team faced this question and more. Their challenge was to integrate terminal operations to meet increased demand. Their challenges were further complicated by the decision to build a new terminal building. The terminal management company, Brussels Airport Terminal Company (BATC), was charged with building and operating the new terminal, integrating 150 companies that work at the airport, including 85 airlines, *and* meeting all of their different information systems and technology needs.

From an information technology perspective, BATC created a single source for operational data, incorporating all of the processes within the terminal. This data source integrates and distributes timely information to and from each operation, including flight, passenger and baggage coordination. The data source ensures airport resources are used efficiently, such as sharing check-in desks between different airlines. Also, it enables different airlines to access their *own* dedicated information for check-in counters, boarding gates, and ticketing areas as well as update the system with any changes. In addition, it gives security officials, customs, state police and private airport security access to the data they require.

With the new terminal and the new systems, BATC is able to capture and analyze actual aircraft movements, manage the manpower and equipment of the airport more efficiently and reduce the paper flow across all airport users. In addition, management and operational staff are now able to access this information quickly, resulting in improved service to customers. The result is a well-managed terminal with timely, accurate, controlled information flowing among users through secure channels.

After the successful completion of this project, the responsible IT division within BATC was made an independent subsidiary of BATC called swITch. swITch added a data warehouse that archives all central database information from this single data source. Airport management uses this information to analyze operations, using databases from Oracle and Sybase of approximately 4 to 5 GB in size, with approximately 13 million records. This data warehouse is running on a Sun Solaris platform.

Increasing User Access to Information

BATC still had one remaining issue: how to increase end user access to information. In a traditional end user versus IT structure, the end user would define his query without understanding the technical impact of his choices (e.g., do I have to take into account canceled or diverted flights? What is a

diverted flight for the database?). Conversely, the IT specialist would implement the user's specifications without knowing the decision the user will take based on the figures.

*"We needed a tool that would hide the technical complexity of
the database so that power users could query it directly and understand the impact of their choices on the result they'll get."* Alain
Dejalle, Project Manager for swITch

swITch also found that their most experienced Sybase
DBA was spending a significant part of his time generating
queries for end-users. *"Analyzing the [long awaited] query
results always leads the user to additional questions ... and report
requests.. The goal of such a query and reporting tool is to allow the
end-user to get the information he/she needs while letting the database experts focus on their job – running the airport."* Alain
Dejalle

Because the end user tools needs were so critical, swITch
conducted a thorough investigation of the products available.
In 1995,swITch reviewed 35 query and reporting products.
They selected four of those to be evaluated. The evaluation
consisted of a one-week test pilot against their own data. They
selected Brio Enterprise. *"BATC is known for its very thorough
selection process regarding IT products,"* Bert Verelst, Sales Manager for Axio Systems, Brio Technology's Distributor in Bel-
gium.

*"Brio Enterprise is very versatile, flexible and is less depen-
dent on IT personnel. Other [products] have a protected layer, with
predefined objects. We wanted control to be in the hands of the user,
according to his or her knowledge. With BrioQuery, you can add
new objects and queries very quickly."* Alain Dejalle

The evolution of their data warehouse and BrioQuery
really contained two aspects. *"First, you need to discover the
tool. Second, you need to discover the database. We found learning
the tool to be very fast, very user-friendly. What takes time is discovering the optimal way to use the repository. IT needs to review
and test complex queries,"* Paola Petre', Data Manager for BATC

For people who do not want to get involved with the extraction of data, predefined queries based on the users' needs are developed.

"Brio enables us to distinguish between the production of data and the analysis of it." Paola Petre', Data Manager for BATC

BATC's operational personnel and staff were able to discover the contents of the database without going through the technical people.

Using the Web

"The Internet is changing the way we deliver information. Now we have one vehicle for information delivery. They will receive information on a daily basis via the Web," Alain Dejalle. BATC plans to have their Intranet in production by September 1997. However, BATC does not plan to stop there.

"We want to expand our Intranet to include an extranet. We handle a lot of data, which are of common interest for the whole airport community. We could distribute the information to numerous partners via Brio's Web products [Brio.Insight]; for example, handlers, airlines, the police, customs control, tax free shops, maintenance, and cleaning." Paola Petre'

"The first lesson we learned during this process was that from a database perspective we had overestimated the quality of the data. Because the nature of our business is so time critical—daily operations, passengers, aircraft—until the airline departs, we realized we needed to increase the quality of the data we distribute." Alain Dejalle

In the future, BATC would like to see less expensive extraction tools. *"We found the extraction tools difficult to implement. They also had high general overhead. To implement most other products at BATC, would have meant investing a lot in IT as well as additional consulting fees. We were able affordably to implement Brio with our existing internal resources. We wanted to keep the complexity of the implementation limited to the resources we had available."* Alain Dejalle

Delicato Vineyards

As you shop for a bottle of Delicato wine, you may not know what's behind their distinctive Blue label. In the complex, competitive world of vintners, however, Delicato Vineyards established itself as a full-service, custom producer of wine and wine-making services. Other wineries contract with Delicato to purchase products such as grapes or wine and to perform services such as crushing, processing, and storing wine. In addition, Delicato also sells wine in their winery tasting room and to distributors, who handle over a million cases of wine annually.

For Delicato Vineyards, a family-owned wine business in operation for over 60 years, this market niche has proven to be very successful. Today, Delicato is the USA's 4th largest wine exporter, 12th largest case goods producer and 8th largest winery, producing an average of 40 million gallons annually. The company also owns the country's largest premium wine grape vineyard, a 12,000-acre property located in Monterey County, California.

As Delicato grew as a company, so did its need to effectively understand and track the manufacturing process. They needed more information to respond to its customers' demand for information. They needed to address unique business requirements and government regulations specific to the wine industry. It is this information that has helped fuel Delicato's success. *"We must be able to identify all our product at any time—all the way back to the grape,"* Rita Graham, Manager of Information Systems at Delicato Vineyards.

Over the past thirteen years, the company developed in-house COBOL application software to manage its operational data. With a rapidly growing business, and an ever changing market, Delicato realized that their need for decision support quickly outpaced the capabilities provided by their system.

Delicato needed information to balance grape supplies with customer contract demands, project cash flows, produce profit analysis for its products, and develop production forecasts based on sales trends, etc. *"When we gave management their requested reports, which had taken hours to program, they invariably asked another question. In effect, the system that had given Delicato a tremendous advantage over our competitors was becoming impossible to manage and maintain."* Rita Graham

In the spring of 1995, Delicato implemented a data warehouse (Oracle on an NT server) using Brio Technology's Brio Enterprise as the decision support tool. As a result, report development moved from the IT department to the desktops of the users. *"We were beginning to analyze data on the fly. As quickly as we could ask the questions, BrioQuery([the query, analysis and reporting tool within Brio Enterprise] would provide the answers."* Rita Graham.

"The biggest impact of purchasing Brio Enterprise was learning that we didn't have the data integrity we thought we had. We began a corporate-wide 'scrubbing' of our systems (processes and software) to provide more meaningful results. We were in another cycle again, but this time systems were improving at a very rapid rate. Recognizing the power of the new tools, the organization demanded more and more from BrioQuery. It became a 'household' word. 'Can we get a Brio report to do x?' BrioQuery has earned its acceptance as part of our information processing culture," Rita Graham

Graham says that when a company implements a data warehouse, they will see if the data in the transactional systems makes sense or not. *"When you begin querying your own data, you will change the way you do business, I guarantee it,"*

One Stop Shop on the Web

In mid 1996, Delicato began evaluating the use of a corporate Intranet as an information delivery mechanism (primarily to the desktop of executives). *"Our goal was to have a 'one stop shop' for the executives. We needed a way to present corporate information developed on the desktop along with data warehouse information."* Rita Graham

The IT group experimented with exporting information to HTML, but found it to be a very labor-intensive process. The project languished for six months, until Graham saw information about Brio's Web products. *"The Web implementation was extremely smooth—in a matter of hours we had the tool running—within a week we had published and used the software to automatically update over fifty decision support models."* Rita Graham

Delicato has over 150 reports on its corporate Intranet today. *"On our Web site, we include descriptions about reports. It describes what a report means. When a user is reading a report, they need to know more about where the data comes from. Our report list is growing daily as users embrace the concept of instant point-and-click access to their data. We expected productivity improvements within the IT group, but were pleasantly surprised by end user time savings. Time that is now being used to focus on our customers."* Rita Graham

Delicato Vineyards plans to give Web access to information to its customers with Brio.Insight. *"In the coming months, Brio Enterprise will take its place on our Extranet...a system developed to give our customers the same easy access to their specific information. We believe that will place us light years ahead of our competitors in providing customer service,"* Rita Graham

Chapter 12

Comshare, Inc.

PUTTING DECISION SUPPORT TECHNOLOGY TO WORK FOR EFFECTIVE DECISION MAKING

12-1 COMPANY PROFILE[1]

Established in the United States in 1966, Comshare Inc. provides software and support to customers worldwide. Comshare has direct sales and support offices in the United States, Canada, the United Kingdom, France, and Germany, and is represented in approximately 40 other countries through agents.

The "Whole Product" Approach

Comshare is a full-service vendor. Its infrastructure includes customer helpline services, implementation services, and training programs provided through a worldwide network of offices and appointed agents. Two hundred consultants, with both product and industry expertise, work closely with customers. These are elements of Comshare's "whole product" approach (see Figure 12-1).

---

[1] This chapter was contributed by Comshare, Inc. and is copyright by them. It was written by Dr. David King and Doug Hockstad of Comshare, Inc.

Figure 12-1: Whole Product Solutions

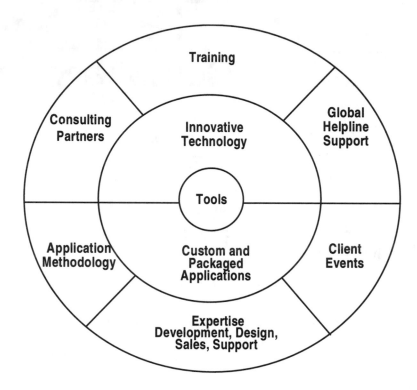

The Decision Support Company

Decision support applications transform data from an organization's business transaction systems and data warehouses, such as general ledgers, sales databases, and numerous other sources, into business-critical information which can be used to make planning and management decisions.

Comshare was a leader in the executive information system movement and now is involved in the definition, design, and implementation of a new generation of decision support applications.

Comshare provides planning, analysis, and operational applications for the financial services, utilities, manufacturing, retail and consumer goods industries. Comshare applications include:

- Enterprise budgeting
- Product and customer profitability
- Key performance indicators
- Merchandise allocation
- Merchandise planning and performance analysis
- Sales analysis
- Sales and margin planning

12-2 COMSHARE'S DECISION SUPPORT APPLICATIONS

Built-In Value-Added Functionality

Comshare provides the following value-added functions for supporting decision making:

- *Built-in Decision Support Intelligence* that increases functionality while reducing the effort and expertise required by the user.
- *Automatic Information Visualization Techniques* that do not require development or customization.
- *Monitoring Capabilities* that use the built-in intelligence of the application to provide functionality.
- *Decision Support Processes* that reduce implementation time.

Comshare's tools and applications "lead" the user to areas of information, rather than forcing the user to search for those areas. This "guided analysis" includes:

- *Detect & Alert*® — Automated "agents" perform routine surveillance of areas of interest. If the user knows what to look for, but doesn't want to spend the time daily to look for something that may or may not occur that day, Detect & Alert agents are used.

- *Advanced Exceptions* — As in most products, color coding draws attention to a number. However, even if a number is satisfactory, it is tagged with a symbol to indicate hidden problems at deeper levels of the hierarchy. For example, the Eastern Region might be color-coded green, indicating satisfactory performance. However, with Comshare's advanced exceptions symbols, that same number might be "tagged" with a bomb, indicating that a problem exists at some lower level, like New York, or Boston. Selecting the bomb directs the user immediately to the problem.

- *Overview* —Visualization technology allows users to see "the whole picture" and where the problems lie at a glance. The overview visualization capability gives users the knowledge of whether problems occur in clusters (indicating larger potential problems) or are just an anomaly.

- *Q&A* — Process management, in the form of a Question & Answer interface, guides the user through all the steps of a process, ensuring that all important questions are asked.

Scenario Building

Scenario building assists decision making. Each decision alternative can be modeled for its potential impact. Since strategic decisions have a long-range impact, most scenarios are based on forecasts of what the impact will be on the future performance of the business.

Data warehouses usually prohibit write-access by end users. The read-write capability of Comshare applications allows these "what if" analyses to be run interactively, stored for comparison, and deleted when no longer needed. Because planning scenarios are based on assumptions and projections, they are often transient and do not need to be recorded permanently.

Information Visualization

Users must be able to analyze the relationships among many types of business elements over time; for example, sales, profit, products, regions, and channels. Comshare's application software, allows information to be "sliced" by product, region, customer, measurement, and time. The user can augment the business model with personalized analytical functions such as trends, averages, ad hoc summaries, variances, and ratios. This ad hoc analysis is critical because it is rarely possible to anticipate all the desired analytical views needed by the many diverse users.

The user's mental model of the data is multidimensional. The user needs to navigate easily from high level summaries to increasing detail in an intuitive way, guided by the user's own knowledge of the business and the problem. Users become self-sufficient in navigating the data analytically and comparatively.

Monitoring: Data Mining

Monitoring takes on special importance once a decision is made and a plan is in place, because management needs to guide execution. The flood of data from the data warehouse and the other data sources creates a significant challenge for managers and executives. These users no longer have the luxury of spending time looking through the data for what is relevant. Rather, the relevant information must find its way to those who need it

Detect and Alert®, technology, described above, reduces information overload. Robots transform decision support applications from analysis and reporting to personalized alerting. Detect and Alert monitors search for key trends, variances and exceptions to notify users of deviations from plan. Monitors can be used to identify loss of market share, new competitors, a change in a competitive strategy, a new market trend, and additional opportunities.

The Detect and Alert robots have the ability to perform calculations and comparisons so that the user is not limited to mining the raw data. If exceptions are identified, they are reported back to users through Comshare's Commander Decision application. (see Section 12-3, below)

12-3 Comshare's Decision Support Application Portfolio

Comshare packages typical applications that are useful across industries. For example, there are aspects to budgeting that are common to every company. By packaging these functions together, companies gain the expertise and practices common to their industry, but retain the flexibility to customize the application to meet their needs. Comshare's applications allow customization. For example, EIS, product profitability, and product costing are all customized applications for individual companies. Comshare's suite of decision support tools contains built-in decision support application-specific functions.

Comshare's Packaged Applications

Commander BudgetPLUS™ is an integrated budgeting, analysis, and reporting application designed to improve productivity, shorten the budget cycle, and enhance the quality and usability of planning information. Unlike spreadsheets, Commander BudgetPLUS manages and controls the entire budgeting process across the enterprise, reducing the time and effort needed to complete the budget cycle. BudgetPLUS offers access to planning information for the whole spectrum of business users. BudgetPLUS provides more flexibility than conventional budgeting applications, and more accounting intelligence than spreadsheets.

Commander BudgetPLUS's built-in accounting intelligence accommodates multiple company structures, script-free consolidations, currency conversions, and calculation and posting of allocations. It solves the problems of coordinating bottom-up with top-down budgeting. Its graphic organization structure allows users to keep up with organization changes.

Most important, executive reviewers use Commander BudgetPLUS to evaluate proposed investment plans from any business perspective — by product, by channel, by market or business unit — so planning is based on priorities, and the budget aligns with long-term strategic plans. Executives and line managers can perform direct queries and drilldowns for intuitive ad hoc analysis.

Commander™ *FDC* is a schedule-based application that handles collection, consolidation and reporting of financial data for public, statutory, and management reporting on networked personal computers. It is a solution for the common problems associated with international currency translations, inter-company eliminations, account reclassifications, and changing reporting needs. Commander FDC collects financial data from general ledgers, spreadsheets, and other sources; manages the data in a shared, secure database; produces financial reports; and delivers data and reports. FDC has built-in accounting intelligence to handle general ledger captures, journal entries, and audit trails automatically. It provides point-and-click access to business reporting for accountants. Its interface to the financial decision support database is spreadsheet-oriented.

Companies using FDC report up to 75% reduction in their closing cycle times. FDC eliminates manual re-keying of data. It simplifies reorganizations and restatements. Even more important, the use of FDC sharpens a company's focus on profitability. Reporting financial information by product line or line of business provides insight into critical success-factors.

Comshare's Arthur™ Enterprise Suite, (AES), is designed specifically for the retail industry. It is the first truly complete set of retail decision support applications. The Arthur Enterprise Suite allows the retailer to review results, plan future seasons, and react swiftly to actual performance. It integrates the business processes of planning, assortment planning, allocation, and performance analysis.

The suite provides a detailed step-by-step methodology for managing the merchandise cycle. This methodology is drawn from the experiences and success of current Arthur users.

Components of the Arthur Enterprise Suite

Comshare's retail applications are a family of Full Lifecycle Decision Support applications. Comprised of base modules that mirror the business process of a retail organization, the Arthur Enterprise Suite allows retailers to benefit from industry-wide best practices embedded within the applications. Applications are also customizable. User organizations can also embed the skills of their own experts into the business process, so that they can exploit their own unique business practices.

Arthur Information Manager™ lies at the heart of the suite. This database and its associated tools allow parallel processing, handle large volumes of data; and provide speedy loading, calculating and tracking of information. The Arthur Information Manager deals specifically with retail problems of massive detail; short processing windows, frequent reorganizations of product and location classifications, and complex calculations like open-to-buy, and forward cover.

Arthur™ Planning creates detailed merchandise plans. Goals can be pushed down rapidly to lower levels of detail. The impact of a change at a detailed level can be quickly viewed at the summary level. Gaps between desired sales targets and planned targets can be identified, and resolved. The impact of intake timing, pricing, markdowns, or promotions can be determined.

Arthur™ Assortment Planning provides the ability to take the product plan through the merchandise selection process, bridging the gap between plan and purchase order. Buyers and planners can see the results of their planned purchases. Collections can be built, color or price stories detailed, and deliveries targeted. The range review can be fact-based. Buyers and planners can quickly determine if their planned assortment is in balance with company objectives.

Arthur™ Allocation assesses store performance for each product. It uses the assortment plan as the basis for distribution and blends in current performance to optimize product deliveries. Allocation allows retailers to match the product to each store's current personality and capacity. Using Arthur Allocation, retailers move from planning into the in-season process.

Arthur™ Performance Analysis enables users to see trends over the years, on a store-by-store basis. With exception highlighting, trends emerge, and the facts about past performance become clear.

Comshare's Custom Applications

Comshare has long specialized in helping companies build their own, specialized performance measurement applications. We have built much of the common functionality directly into the application building environment.

Commander Decision™ is a decision support product for analysts, managers, and executives. It is a planning, analysis and reporting system that promotes innovative thinking, helps identify alternative courses of action, and monitors progress. Commander Decision supports the delivery of customized, enterprise-wide decision support applications.

Commander Decision allows business users to view business as charts, as maps, as exceptions, as ad hoc queries and calculations, and as personal alerts.

Commander Decision includes Comshare's Detect and Alert® technology (discussed earlier in this Chapter). Advanced Exceptions, Overview, and Q&A are also available.

Commander Decision is a 32-bit software product that can accommodate Windows 95 and Windows NT 3.5 desktop users all within a single application. It exploits technologies such as OLE2 and OCXs, for openness.

Commander DecisionWeb™ allows delivery of Commander Decision applications to remote users who have only a Java-enabled Web browser on the desktop. Commander DecisionWeb mirrors the Commander Decision client-server desktop, enabling users to perform hands-on analysis of multidimensional data. DecisionWeb is designed to provide a client-server style interface with active applications.

Commander Sales Analysis™ **(CSA)** is a sales tracking and analysis application built with Commander Decision. It's allows such activities as tracking sales and profit, comparing actual results against planned targets, and monitoring growth trends and product contributions by sales representatives, account managers, marketers, business unit managers, and sales executives. CSA uses question-and-answer-based analysis of products, customers, promotional effectiveness, and markets, they gain insight that allows rapid, effective decision making based on current performance.

12-4. COMSHARE'S THREE TIER ARCHITECTURE

In developing custom and packaged applications, Comshare adopted a three-tier architecture. The architecture provides the ability to create new applications in a timely fashion and to modify or enhance existing applications. While the specifics vary from one decision support application to the next, the diagram in Figure 12-2 provides an overview of the basic components underlying the three-tier architecture of our newer decision support applications

Figure 12-2 Comshare Application Architecture

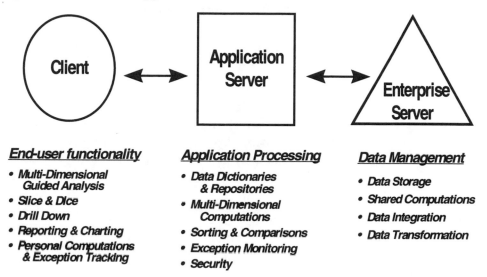

End-user functionality

- *Multi-Dimensional Guided Analysis*
- *Slice & Dice*
- *Drill Down*
- *Reporting & Charting*
- *Personal Computations & Exception Tracking*

Application Processing

- *Data Dictionaries & Repositories*
- *Multi-Dimensional Computations*
- *Sorting & Comparisons*
- *Exception Monitoring*
- *Security*

Data Management

- *Data Storage*
- *Shared Computations*
- *Data Integration*
- *Data Transformation*

Client

Application clients provide graphical user interfaces to guide and support end users with various planning, analysis and reporting tasks. Some applications have multiple clients each designed to support users differentiated by their roles, interests and skills. In some cases the client is spreadsheet-based. In others the client is a performance measurement system designed to support the managerial user.

All clients are Microsoft Windows-based and run on the end-user's desktop. More recently, clients have been built as 32-bit OLE containers with features and functionality provided by individual OLE custom controls (OCXs) and DLLS.

OCXs are self-contained OLE servers whose services are exposed through a well-defined object interface. From a technical standpoint, they are portable across a variety of programming languages and many different desktop applications (not just Comshare's). From an architectural standpoint, the use of OCXs and DLLs allow us to:

- Add new functions and features to a client with minimal impact on existing components.

- Create new clients aimed at new classes of application users or new classes of client services (e.g. the application administrator).

- Produce "intelligent" features (objects) that know how to coordinate the actions of other features (objects). For example, the grid, map and chart objects in Commander Decision are intelligently linked so that a change in one (say an exception on the grid) can automatically invoke a change in another (say the color coding of a geographical region on the map).

Because the Decision Desktop is a "control container," virtually any OCX can be inserted in a Decision application.

Application Server

The Decision Access Module (DecAM) is a multitasking and multithreading program that determines which application engine should be invoked to satisfy a given client request. The various application engines each perform different sets of computational tasks. For example, if a user performs an action that requires a "virtual" member to be dynamically created (e.g., a ratio that doesn't exist in the underlying multidimensional database), then the access module processes the request and creates an answer by first querying the database on the enterprise server, using the application engine to calculate the virtual result, then returning only the information needed for display. The impact is fourfold:

1. it reduces the size of the database
2. it reduces the amount of network traffic
3. it improves the response time

4. it allows adding application-specific calculations that may not exist in the database engine (e.g., % of parent)

The components of the application servers run on a variety of platforms. The application server is at the heart of Comshare's application strategy. It's existence enables mixing-and-matching front-end and back-end components and to add and surface new "business processing" functionality to existing applications without having to re-architect the application. Two cases in point are the addition of a "thin client" version of Commander Decision and the ability to access a variety of back-end databases.

Commander DecisionWeb, described above, acts as a gateway between a Web server and DecAM. That is, the browser converses with a Web Server that, in turn, invokes DecWeb. DecWeb passes the client request on to the DecAM; formats the results returned by the DecAM before it passes them back to the Web server; and maintains the session between the client and the application and enterprise servers (since a Web server lacks the ability to maintain this information). In this way, all of the functionality resident in the DecAM has the potential to be surfaced to end users in a web browser.

A "data source API" (DSAPI) enables the DecAM to converse with a variety of multidimensional databases, including Express, TM1 and Essbase. Relational databases whose tables are in a star schema format will also be available. The DSAPI can be modified to handle additional databases if the need arises. Overall, any of the functions provided by the Application Server will be available to an application regardless of the back-end database.

The Application Server has been augmented with a new "Calculation API." This API makes it possible for application builders to extend the range of "server-side" arithmetic functions that can be calculated by the Application Server with their own specialized computational functions. For example, an application builder could add a specialized DLL for performing neural net forecasts and have the Application Server return those forecasts to any client application requesting the forecasts.

Enterprise Server

Logically, the enterprise server consists of a series of components for managing shared application databases and for responding to queries issued by various application servers against those databases. In addition, there are data integration components for transforming, cleansing, and importing data from external systems (e.g., data warehouses and legacy systems) into the application databases.

Each back-end database contains:

1. metadata defining the dimensions, hierarchies and dimension members (both static and calculated) in an application;
2. the input data; and
3. calculated results[2].

In contrast to the computations performed by an application engine on an application server, the calculated results stored in a multidimensional database on an enterprise server take up physical storage space, and are those needed and shared by a range of users or applications.

For all applications, the data integration component is the Data Integrator, also referred to as ADL. ADL is used not only to import data into an application database from various external sources but also to cleanse and transform the data before it is imported. ADL runs on a wide range of workstation, server and mainframe platforms.

---

[2] Except for TM1, which calculates results on the fly

The core of Comshare's applications is multidimensionality, regardless of the specific functional area addressed. As a result, the physical design of the enterprise server is currently (1997) built around a multidimensional database rather than a relational database. Relational databases lack native multidimensional support. Over the next several years, this will change. Already, databases such as Microsoft's SQL Server 6.5 have new operators such as "Cube By" and "Rollup" that support simple multidimensional operations. While these operations are not sufficient to support complex multidimensional applications, they can form the basis for less sophisticated multidimensional applications when combined with specialized application server components. Comshare's application server is being enhanced to handle a variety of multidimensional calculations for data from multidimensional and relational databases. In fact, Comshare has announced relational versions of existing products, including its budgeting package BudgetPLUS.

Developing New Applications: An Example

In theory, component architectures, like Comshare's Application Architecture, offer the opportunity for rapid application development (RAD). To see how the theory works in practice, consider the development of our Sales Analysis application discussed above. This application supports sales analysis for business and account managers, as well as business and trade analysts. The application is designed to readily answer multidimensional questions like:

- What is customer profitability by product?

- What is product contribution this year compared to last?

- How are my customers doing relative to plan?

To answer questions of this sort and to meet the information needs and skills of end users, the application required a specialized interface, calculations and rules, and database content. The application was developed by utilizing, enhancing, and supplementing various components in the three-tiers of Commander Decision.

The client for this application rests on the "question and answer" metaphor in which the end-user generates specialized analysis and reports by selecting from an extensive list of sales analysis questions (like those above). The questions cover a large percentage of the sales analysis queries asked by analysts and managers. The interface also provides the ability to customize and extend the list.

The client for this application was constructed from the Commander Decision client. Commander Decision provides most of the components required to support the "Q&A" metaphor (e.g., list boxes, an extensive repertoire of graphs, multi-dimensional tables,). New objects, however, were needed to handle the "fact log" and "Q&A Show." These objects were developed using 3rd party OCXs rather than adding this functionality to Decision from scratch.

The application and enterprise servers working in concert provide the "answers" to the questions posed from the Sales Analysis client. The answers to many of the questions rest on straightforward computations and comparisons that are already provided by the servers. Others do not. A case in point is "% of parent," which requires the values of the members at a lower level of a hierarchy to be compared to the value of their parent member. For example, "% of parent" is used to answer: "What is the % of 2 liter cola sales to total cola sales?" To support these new computations, we could have enhanced either the application server or the enterprise server. We chose the former because it had less impact on other components in the architecture. The new computations and comparisons were simply added by enhancing the list of computations and comparisons supported by the application server.

Most of the data for this application originates from legacy systems (like General Ledgers). Before Sales Analysis can provide answers to end user queries, the data needs to be cleansed, transformed and loaded into the multidimensional database. This is done with the "data integration" component of the enterprise server (Comshare's ADL). The components of the enterprise server did not need to be modified to develop the application.

As the Sales Analysis application illustrates, the difficult part of developing an application is not writing the code. Comshare's component architecture enables developers to add new functionality by modifying existing components, incorporating components provided by 3rd party vendors, or creating new components of our own. Instead, the hard part lies in creating the metadata for the application—the data, multidimensional structures, rules, analysis and reports that drive the application. The metadata represent the knowledge of best practices and expertise required by an end user to perform a particular functional task.

Evolving Toward the Distributed Component Future

In the past, decision support applications were implemented as host-based systems. Only a few years ago host-based systems gave way to two-tier client/server systems. Now (1997), the two-tier systems are giving way to three-tier and n-tier architecture. What about the future?

Comshare's decision support applications are architected in an open, modular fashion with industry standard component interfaces and communication protocols. The interfaces and protocols of the application and enterprise servers rely on call level interfaces and peer-to-peer communications both of which are system dependent. CLI and peer-to-peer communications are currently employed because these industry standards are supported by the Microsoft and Unix environments where our applications run. Ultimately, the goal is to have highly configurable, high performing, component-based systems capable of transparently operating in distributed heterogeneous computing environments.

It has long been claimed that object-oriented interfaces and communication protocols will enable the design and implementation of such systems. Several competing (distributed) object model standards are available in 1997.

From Comshare's perspective, we really don't care who prevails. What the Web, Java, and ActiveX provide is a new platform and the opportunity to mix-and-match components according to application requirements. The aim is to develop applications that incorporate "best-of-breed" components in a seamless and transparent fashion, so end users need not be aware of the underlying architecture and technologies.

12-5 CUSTOMER SUCCESS STORIES

Transco — Commander Decision

Transco, part of BG PLC, is the pipeline and storage division of the UK's gas business. It is responsible for delivering gas to 19 million customers safely and efficiently. To ensure the timely flow of cost information to the managers and analysts charged with making the company successful, Transco uses Commander Decision.

Major change has been part of Transco's everyday life since it was formed in 1994. After one of the largest corporate restructurings on record, it slimmed down and reorganized itself to compete in a challenging business.

"The Regulator requires significant and continuing decreases in our operating costs to insure that our customers' prices also fall. To do that and still give an adequate return to our shareholders, we must have very tight control over costs," Chris Le Fevre, Director - Special Projects, Transco.

Information is absolutely critical.

"If we don't know what the costs of our products are, how do we know how to price them?" Colin Johnson, Manager District Operations, Hadrian District, Transco:

To really understand costs, the company needs to look at costs from a multidimensional perspective. *"As a regulated business, we're operating to a five-year formula period, so it's very important that we get our projections on a common basis and look at the potential impact of different levels of demand for gas."* Richard Cribb, Business Finance Analyst, Transco

These needs became a mandate for Transco's finance group to deliver cost information quickly to a spectrum of users. To meet the requirements, they needed a client/server technology which would integrate with existing systems, such as the activity-based costing system and the Oracle database, where much of the data for the application is stored—including data from payroll, supply systems, and creditor information. They needed to offer options for spreadsheet users and non-spreadsheet users alike, and they needed a product that could handle their volume and deliver quick response for users. After a systematic evaluation, Transco selected Commander Decision.

Transco's Decision application is now used by 150 people, from the Director to financial analysts and first line managers throughout the United Kingdom. Commander Decision provides Transco's users with access to cost information, drill-down, and multiple views of information. Users can pose "what if" questions; for example, a district manager might ask: what if our emergency workload goes up by 5%?, and see the effect on costs as a result.

"I like the way you can decide what you want to see and change the perspectives very quickly. And we can drill all the way down to the original item from the general ledger. We can also look at key indicators very quickly to see trends," Chris Le Fevre.

"Using Decision, we can roll out applications very quickly all over the country with our team based here in Solihull, in Britain's West Midlands... We have met user requirements and within our promised deadline. Maintenance is manageable, as well, because there is very little scripting, so if a change occurs to a product or

structure in the underlying database, what the user sees on the desktop changes automatically." Richard Cribb

"Commander Decision is clearly helping us make better decisions The application gives us a unique opportunity to work directly with our cost base so we can see the effects of decisions out in the field. This application allows us to give all of our users a single source of the truth and promotes awareness throughout the company of exactly how we're doing." Colin Johnson

Fluor Corporation — Commander FDC

Fluor Corporation is the world's largest engineering, construction, maintenance, and diversified services company, with approximately 59,000 employees working in more than 80 countries. Using Comshare's Commander FDC, Fluor streamlined its financial consolidation processes and created an interactive database to speed analysis of financial information.

Fluor's accounting group used a network of Lotus spreadsheets and a mainframe consolidation system for its worldwide financial results. The system required extensive and repeated manual rekeying of data to get a consolidated trial balance, and more rekeying for each succeeding step in the financial reporting process. The result was time-consuming, error-prone labor to create consolidated financial data that was not easily accessible for analysis. The accounting group found that Comshare's Commander FDC offered the consolidation logic, the Lotus interface, and the facility for building and maintaining multiple organization structures that they were looking for.

Michael Van Houten, Fluor's Director of Corporate Accounting, is responsible for the financial consolidation of over 400 companies. *"One process leads to another. We start with consolidating actuals for tax and statutory reporting; then we prepare outlooks or forecasts for management. When we found an interactive application where we (and others) could actually use the database for succeeding steps without rekeying all the data each time, that was a big plus. We're now using FDC to do budgeting, forecasting, and cash flow modeling as well as consolidation."* Michael Van Houton

The accounting group worked with Comshare consultants to implement FDC.

"Now, two days after receiving the 400+ financial statement packages, we are ready to release preliminary earnings results. From that point on, we save a lot of time in the subsequent processes, because we can use adjusted figures as a starting point for our forecasting without rekeying data. We can provide management with forecasts much faster than before." Michael Van Houten

Replacing the mainframe system with a PC-based application allowed Fluor to eliminate error-prone rekeying of data and cut the turnaround time for management reporting. A standardized approach to data collection has also paid off.

"We have given a standard data collection template to all of our companies, so that all the companies are now supplying us with consistent information. This saves us a lot of work compared to the way we used to get the information. When we found an interactive application where we could actually use the database for succeeding steps without rekeying all the data each time, that was a big plus." Michael Van Houten

"We're continually evaluating our work processes and finding ways to eliminate unnecessary steps. With FDC, you can change things, cut a corner here and there, and increase productivity. Our accountants are very competent using Lotus. With FDC in place, we don't need a programmer to debug the changes we make when we improve a process," Michael Van Houten.

Lockheed Martin — Commander BudgetPLUS™

Lockheed Martin wanted to improve the quality of their budget information while they cut the number of staff hours needed to develop it. No they are doing both with Commander BudgetPLUS.

Headquartered in Bethesda, Maryland, Lockheed Martin is a highly diversified global enterprise engaged in the research, design, development, manufacture, and integration of advanced-technology products and services. Over 19,000 Lockheed Martin employees in 200 operating companies are engaged in a diverse set of activities including defense projects, aerospace ventures, and systems integration projects for federal, state, and local governments and commercial organizations.

Providing high-quality budget information to managers all over the world presented a change. In the Finance department, *"we're working to hold the line on staffing, and yet to improve the quality of information we provide to the rest of the company. To do that, we needed to improve reporting productivity and help department heads manage cost more effectively."* Tom Barranger, Manager Corporate Financial Systems, Lockheed Martin.

Lockheed Martin's corporate headquarters selected Comshare's BudgetPLUS application software for corporate budget development, analysis, and reporting. Using Commander BudgetPLUS, Lockheed's financial systems group is linking all corporate headquarters operating departments and managers worldwide. The application will provide for electronic submission and review of financial plans for budget development and budget and cost reporting. In choosing Commander BudgetPLUS, Barranger's team evaluated leading alternative products thoroughly. *"Commander BudgetPLUS is a true client/server product which gives us the speed and reliability of a multithreaded application. We needed that because we're a large organization, and our users need consistently fast response, especially at budget deadline time."* Tom Barranger.

Another factor in the decision was lockheed Martin's existing relationship with Comshare. *"We know from experience that we could work effectively with Comshare's consultants."* Tom Barranger.

A team of three is implementing the corporate budgeting system. *"We are allocating our corporate overhead costs across our operating companies and providing information to our headquarters staff using Commander BudgetPLUS. We will also be using it to produce a whole series of federal reports, including incurred cost submission reporting."* Tom Barranger.

Lockheed has been using Comshare's Commander FDC™ product for financial consolidation and reporting since 1991, prior to the corporate merger of Lockheed Corporation and Martin Marietta Corporation. Barranger's group is integrating data from the general ledger with sales and profit data stored in the Commander FDC data base; data from these two sources resides in the Commander BudgetPLUS OLAP database, creating a rich store of corporate information for ad hoc analysis by directors and vice presidents across the enterprise. The delivery vehicle for this information is Comshare's performance measurement application, Commander Decision ™, which delivers the information from Commander Budget-PLUS's OLAP database for direct desktop use by executives.

"The Commander BudgetPLUS application is allowing us to improve our reporting productivity and to manage costs more effectively. We plan to deliver budget variance reports within a day of closing, for example." Tom Barranger.

Additional ad hoc reporting capabilities for executives and managers are expected to be available in the next phase of the project. *"You don't have to be a financial person to work with BudgetPLUS - anyone can use it. Our managers can make their dollars go further if they can access more accurate cost information, earlier."* Tom Barranger.

Ross Stores — Arthur Allocation

Ross Stores is growing off-price retailer that prides itself in a unique mix of merchandise at each store. Headquartered in Newark, California, with well over 300 stores across North America, Ross Stores is a familiar name in the retail industry. As an off-price retailer, the company's focus is on providing value with a full line of clothing, home accents and gifts, and even sporting goods. Sales for 1996 were $1.6 billion.

In order to stay on top of day-to-day operations, as the company grew, so did its allocation team. With over 300 stores nationwide, Ross Stores needed an automated allocation system to stay competitive. They chose Comshare's Arthur Allocation – part of Comshare's Full Lifecycle Decision Support system for retail, Arthur Enterprise Suite.

"Ross Stores creates a 'treasure hunt' environment in our stores. We want customers to find that gem of an item they've been looking for. It's an impulse-oriented philosophy. As a result, we get a smattering of different types of merchandise in every store. It is critical, when we do allocations, that we are able to look at a store's style and the store's merchandise mix. Creating such a mix is intrinsic to Arthur Allocation. Retailers won't find that capability anywhere else." Steve Davis, Manager of Merchandise Systems Development at Ross Stores.

Ross Stores has been using Arthur Planning for over six years. Steve Davis manages the development of all MIS projects relating to the merchandising pipeline. He was in charge when the company decided to completely redo its in-house merchandise allocation system.

"We are a company that looks for growth opportunities, new stores, new merchandise, and new ways of providing decision support to our merchants. So, when Comshare announced its intentions to expand Arthur's capabilities to handle allocation, we embarked on a joint development project as a natural extension of our relationship. We knew the product was going to do exactly what we wanted it to do by design. Our partnership with Comshare gave us that assurance. Our previous allocation system was seven years old and no longer keeping up with our needs." Steve Davis

Ross Stores Allocation Planners were performing more than half of all allocations manually. Calculations and data entry were done by hand. The process was time consuming and reactive.

"As we continued to add more stores, we had to add more people. What we really needed was an automated system." Steve Davis.

Ross Stores needed an automatic allocation system powered by the industry's best practice and the technology and retail application expertise Comshare provides. As a result, Ross Stores and Comshare partnered to create Arthur Allocation.

Here is how the system works: Ross Stores gets "real time" updates from stores so that sales information is nearly instantaneous.

"We operate in both Local Area Network (LAN) and Wide Area Network (WAN) environment.," Steve Davis.

Users are spread all over the United States, with Buyers and Merchandise Analysts in New York and Allocation Planners in California. In 1997, the Ross Stores' Arthur Allocation system is accessed by a team of 40 allocators, responsible for the allocation of over 300 stores with over 1,000 classes allocated at one time.

The benefits to Ross Stores are: improved turn time, human resources better spent, and improved quality of decision making, all in support of the company's growth.

"We are determined to expand the number of stores as well as the depth of selection. Arthur Allocation helps us manage that expansion without having to continue to add new people. The time saved is incredible...The quality of the allocation is exceptional and we can perform 'what if' analysis of our allocations on the fly. That capability alone puts retailers on the leading edge of decision making. " Steve Davis

CONCLUSION

The Fact Gap

While the data warehouse architecture provides for query and reporting, there exists an analysis, or fact gap in this paradigm. Even with technologies like spreadsheets, query tools, OLAP databases, and central data repositories, users still are faced with problems. For example, the data may not exist, even in the data warehouse; there may be too much data; end users may not have control over the types of analysis, presentation, business rules, modification that can be accomplished; tedious, time consuming tasks may be required (such as re-keying data from various reports into another spreadsheet); or the application may not respond quickly enough to the changing needs of the organization, driven by acquisitions, re-organizations and new product introductions.

Comshare's application software fills this gap by extending the utility of the investment in technology within the organization providing the end user with the decision support capabilities required for effective decision making. (Figure 12-3)

Figure 12-3: Fact Gap (Source: Gartner Group

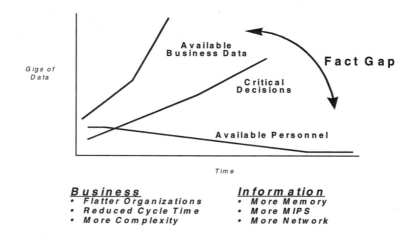

Chapter

13

Seagate Software:

Business Intelligence for the Intelligent Business

13-1 COMPANY BACKGROUND[1]

Seagate Software, a subsidiary of Seagate Technology, Inc., develops and markets tools and applications for information management and infrastructure management, including network, systems, and storage management. Its software solutions are designed as integral components of a total data management product strategy supporting all major operating environments.

The parent company, Seagate Technology, provides products for storing, managing and accessing digital information. Seagate develops and manufactures disc and tape storage devices, magnetic recording heads and media, precision motors, microelectronics, and data access and management software. With nearly $9 billion in revenue, operations in 22 countries and over 110,000 employees worldwide, the Scotts Valley, California-based company is the world's largest manufacturer of disc drives and related components.

---

[1] This chapter was contributed by Seagate Software and is copyright by them. It was written by James Lucy.

Within Seagate Software, the Information Management Group (IMG), (offices in Vancouver, BC, London, England, and many others worldwide) offers a suite of business intelligence products and services. To provide customers with world-class business intelligence systems through seamless, desktop-to-enterprise software solutions, Seagate acquired Crystal Services, maker of the Crystal product line of desktop data reporting tools and decision support applications in May 1994 and acquired Holistic Systems Inc., developer of Holos high-end business intelligence software in June 1996.

Seagate Software's products and services are marketed worldwide through distributors, value-added resellers, system integrators, retailers, and OEMs, and directly to large corporate users. The company has established strategic relationships with such companies as Microsoft, IBM, and Hewlett-Packard.

13-2 SEAGATE SOFTWARE'S BUSINESS INTELLIGENCE MARKET

Seagate Software's business intelligence products include Seagate Holos, Seagate Crystal Info, and Seagate Crystal Reports. The spectrum of business intelligence needs in any large organization – from EIS to decision support to OLAP -- can be met by this complementary set of products. Applications include budgeting and forecasting, financial consolidations, strategic planning, product line profitability, activity-based cost analysis, financial modeling and analysis, customer service, human resources management and marketing promotions.

Companies who have successfully applied Seagate Software solutions to their business challenges include Advanta, Ameritech, AT&T, B.C. Hydro, British Telecom, Cisco Systems, CP Rail, Dell Computers, Walt Disney, Eurotunnel, Federal Express, Fidelity Investments, Hewlett-Packard, KPMG Peat Marwick, MBNA, Nike, Nissan, Northern Telecom,

Pacific Bell, Southwestern Bell, Subaru, TCI, Transamerica Financial Services, and the University of Massachusetts. Seagate Software products are being used in diverse industries including electronics, finance, health care, oil and gas, publishing, retail, telecommunications, transportation and utilities.

Seagate's Enterprise Business Intelligence Philosophy

Users of information technology systems often have a difficult time measuring business intelligence benefits, which seem "intangible" or "hard to justify" because they are technology-driven systems. Seagate Software believes that "bottom-line" benefits of a system must be measurable to be worth the investment. Though it may be difficult to quantify the real gains of systems that keep people better informed, streamline the reporting cycle, and facilitate communication throughout the organization, it should be possible to assign numbers to systems that deliver information that allows, for example:

- call center managers to reduce wastage
- purchasing managers to negotiate better supply prices
- direct marketers to target effectively
- traders to better understand the structure of their deals
- product managers to make better pricing decisions

The closer a system is to the operational edge of the business, the easier it is to draw a direct line from the system to the real, "bottom-line" benefit. While the nature of enterprise business intelligence systems varies among organizations and industries, it should always be possible to show that such systems deliver real benefit and competitive advantage.

Seagate Software believes that business intelligence systems belong on the desks of all levels of staff across the organization. It is only by delivering information directly to the people who can make a real difference to the business that these systems can realize their full benefit.

The current popularity of data warehousing shows that companies are eager to make available, and thus benefit from, the large volumes of low-level, detailed data that usually exist. However, if this data is to be delivered efficiently to its users, then it must be summarized, analyzed and presented in a form that can be assimilated by them as part of their daily routine. This requires an understanding of exactly what each group of users needs and how the information can be best delivered to them.

The most successful business intelligence implementations use small teams of hybrid "analyst-developers" to deliver appropriate functionality to users quickly and effectively. These teams must have a good grounding in the technology and what it can deliver. They must also be able to help the users understand what is possible and how it can be best used to serve them. Most importantly, they must work in partnership with the users to deliver benefit to their company as a whole.

Key Components of Enterprise Business Intelligence

Useful business intelligence systems, in addition to offering a holistic approach to business needs, typically include the following technology components:

- OLAP—Online Analytical Processing tools, which incorporate multidimensional capabilities, offer the ability to view and manipulate data in a way that matches an individual's perception of the business, not the way the data is stored in the underlying systems. OLAP technology, a key feature of Seagate Holos and Seagate Crystal Info, is perhaps one of the primary factors influencing the explosion of data warehousing today.

- Query and Reporting Tools—Today's query and reporting tools make it possible for people to ask for business information in business terms with a minimum of SQL and other programming language requirements. In addition to the reporting capabilities built into Seagate Holos, Seagate Software offers Seagate Crystal Reports and Seagate Crystal Info desktop tools.

- Agents—Software constructs that allow users to specify the kind of information they want to access, and empower the computer system itself to go and find it, analyze it and report back about what is found. Agent technology is incorporated into Seagate Holos software.

- Statistical Analysis Tools—Seagate Holos incorporates an unusually wide range of statistical analysis and forecasting capabilities with emphasis on ease of use and accessibility.

- Data Discovery (Data Mining)— Products in this category apply statistics or artificial intelligence to interpret large amounts of data. Techniques like CART and CHAID, approaches such as neural networks or decision trees, and a wide assortment of specialized tools make prediction, estimation and forecasting a scientific process. Seagate Holos provides an increasing range of these capabilities.

- Web-Based Discovery—The burgeoning use of the World Wide Web has resulted in products to input, access, and analyze data over the Internet and corporate intranets. All Seagate Software business intelligence products are Web-deployable.

The Seagate Software Advantage

Seagate Software's desktop-to-enterprise vision is designed to offer users a comprehensive approach to meeting their business information needs. The products together support the spectrum of business intelligence activity, starting at the desktop and extending to the overall enterprise, from simple end-user access and reporting, to complex queries, to sophisticated analytic manipulation of data and reports.

Seagate Software support services include training, documentation, telephone and on-site support, application development and consulting services. The company has formed partnerships with consulting organizations and hardware and software vendors to ensure well-supported installations. Descriptions of several of Seagate Software's products follow.

13-3 PRODUCTS

Seagate Crystal Reports

The world's first Windows report writer is today the leader in query and reporting, with over three million units shipped. It has become so popular, there is even a *Crystal Reports for Dummies* book. A developer and end-user tool with Standard and Professional versions, Seagate Crystal Reports allows users to design all types of reports and integrate them into database applications. Users can access most types of PC and SQL data. There is comprehensive user and developer documentation, and an interactive learning CD is available.

Seagate Crystal Reports, available in 32-bit and 16-bit versions, is designed to extract critical business data and transform it into presentation-quality, information-rich reports. Over 150 software vendors, including Microsoft, PeopleSoft, and Oracle, bundle Seagate Crystal Reports in their retail software programs. Seagate Crystal Reports accesses more than 30 data sources and is designed to save time in creating and distributing reports and to let developers seamlessly integrate reporting into database applications.

Figure 13-1: Seagate Crystal Reports Provides Report Capabilities Across the Enterprise.

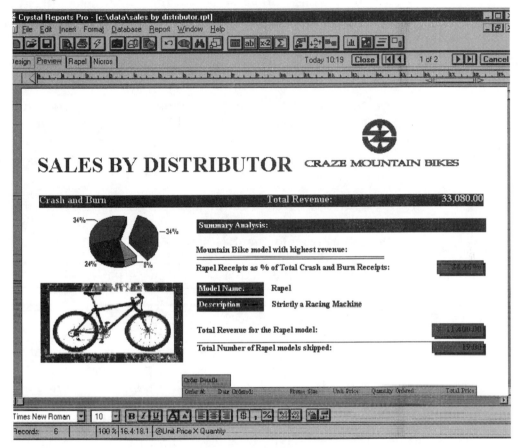

Its modular design allows the Crystal Reports Engine to be used to integrate reporting into database applications and distributed with a free runtime. Integration can be done using direct API calls, or by using any of the following interfaces: ActiveX (OCX/OLE) Control, Visual Basic Custom Control (VBX), Microsoft Foundation Class Library, Delphi Visual Component Library (VCL), Informix-New Era Class Library, or the new Automation Server Interface, which provides object-oriented access to the entire Crystal Report Engine.

Seagate Crystal Reports is used:

- by business professionals to report or query directly from a data source
- by IS personnel to provide reports to users
- by software vendors and developers to include reporting in database applications

Seagate Crystal Reports also offers access to information across the Web. The Seagate Crystal Report "thin-wire" architecture improves response time and reduces Web traffic. Users can pull reports from the Web server to their browser a page at a time as desired.

Lightweight ActiveX and Java plug-ins allow viewing reports in their native format in almost any browser, and cross-platform deployment is simple. For flexible reporting within Web-deployed applications, Seagate Crystal reports can be integrated directly into Active Server Pages.

Seagate Crystal Info

Seagate Crystal Info is a three-tier client/server enterprise analysis and reporting system designed to give business users immediate access to decision-making information, while giving IT professionals security and control over the data and the system. Its design gives people the freedom to query data themselves, or analyze shared reports created for them, while ensuring data security is maintained. Business users automatically receive information on time, without creating high volumes of network traffic or overloading the database.

Benefits of Seagate Crystal Info include desktop reporting and analysis – users may access decision-making information in e-mail style folders containing shared reports, cubes, and Windows executables, or create presentation-quality ad hoc reports using the Crystal Reports Designer. Through a point-and-click interface, Crystal Info users may schedule reports based on the clock, on events (e.g., data warehouse update), or on custom business calendars. HTML reports are used to update a Website automatically.

Seagate Crystal Info includes clustering technology to increase both performance and scalability. APS (Automated Process Scheduler) Clustering allows multiple APSs to act as one "virtual APS." As a result, the number of users the system can support by simply adding new machines can be increased. In addition to scalability, APS Clustering makes Seagate Crystal Info more fault tolerant by providing high availability. If an APS goes down for some reason, any user connected to that APS is automatically switched over to an active APS that is part of the cluster. Clustering technology also improves system performance by distributing the workload across several machines.

Overall, clustering technology in Seagate Crystal Info offers the following advantages:

- Improved Scalability -- As more users, objects, and jobs are added to the system, additional APS machines can easily be added while a cluster continues running.
- Workload Allocation -- Requests received by an APS machine are broadcast to the rest of the machines in the cluster; all the APS machines in the cluster can participate in fulfilling requests.

Seagate Crystal Reports' Web capability includes Smart Viewers, thin-client browser add-ins that provide platform-independent reporting functionality without the need for application set-up on client desktops. Users of browsers that support ActiveX or Java can view reports on a Web site or within a Web application in native Crystal format for maximum presentation quality. Reports can be downloaded a page at a time using thin client Page-on-Demand technology. Automatic Smart Viewer downloading simplifies deployment. Smart Viewers for Frames and Plain HTML allow users to view reports from any browser.

Seagate Crystal Info provides several alternatives for accessing information. Users can view and manipulate shared reports, spending less time gathering information and more time analyzing it for decision making. Select users who require additional ad-hoc capabilities can be given access to Seagate Holos' OLAP technology to create multidimensional views of data to explore inherent trends and relationships. By presenting data in a spreadsheet-style interface, Seagate Software's OLAP technology makes it easier to examine key business drivers such as variations in unit sales per product per region, or revenue per employee per site, enabling more informed business decisions.

Other users across the organization can be given access to the reporting technology of Seagate Crystal Reports. The Crystal Reports Designer provides intuitive Experts for creating presentation-quality reports from PC, SQL, ODBC compliant, and multidimensional data sources. Integrated graphing, a formula editor, and a gallery of report styles help specified users create and share reports. Both of these technologies are integrated into the Seagate Crystal Info 3-tier architecture.

Seagate Holos: Overview

Seagate Holos is an application development environment and delivery vehicle engineered for large-scale, custom business intelligence applications. By combining full relational and multidimensional OLAP, modeling, business rules, statistical analysis, forecasting and data mining, Seagate Holos offers capabilities for developing and delivering sophisticated business intelligence applications aimed precisely at each business requirement.

Seagate Holos is available on a wide variety of servers, including NCR WorldMark; Digital VMS on VAX and Alpha; Digital UNIX; ICL DRS6000; IBM RS/6000; HP 9000 (800 series); Sequent Symmetry; Sun Solaris; and Windows NT (Intel and Alpha). It can be accessed through MS Windows, MS Windows NT, or Apple Macintosh client desktop environments. Seagate Holos provides full dynamic SQL links to most popular relational databases, including Ingres, Informix, Microsoft SQL Server, Oracle, Rdb, Red Brick, Sybase, Teradata and many others through ODBC in both the UNIX and Windows NT environments.

Data of all kinds, in any computing environment, can be accessed, assembled and analyzed by Seagate Holos through its support for all popular data access and communications methods. Seagate Holos supports many open systems interoperability standards, leveraging existing investments in client/server architecture and relational database technology.

Seagate Holos's History in Business Intelligence

Seagate Software's Holos product originated in the business intelligence marketplace in 1988, and has a number of firsts to its credit. Holos was developed by Holistic Systems, which Seagate purchased in 1996.

- Seagate Holos software was the first product to combine EIS and OLAP technology in a single, integrated offering. Some EIS purists at the time criticized the approach as being "improper" EIS. Indeed, a number of industry experts suggested that EIS and DSS (i.e., the OLAP of the time) were so radically different that they should never be mentioned in the same breath.

- Seagate Holos was the first business intelligence product to use the "client-server" model. As the term did not exist at the time, it was called "cooperative coprocessing," which later became an accepted term for one form of client-server architecture.

- Seagate Holos was the first business intelligence product designed to integrate its OLAP engine directly with standard relational databases. Seagate Holos does not mandate a proprietary OLAP database—it is flexible. When Holos was first introduced, this ability to work with any relational database was not described as Relational OLAP (ROLAP) because the term had not been invented, but Holos was delivering both ROLAP technology and consequent customer benefits as early as 1988.

- Seagate Holos has taken the next step in OLAP technology, Compound OLAP, described later in this chapter.

Although the original form of Seagate Holos was designed in 1987, it has remained at the forefront through continuing development and through its initial choice of the right architecture. As a result, Holos applications written in 1988 continue to run on current versions with minimal changes.

Features and Benefits

Seagate Holos is a system for both application delivery and application development. Seagate Holos accesses corporate and other data at its source in the data warehouse, data mart or other location, analyzes and adds value to it in many ways, and then presents information in an environment that allows the insight and knowledge of the user to be augmented by the analytical power of the Seagate Holos system. Seagate Holos' Compound OLAP Architecture deals effectively with the explosion in the quantity of data and in the complexity of its structure in large organizations today.

Seagate Holos is a tool that crosses established application category boundaries. Seagate Holos could be called an executive information system, because it can deliver high-value, well-presented information suitable for use by senior managers. Seagate Holos is also a decision support system, because it allows the creation of models of the business, the testing of alternative scenarios, and the statistical forecasting characteristic of such systems. And Seagate Holos is an OLAP tool, because it delivers multidimensional querying, reporting, and analysis.

The user's view of Seagate Holos is likely to be within one or more Seagate Holos applications, running in a familiar

Windows or Macintosh environment. Seagate Holos can also be accessed from other desktop applications, such as Microsoft Excel, Seagate Crystal Info, Seagate Crystal Reports, or through the World Wide Web. The capabilities and look-and-feel of the Seagate Holos application are entirely under the control of the application developer, so the application can be precisely tailored to meet an organization's needs.

Generally, users will have available to them a variety of "reports", although a Seagate Holos report bears little relation to the traditional idea of a report. A Seagate Holos report is actually a starting point for a multidimensional exploration of the data, with analysis, what-if, forecasting and data visualization tools to help along the way.

Figure 13-2: Seagate Holos Data Expressed in an Excel Spreadsheet

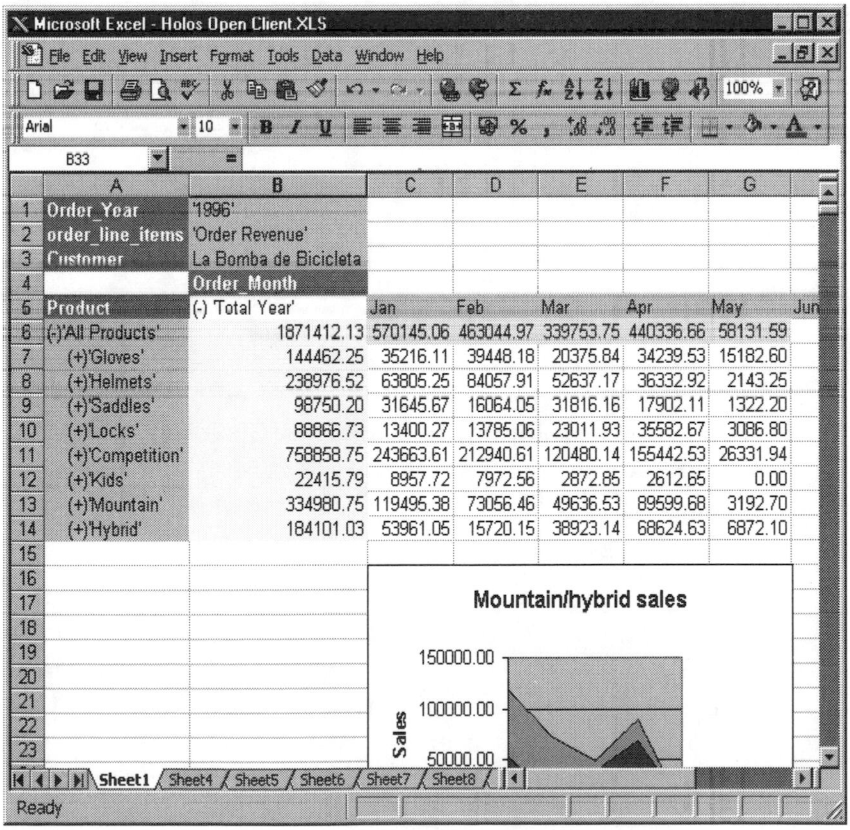

Figure 13-3: Seagate Holos Reports Can Be Tailored to Almost Any Requirement

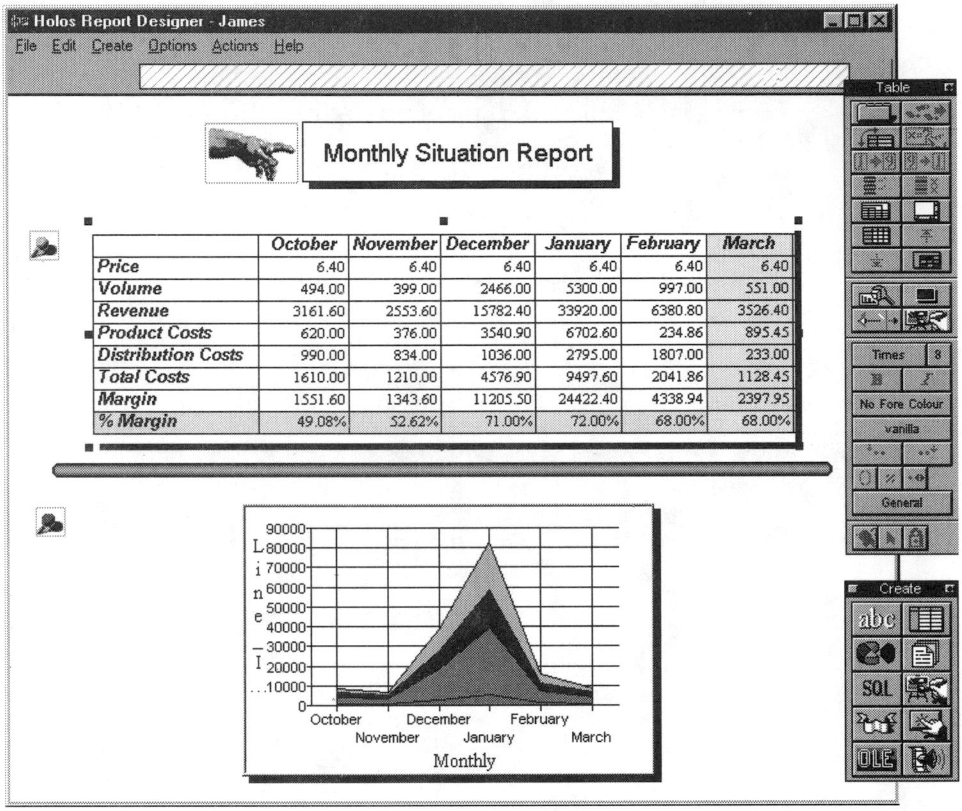

Seagate Holos works together with the other business intelligence solutions from Seagate Software, Seagate Crystal Info and Seagate Crystal Reports, to provide complete desktop to enterprise coverage of the business intelligence needs of any organization.

At the core of the Seagate Holos system is the Holos Server, which controls and contributes to the operation of the Holos Client. The overall Seagate Holos system is almost infinitely configurable and can be made to look and perform exactly the way a user wants it -- the thousands of Seagate Holos applications that exist cover a very wide range of applications, and are all very different in appearance.

Analysis

A business intelligence system needs to add value to the raw data it gathers. Seagate Holos manipulates and represents data multidimensionally. This basic requirement of OLAP systems reflects the business user's view of the organization, rather than the way in which underlying data is stored. OLAP tools vary considerably, however, in the flexibility and performance of the multidimensional storage mechanisms. The Seagate Holos Compound OLAP Architecture places no limits on data volumes, and provides scalable performance through parallel processing.

A business intelligence system needs to allow the creation of business rules that reflect relationships between business information, and thus allow business models that can then be used for forecasting and other forms of analysis. Organizations will typically have a reporting and financial hierarchical structure, and the business intelligence system must reflect this structure. Seagate Holos has special-purpose financial consolidation routines, along with a graphical tool for manipulating these hierarchies to respond to frequent organizational change.

Once a model of the business operation has been created, it is possible to explore the behavior of that model using target analysis, risk analysis, and many other statistical tools. With increasing accessibility of large volumes of data, data mining is becoming an important aspect of business intelligence systems. Seagate Holos provides these analysis tools including data mining techniques based on neural networks, together with pattern recognition methods.

Figure 13-4: Data Mining Via Neural Networks in Seagate Holos

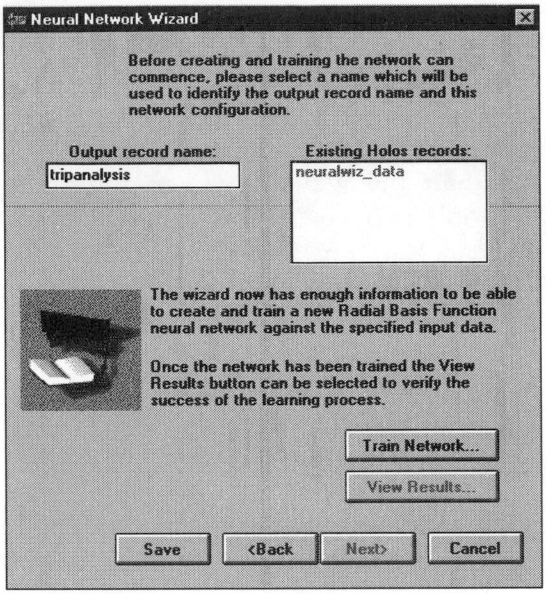

Interaction

The user's working environment, the way information is presented, and the tools provided for working with and exploring the information are the final, vital ingredients of the business intelligence system. Seagate Holos can deliver Holos information to practically any desktop. Any Java-enabled web browser, any ODBC-capable desktop application, or the Windows and Macintosh compatible Seagate Holos Client can be used.

Seagate Holos Language

The Holos 4th Generation Language underpins all functionality of Seagate Holos, and is what enables Seagate Holos applications to be customized to the user's unique business processes. In the real world, applications need to be connected into the existing application environment and derive benefits from the legacy that is there. This cannot be achieved seamlessly and in detail without the flexibility of a language.

Figure 13-5: The Desktop Designer in Seagate Holos Enables Custom Creation of an Environment.

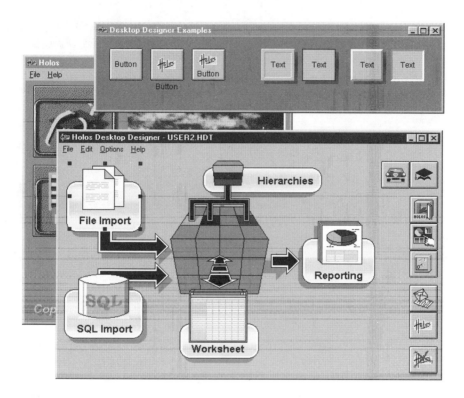

Seagate Holos Clients

Holos Reports are the primary way to deliver information to the user. Reports in Holos are much more than a static representation of information. A Holos report user has available a wide range of capabilities including analysis, forecasting and drill-through. Thus, a particular report is a starting point – it is just a "view" of the information from which many other views can be accessed, as they suggest themselves to the information consumer.

Figure 13-6: The Holos Worksheet

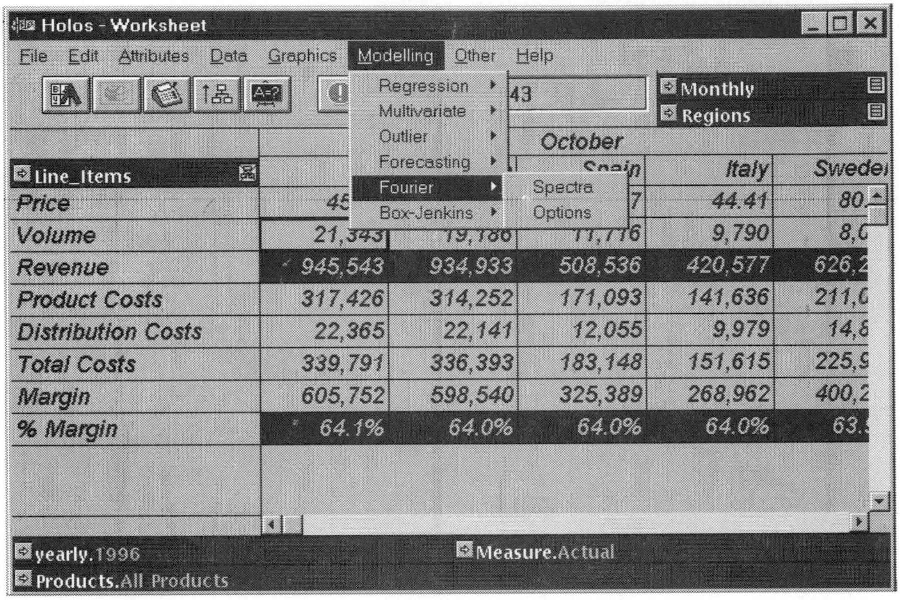

The Holos Worksheet offers a way of working with data that is familiar to many spreadsheet users. In addition, the Holos Worksheet is specifically designed to work with multidimensional information, and has transparent access to the Holos Server.

The Data Filter allows creation of a set of criteria that define information of interest to the user -- "Show me all sales that yielded more than 50% profit," for example.

Graphical tools are designed to simplify the development process. The Application Manager, Data Manager, Dialog Designer, and Desktop Designer combine to make application development efficient for the application developer.

Figure 13-7: The Data Filter in Seagate Holos Allows Custom Selection of Data.

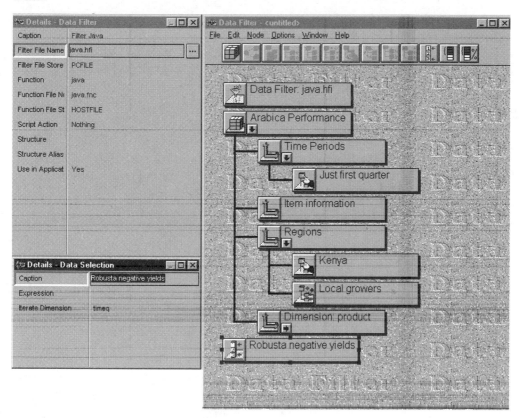

Seagate Holos Open Client Interface

The Seagate Holos Open Client Interface makes Seagate Holos information available to any desktop application that supports ODBC. Applications developed in Visual Basic, or common productivity tools like Microsoft Excel, can obtain data from the Seagate Holos Server in a format that permits multidimensional manipulation and display.

An Excel Add-in is provided to allow multidimensional data selection, navigation and analysis within the familiar Excel environment. Seagate Crystal Reports and Seagate

Crystal Info can also use the ODBC interface to obtain reporting data from Seagate Holos.

Seagate Holos on the Web

For many business intelligence applications, Internet technology offers a compelling way to meet users' information needs. A Web browser can now be found on almost every business desktop, providing intuitive ease-of-use and access to vast quantities of information. The Seagate Holos Web Gateway delivers Seagate Holos capabilities through a Web browser. Interactive Holos Reports including tables and graphs can be created; graphs are implemented as Java applets.

To increase flexibility, the Web Gateway includes the Holos Web Toolkit, a set of Seagate Holos utilities that start by giving simplified access to standard report navigation like drilldown and drill across. The Toolkit goes further, though, and encapsulates much of the more advanced Holos report capabilities in a simple way -- so, for example, it is possible to perform Holos data mining from within the Web browser.

A QuickStart application offers a way to deliver Seagate Holos information from an existing Seagate Holos application over the Web, allowing simplified selection and orientation of report data. The QuickStart application can also create static HTML versions of Holos reports, suitable for distribution via E-mail.

The architecture of the Seagate Holos Web Gateway offers these key benefits:

- Scalability -- The Seagate Holos WebBroker passes incoming requests to as many Seagate Holos Server processes as are necessary, and provides load-balancing between them.

- Compatibility -- with almost any Web Server. Communication with the web server is via CGI, implemented on practically all web servers.

Figure 13-8: A Holos Graph Displayed Via a Web Browser

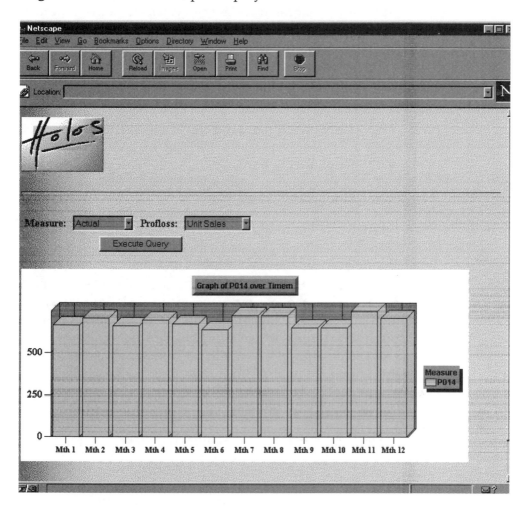

Seagate HOLOS Compound OLAP Architecture

Much of business intelligence involves working with multidimensional data, because that is the way people perceive their business function and expect to manipulate the corresponding data. The main division within the spectrum of approaches to OLAP is between Relational OLAP (ROLAP) and Multidimensional OLAP (MOLAP). Before the user can implement a business intelligence system in some products, there has to be "buy in" to one or the other technique. In a typical organization, the range of business intelligence needs is wide, and can change rapidly. It could well be that the best approach for one application is completely inappropriate for another.

Seagate Holos' previous Hybrid OLAP design made it possible to combine the best features of both ROLAP and MOLAP. Seagate Holos now goes a step further with Compound OLAP Architecture – called by its developers "OLAP for the Real World."

With the Compound OLAP Architecture, any number of individual OLAP "cubes" can be joined, with the result treated as a single cube. Various relationships between individual cubes and the overall OLAP store can be achieved -- "racking" of cubes allows the joining of peer cubes along a backbone dimension, while "stacking" allows a conditional read-through and write-back relationship between cubes -- effectively, a "data valve." A single Compound OLAP cube can contain any combination of racked and stacked cubes. This free combination of cubes will become as fundamental a part of OLAP as joins are in the relational database world.

The Compound OLAP Architecture delivers:

- Scalability and parallel processing -- Typical OLAP implementations are now handling volumes of data that start high, and keep on growing. Parallel processing, including calculation and data loading, is one way to make such large data volumes feasible. The way parallel processing is implemented in the Compound OLAP Architecture provides scalability, too, because it is possible to exploit additional processing and storage resources efficiently. Any limit on the volume of data that can be handled will arise from physical storage and processing constraints, not from Seagate Holos.

- Separation of the logical OLAP view from the physical implementation -- Typically, the preferred logical view of OLAP data is as one giant hypercube including all the data and all the dimensions. Physically, in real-world OLAP applications, it is not practical to implement this. The Compound OLAP Architecture delivers the giant hypercube view to analysis tools, while allowing the physical implementation to take account of resource constraints imposed by the hardware or operating system.

- The ability to handle real-world data -- Real world data is not all the same. Some data is sparse, some dense. Some data is fast changing, some static. There may be many dimensions with multiple hierarchies, or just a few. The Compound OLAP Architecture allows all these variations to be handled efficiently.

The Compound OLAP Architecture meets two fundamental challenges for OLAP systems:

- the explosion in data volumes
- the complexity and varied nature of the data to be handled

These challenges make simplistic solutions based on a monolithic black-box multidimensional database, or on a high-capacity but low-performance relational system impractical. Say Seagate Software's visionaries, "... Someday, all OLAP will be this way."

13-4 Case Study: Ameritech - Data Warehousing For Sales Force Management

Ameritech's Consumer Services division accounts for over $6 billion of the Chicago-based telecommunications giant's revenues of $14.9 billion (1996 figures). As of early 1997, Consumer Services handled some 13 million access lines in the Midwest's five-state region.

Like most regional telecom firms facing increased competition for local customers, its customer-oriented focus is a lot more than lip service. Ameritech championed the idea of a data warehouse because the company saw it as an opportunity to improve customer support. The company wanted information about customers' orders to be available throughout the sales channel as soon as the orders were placed, not just when the orders were completed and billed.

Needed: More Timely Sales Reports

Ameritech had determined that its sales reports simply were not current enough. Even though Ameritech's 5,000+ sales agents received sales reports electronically (with monthly paper-based reports going to more than 100 managers), this did not give the sales force the up-to-date information it needed to answer questions like, "What's the status of the orders I entered yesterday?" or "How many Caller-ID units have we sold this month in total, by sales team?"

Until 1996, Ameritech relied solely on mainframe-based reports that were both hard to maintain and expensive. So, in early 1996, sales management convinced Ameritech to fund a new POST (Paperless Online Service Tracking) system. With impressive speed, the company established a team consisting of both in-house and outsourced personnel, and development was fully underway by March.

Consultants did the back-end work, performing the analysis (most of the source data remains mainframe-based) and designing the new data warehouse, an Oracle 7.3 database running on a Sun SPARCserver 2000. Within five months, a beta version of the system was operational and was launched at a single sales office. All 23 offices were "live" by February 1997. Then, the existing paper reports, which had been run in parallel, were phased out.

The system accommodates between seven and eight million transactions monthly and is updated nightly. The Seagate Holos part of the update takes an average of 1.5 hours nightly. The Oracle data processing takes between four and five hours, as Oracle has to add information from the order entry system and perform several types of reconciliations (the data cleansing). The 600 gigabyte Oracle data warehouse keeps data for the previous three months and the current month. Every month, Ameritech rolls off the oldest month to keep the database size manageable so that it can be updated overnight. History, however, is maintained in Seagate Holos. Ameritech plans to keep one year's worth of structures online.

Seagate Holos Reports

Ameritech has so far developed two major reports using Seagate Holos software. The main report contains daily and month-to-date quantities by product group. It matches the monthly objective with daily and month-to-date revenue, calculates percentage objective achieved, and estimates the percent achieved for month-end based on the current pace of orders. Month-to-date revenue ranking within the office and state is provided, along with the number of orders updated and errored, service order accuracy and the number of orders that are still pending completion.

From this report, a manager can drill into the Oracle database to check on the status of orders or on any errors that have been generated, as well as order tallies for the individual sales reps. This report can be viewed for any day of the month, and for current as well as previous months, and it is consolidated from sales reps to team, office, state and regional totals.

The second report contains month-to-date gross quantities and revenue, adjustments, and net quantity and revenue by product code. Quantities and revenue allow drilling down to show the order type, and adjustments allow drilling down to show the adjustment reason. This monthly report can be viewed for current as well as previous months and follows a similar consolidation scheme.

Prior to the POST roll out, users were given training, with at least five individuals from each sales office's customer care center attending two-day POST system classes. Seagate Holos, the main front-end analysis tool, has become Ameritech's standard, multidimensional analysis engine. Because the Seagate component is quite intuitive, managers were taught how to use it in about a half day.

The dynamic nature of the Seagate Holos reports, coupled with the multidimensionality of the business data being analyzed, turns these two reports into what is really thousands of different views of the information, suited to the individual user's requirements. This yields the benefit of very rapid implementation and response to changing requirements, as well as a modest maintenance effort over time as the application evolves. These characteristics are important to many businesses, but especially in the rapidly changing competitive landscape of the telecommunications industry.

Security for the new POST system is efficient. The 5000 sales reps may view their own results only through a simple Visual Basic application. Visual Basic is also used to update static data such as data about the sales reps themselves and product tables. However, the 400 or so managers who use Seagate Holos and who attended training have access to all of their own sales reps' information and can also view results from other offices and channels, but only at the office level of detail.

Ameritech's vice presidents and directors generally have little interest in drilling down to individual rep performance, so they have access to summary data for all offices in all channels. Administrative staff have access to everything (all reps in all offices and channels). In addition, managers are reporting that they have been using the new reports for coaching. The combination of drilling down and more timely information makes it easy to identify not only sales reps who are not selling well, but also reps who prefer selling certain products, and so on.

Futures

Ameritech already has plans for additional Seagate Holos development. Upper management has put in requests for more summary data. Improved integration (and faster processing) with the feeder systems, tie-ins with call-volume management, and tie-ins with the sales force scheduling system are also planned.

Ameritech's vision and delivery are impressive, and the company's application is a textbook example of how data warehousing can be used effectively for sales force management. POST is now being integrated with a new departmental EIS, along with marketing, financial and network information, for additional usefulness.

13-5 CASE STUDY: B.C. HYDRO – FRONT-ENDING A DATA WAREHOUSE

British Columbia Hydro and Power Authority serves more than 1.4 million customers in British Columbia. The third largest utility in Canada, B.C. Hydro generates between 45,000 and 50,000 gigawatt-hours of electricity annually, which reaches customers through an interconnected system of over 70,000 kilometers of transmission and distribution lines. B.C.

Hydro has about 5,000 employees, at headquarters in Vancouver and in regional offices all over British Columbia.

In the early 1990s, B.C. Hydro began the process of improving users' access to business data. At that time, tools available in their existing mainframe environment required considerable technical knowledge to run even the simplest reports, and user demand for information was increasing rapidly. Fueling this effort was the fact that the company has been headed in new directions: the Canadian energy industry is facing rapid change, including the introduction of competition to a field that has essentially consisted of nationally protected monopolies. Availability of business information for timely business decision-making would be a critical factor to future business success.

In the summer of 1995, a B.C. Hydro team developed a business case that outlined their problems and investigated ways to build an enterprise-wide data warehouse for financial information. The team decided that front-end data access would be a key focus of their efforts, and, in order to deliver the variety of information users needed, determined that multidimensional analysis would be a requirement. Faced with a changing business, they needed more than a tool to efficiently deliver today's information to the users — they wanted a tool to create systems that could grow and change with the company.

The B.C. Hydro team also determined that the tool selected must handle two approaches: the new system must address the needs of "power users" who were comfortable with the existing environment and could write their own SQL queries, and it also needed to make information accessible to the large number of users without technical expertise who wanted a user-friendly interface. These users needed to be shielded from the complexity of the data but still had to be able to retrieve, analyze and manipulate complex information.

By the end of 1995, the team had looked at more than a dozen front-end products, using well-defined and specific criteria for reporting and results manipulation, which had undergone further refinement after a Request for Information was issued. B.C. Hydro's investigation was complicated by complex data hierarchies that are imbalanced, and they found that not many products could address this issue without employing a work-around. Their search was further narrowed in January, 1996 to six products covering a good cross-section of the market.

In early 1996, after further comparisons, the team was able to narrow the selection down to Seagate Holos and one other product for benchmarking. The B.C. Hydro team gave each company's representatives three days to produce a mock application, built to B.C. Hydro's specifications and using actual data. The mock applications were then turned over for two days of testing to 10 to 15 business analysts from B.C. Hydro's individual business units and users from the company's budget management group.

An interesting twist to this benchmarking effort was that it happened to fall during the company's planning cycle; thus, the data used with these prototypes being actual, current data, the real-life applications were very welcome indeed. *"The users weren't too happy when we took the products away,"* recalled a team member.

B.C. Hydro started the benchmarking without any experience on Seagate Holos, which was the first to be benchmarked. Since the B.C. Hydro team knew the capabilities of the other product, many of the functions they asked Seagate Holos to execute were ones they knew the other software tool could provide. Seagate Holos surpassed their expectations.

During their exploration of the two products, the B.C. Hydro team found that the more they saw of Seagate Holos, the more they appreciated its potential for developing their enterprise-wide applications. Seagate Holos fulfilled these key conditions for B.C. Hydro:

- Simple storage requirements
- Data refreshed quickly
- Seamless integration with their relational database
- Very thin client so that users could easily multi-task
- Reporting interface that provided a great deal of control and flexibility
- Customizable user interface that could suit the needs of executives and non-technical users, as well as those with technical expertise. *"Many of our users just want data dropped on their desktops,"* noted a team member. *"They don't want to have to build it or wait for someone else to build it for them."*

Once the benchmark tests were completed and the development team had compiled and compared the results, users made recommendations at the end of February. Seagate Holos was selected as the front end to B.C. Hydro's financial data warehouse, and the company began the purchasing process in mid-March, 1996. Seagate Holos arrived in April, and by late July the first pilot application was rolled out to the user community.

Today, B.C. Hydro has a financial data warehouse running on an HP 9000 Model K460 using Informix RDBMS and Prism Warehouse Manager. Data is extracted, integrated, transformed and summarized from the many different mainframe sources down to the HP platform, and Seagate Holos is the primary information delivery tool, providing access and multidimensional analysis of warehouse data.

The Seagate Holos users at B.C. Hydro are looking at financial data for cost control; some are managing their own business units and some are monitoring the business of the entire company. The pilot application was initially deployed to approximately 20 financial and business unit analysts; the final application is likely to be used by approximately 100 users.

Before B.C. Hydro started using Seagate Holos, it would often take a business systems analyst several iterations, and even days, to generate the complex SQL queries needed to satisfy the non-technical analyst's or manager's reporting requirements. With the Seagate Holos front end to the data warehouse, a non-technical analyst can produce that same report, manipulate the data, and format a report without any technical involvement in just a matter of minutes.

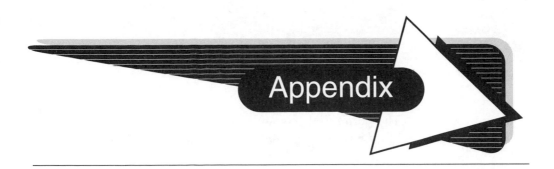

Codd's 12 Rules for OLAP

In a 1993 white paper, E. F. Codd formulated 12 rules that he believes are needed for on-line analytic processing. These rules were summarized in Table 1-5, which is reproduced here as Table A-1. They are intended to serve as a checklist for evaluating OLAP tools.

Table A-1: Codd's 12 Rules for OLAP

1. Multidimensional view	7. Dynamic sparse matrix handling
2. Transparent to the user	8. Multi-user support
3. Accessible	9. Cross-dimensional operations
4. Consistent reporting performance	10. Intuitive data manipulation
5. Clientserver architecture	11. Flexible reporting
6. Generic dimensionality	12. Unlimited dimensions, aggregation

The purpose of this appendix is to expand on each of these rules based on Codd's paper (Codd and associates, 1993).

1. *Multidimensional view.* Business models (and user's views of information) are multidimensional. OLAP software should allow users manipulate multidimensional data easily and intuitively.

2. *Transparent to the user.* OLAP should be provided in an open systems architecture. The user should not know (or care) whether or not the front end which they see is based on OLAP. The analytical tools can be embedded anywhere without affecting functionality. The OLAP tool should not introduce new complexity.

3. *Accessible.* An OLAP system should only access data required for the analysis and should not access data not needed.

4. *Consistent reporting performance.* Reporting performance should not degrade as the number of dimensions or the size of the database increases. By keeping performance independent of size, people do not strategize to avoid problem expansion, thereby reducing the value of the content.

5. *Clientserver architecture.* With data required for on-line analytic processing stored in warehouses that act as servers and users having PCs for clients, OLAP tools should be able to operate in a clientserver environment. The tools should be sufficiently intelligent that a variety of clients can be used with minimum effort and programming.

6. *Generic Dimensionality.* Data structures, formulas, and reporting formats should not be biased toward any one data dimension.

7. *Dynamic sparse matrix handling.* Data for analytic processing tends to be sparse. That is, most cells in a multidimensional model are empty. The OLAP tool should be able to adjust to the sparseness of the particular matrix and choose the best access method (such as B-trees, hashing, or direct calculation) depending on the matrix. Failure to adjust to the data can lead to working with data sets that are needlessly large and/or slow. By reducing the amount of data that needs to be processed, analysts are able to work on problems they previously avoided or oversimplified because they perceived them as too complex.

8. *Multi-user support.* Concurrent retrieval and update access, integrity, and security should be provided so that several people can work simultaneously with the same model and data.

9. *Cross-dimensional operations.* Cross-dimensional calculations refer to calculations performed across multiple dimensions such as are encountered in rolling up hierarchical results in a budget calculation.

10. *Intuitive data manipulation.* The user's view of the dimensions in the analytic model should contain all the information needed to manipulate the data.

11. *Flexible Reporting.* Because data analysis is simplified when data that are to be compared to one another are presented in proximity to one another or grouped logically with respect to the enterprise, it should be possible to present information as the users think about it rather than in a rigid format. This flexibility should be true from one dimension to all the dimensions in the model.

12. *Unlimited[1] dimensions and aggregation levels.* Analytic models may involve 15 to 20 or more dimensions. OLAP tools should be able to handle this many dimensions and should allow each analyst to aggregate data in any dimension in any way that is needed.

---

[1] Note that Codd's Rule 12 calls for "unlimited" dimensions, but that he limits the number to 20 or less.

References

Ackoff, R. L. (1967). "Management Misinformation Systems." *Management Science* , Vol. 14, No. 4, pp. B147 - B156.

Ambrosio, J. (1992). "Information Warehouses: One Size Does Not Fit All." *Computerworld, Vol.* 26,. No. 16, pp. 71,74.

Anahory, S. and Murray, D. (1994). *Data Warehousing in the Real World*. Harlow, UK: Addison-Wesley, Chapter 16.

Anonymous (1994). "How to Build and Design Data Warehouses to Improve Information Access." *I/S Analyzer*. Vol. 33, No. 11, pp. 1 - 16.

Anonymous (1996). "Interview with Meta Group's Karen Rubinstrunk." *DBMS*, February.

Anonymous (1997). *White Paper: Putting the Data Warehouse on the Intranet*. Minneapolis, MN: Information Advantage, Inc.

Babcock, C. (1995). "Slice, Dice, and Deliver," *Computerworld*, November 13, p. 130.

Bennett, J. L. (1977). "User-Oriented Graphics: Systems for Support of Unstructured Tasks". *User-Oriented Design of Interacftive Graphics Systems*. S. Treu(editor). New York: Association for Computing Machinery, pp. 3 - 11.

Bennett, J. L. (1983). *Decision Support Systems: Current Practices and Continuing Challenges*. Reading, MA: Addison-Wesley.

Berresford, T. R. and Wetherbee, J.C. (1979). "Heuristic Development: A Redesign of Systems Design." *MIS Quarterly*, Vol 3. No. 1, March, pp. 11 - 19.

Bostrum, R. P. (1989). "Successful Application of Communications Techniques to Improve the Systems Development Process." *Information and Management*, Vol. 16, No. 5, May, pp. 279 -285.

Bostrum, R. P. and Heinen, J.S. (1977). "MIS Problems and Failures: A Socio-Technical Perspective: Part I." *MIS Quarterly* Vol. 1, No. 3, September, pp. 17 - 33.

Brooks, F. P. Jr. (1995) *The Mythical Man Month.* Reading MA: Addison-Wesley.

Brooks, P. (1997). "March of the Data Marts," *DBMS.* March 1997.

Bull, C. (1995). "The Ideal File Cabinet." *Information Week*, January 16, pp. 43 - 48.

ButlerGroup (1995). *Data Warehouse- Hype or Reality?* http:// www. butlergroup.co.uk/butgrp/issues/dwiss02.htm, Butler Group (UK) (September 15, 1995).

ButlerGroup (1995). *Total Solution Providers.* http://www. butlergroup.co.uk/butgrp/issues/dwiss06.htm,ButlerGroup (UK), September 15.

Byrd, T. A., Cossick, K.L., and Zmud, R.W. (1992). "A Synthesis of Research on Requirements Analysis and Knowledge Acquisition Techniques." *MIS Quarterly* Vol. 16, No. 1, March, pp. 117 - 138.

Carickhoff, R. (1997). "A New Face for OLAP." *DBMS*, January.

Christman, G. A. (1995). *"Enterprisewide Data Warehousing With INFORMIX-On-Line Dynamic Server, Version 8.0."* Technnotes Vol. 5, No. 3 http://www.informix.com/informix/servicessuperserv/pubs/tech note/tn95v13, Informix.

Codd, E. F. (1970). "A Relational Model of Data for Large Shared Data Banks," *Communications of the ACM* Vol. 13, No. 6.

Codd, E. F., Codd, S.B., and Salley, C.T. (1993). *Providing On-Line Analytic Processing to User-Analysts.* Sunnyvale, CA: E. F. Codd and Associates.

Codd, E. F. (1995). "Twelve Rules for On Line Analytic Processing." *Computerworld,* April 13.

Corey, J. M. and Abbey, M. (1997). *Oracle Data Warehousing: A Practical Guide to Successful Data Warehouse Analysis, Build, and Rollout.* Berkeley, CA: Osborne McGraw-Hill.

Davis, G. B. (1982). "Strategies for Information Systems Requirements Determination." *IBM Systems Journal* Vol. 21, No. 1, pp. 4 - 32.

Demarest, M. (1997). "Building the Data Mart." *DBMS,* July.

DePompa, B. (1996) "Stack that Data," *Information Week.* January 29, pp. 50 - 57.

Eckerson, W. W. (1996). *Leveraging the Web for Decision Support.* A White Paper by Patricia Seybold Group, Boston, MA for Brio Technology, Inc.

Eckerson, W. W. (1997). "Web Based Query Tools and Architectures." *Journal of Data Warehousing* Vol. 2, No. 1, April, pp. 21 - 32.

Fayyad, U., Piatetsky-Shapiro, G., and Smith, P. (1996). "The KDD Process for Extracting Useful Knowledge from Volumes of Data." *Communications of the ACM.Vol. 31, No. 11, pp. 27 - 34.*

Fayyad, U. et al. (1996). *Advances in Knowledge Discovery and Data Mining.* Cambridge, MA: MIT Press, Chapter 1

Finkelstein, R. (1995). "MDD: Database Reaches for the Next Dimension." *Database Programming and Design,* April.

Foley, J. (1997). "Data Warehouse Pitfalls". *Information Week,* May 19, 1997, pp. 94 - 96.

Friend, D. (1989). "EIS and the Collapse of the Information Pyramid." *Information Center,* Fall, pp. 14 - 22.

Gray, P. and Watson, H.J. (1997). "New Developments in Data Warehousing." *Journal of Data Warehousing* Vol. 2, No. 2, pp. 2 - 4.

Grupe, F. H. and Owrang, M.M. (1995). "Data Base Mining: Discovering New Knowledge and Competitive Advantage," *Information Systems Management*, Fall, pp. 26 - 31.

Hackathorn, R.D. (1997). "Data Warehousing's Credibility Crisis." *Byte*, August, pp. 43 - 44.

Hackathorn, R. D. (1993). *Enterprise Database Connectivity*. New York: Wiley pp. 261 - 266.

Haisten, M. (1995). "Planning for a Data Warehouse." *InfoDb*, Vol.9, No. 1.

Hammer, K. (1995). "Anticipating the Cost of Maintenance in Building a Data Warehouse." *Data Management Review*, May.

Harding, E. (1995). "Purina Mills Warehouses a Legacy of Success," *Software Magazine*, November, pp. 39 - 44.

Hildebrand, C. (1996) quoting J. McElreath, J. in "Form Follows Function." *CIO*, November 1, p. 41.

Hurwicz, M. "Take Your Data to the Cleaners." *Byte*, January pp. 97 - 102.

Imhoff, C. (1995). *Seminar on Data Modeling for the Data Warehouse*. New York: DAMA, New York Chapter, March 29.

Inmon, W. H. (1992). *Building the Data Warehouse*. New York: Wiley.

Inmon, W. H. and Hackathorn, R.D. (1994). *Using the Data Warehouse*. New York:Wiley.

Inmon, W. H. (1995). *Data Warehouse Defined*. Special *Computerworld* Advertising Supplement.

Inmon, W. H., Welch, J.D., and Glassey, K. L. (1997) *Managing the Data Warehouse*. New York: Wiley.

Janah, M. (1995). "Stanford Data Warehouse Improves Operations," *Infoworld*, July 31, pp. 61 - 64.

Keen, P. G. W. (1981). "Value Analysis: Justifying Decision Support Systems," *MIS Quarterly, Vol.* 5, No. 1, pp. 1 - 15.

Keen, P. G. W. (1991). *Shaping the Future: Business Design through Information Technology.* Boston: Harvard Business School Press.

Kimball, R. (1996). *The Data Warehouse Toolkit: Practical Techniques for Building Dimensional Data Warehouses.* New York: Wiley.

Kimball, R. (1996). "Mastering Data Extraction." *DBMS*, June, pp. 97 - 102.

King, W. R. (1978). "Strategic Planning for Management Information Systems." *MIS Quarterly* Vol. 2, No. 2, pp. 27 - 37.

Mattison, R. (1996). *Data Warehousing: Strategies, Technologies, and Techniques.* New York: McGraw-Hill.

McFadden, F. R. (1996). "Data Warehouse for EIS: Some Issues and Impacts," *Proceedings of Hawaii International Conference on System Sciences*, IEEE, pp. 120 - 127.

McKeen, J. D. and. Smith, H.A. (1996). *Management Challenges in IS: Successful Strategies and Appropriate Action.* Chichester, UK: Wiley.

Memminger, D. (1994). *Multidimensional Data Analysis: Critical to Business Intelligence.* Waltham, MA: IRI Software.

MicroStrategy, Inc. (1994). *White Paper - Relational OLAP: An Enterpise-Wide Data Delivery Architecture.* http://www.strategy.com/ wp_a_i1.htm.

Mintzberg, H. (1973). *The Nature of Managerial Work.* New York: Harper & Row.

Naumann, J. D. and Jenkins, A.M., (1982). "Prototyping: The New Paradigm for Systems Development." *MIS Quarterly* Vol. 6, No. 3, September, pp. 29 - 44.

Page, S. J. (1995). *Database Models for Multidimensional Data Analysis*. Manhattan, KS: School of Business. Kansas State University.

Park, Y. T. (1997). "Strategic Use of Data Warehousing," *Data Warehousing Journal* Vol 2, No. 1, pp. 24 - 33.

Poe, V. (1996). *Building a Data Warehouse for Decision Support*. Upper Saddle River, NJ: Prentice Hall PTR.

Porter, M. E. and Millar, V.E. (1985). "How Information Gives You Competitive Advantage." *Harvard Business Review*, July-August.

Radding, A. (1995). "Building a Better Warehouse." *Infoworld* November 20, pp. 57- 62.

Raden, N. (1996). "Maximizing Your Warehouse." *Information Week*, March 18, pp. 42 - 48.

Raden, N. (1996). "Modeling a Data Warehouse." *Information Week*, January 29, pp. 60 - 66.

Rinaldi, D. V. "Metadata Management Separates Prism from Data Warehouse Pack." *Client/Server Computing*, March, pp. 20 - 23.

Rob, P. and Coronel, S. (1997). *Data Base Systems: Design, Implementation, and Management*. Cambridge, MA: Course Technologies.

Rockart, J. F. (1979). "Chief Executives Define Their Own Data Needs," *Harvard Business Review*, Vol. 57, No. 2, March-April, pp. 81 - 93.

Rockart, J. F. and Bullen, C. V. (1986). *The Rise of Managerial Computing: The Best of the Center for Information Systems Research, Sloan School of Management, Massachussetts Institute of Technology*. Homewood, IL: Dow Jones-Irwin

Rockart, J. F., and Delong, D. W. (1988). *Executive Support Systems: The Emergence of Top Management Computer Use*. Homewood, IL: Dow Jones Irwin.

Russo, J. E. (1993). "A Pyramid of Decision Approaches." *California Management Review,* Fall 1993, pp. 9 - 31.

Rymer, R. J. (1995). *Data Analysis: New Tools for Expanding Needs*, Boston:Patricia Seybold Group.

Small, R. D. (1997*).* "Debunking Data Mining Myths - Don'Let Contradictory Claims About Data Mining Keep You from Improving your Business." *Information Week,* January 20.

Sprague, R. H. (1980). "A Framework for the Development of Decision Support Systems." *MIS Quarterly* Vol. 4, No. 4, pp. 1 - 26.

Sprague, R. H. and Watson H .J. (1996) *Decision Support for Management.* Upper Saddle River, NJ: Prentice Hall.

Stackowiak, R. (1997) "Why Bad Warehouses Happen to Good People," *Journal of Data Warehousing*, Vol. 2, No. 2, April, pp. 33 - 36.

Stedman, C. (1997). "Quick, Hide the Warehousing Experts," *Computerworld* May, 26, 1997, p1.

Telem, M. (1988a). "Information Requirements Specifications I: Brainstorming Collective Decision Making Approach." *Information Processing and Management*, Vol. 24, No. 5. pp. 549 - 557.

Telem, M. (1988b). "Information Requirements Specifications II: Brainstorming Collective Decision-Making Approach." *Information Processing and Management*, Vol. 24, No. 5, pp. 559 - 566.

Thomson, T. (1996). "World's Fastest Computers." *Byte,* January, p. 44.

Vijayan, J. (1997). "Scaling Up Your Warehouse." *Computerworld*, April 21, pp. 71, 74.

Watson, H. J., Rainer, R.K., and Koh, C. (1991). "Executive Information Systems: A Framework for Development and a Survey of Current Practices." *MIS Quarterly,* Vol. 15, No. 1, March, pp. 13 - 32.

Watson, H. J., Houdeshel, G., Rainer R.K. (1997). *Building Executive Information Systems and Other Decision Support Applications*. New York: Wiley.

Watson, H. J. and Frolick, M. N. (1993). "Determining Information Requirements for an EIS." *MIS Quarterly*, Vol. 17, No. 3, September, pp. 255 - 269.

Watson, H. J. and Haley, B. J. (1997). "Framework for Developing a Data Warehouse." *Journal of Data Warehousing*, Vol. 2, No. 1, pp. 10 - 17.

Watson, R. T. (1996). *Data Management*. New York: Wiley.

Watterson, K. (1997). "Parallel Tracks." *Datamation*, May, pp. 92 - 96.

Weldon, J. L. (1997). A Career in Data Modeling. *Byte*, June, pp. 103 - 106.

White, C. (1995). "The Key to a Data Warehouse." *Database Programming and Design*, February.

Zahedi, F. (1987). "Reliability of Information Systems Based on Critical Success Factors Formulation." *MIS Quarterly*, Vol. 11, No. 2, June, pp. 187 - 204.

INDEX